Snapping Beans

SUNY series in Black Women's Wellness
———————
Stephanie Y. Evans, editor

Snapping Beans

Voices of a Black Queer Lesbian South

JAYME N. CANTY

Cover art: Makala L. Fields "Snapping Beans," 2022

Published by State University of New York Press, Albany

© 2024 State University of New York

All rights reserved

Printed in the United States of America

No part of this book may be used or reproduced in any manner whatsoever without written permission. No part of this book may be stored in a retrieval system or transmitted in any form or by any means including electronic, electrostatic, magnetic tape, mechanical, photocopying, recording, or otherwise without the prior permission in writing of the publisher.

Links to third-party websites are provided as a convenience and for informational purposes only. They do not constitute an endorsement or an approval of any of the products, services, or opinions of the organization, companies, or individuals. SUNY Press bears no responsibility for the accuracy, legality, or content of a URL, the external website, or for that of subsequent websites.

For information, contact State University of New York Press, Albany, NY
www.sunypress.edu

Library of Congress Cataloging-in-Publication Data

Name: Canty, Jayme N., 1984– author.
Title: Snapping beans : voices of a Black queer lesbian South / Jayme N. Canty.
Description: Albany : State University of New York Press, [2024] | Series: SUNY series in Black women's wellness | Includes bibliographical references and index.
Identifiers: LCCN 2023058111 | ISBN 9781438498904 (hardcover : alk. paper) | ISBN 9781438498928 (ebook) | ISBN 9781438498911 (pbk. : alk. paper)
Subjects: LCSH: Lesbians, Black—Southern States.
Classification: LCC HQ76.3.U62 S683 2024 | DDC 306.76/608996073—dc23/eng/20240430
LC record available at https://lccn.loc.gov/2023058111

*This book is dedicated to Dr. Josephine Boyd Bradley,
a civil rights pioneer whose guidance and mentorship
planted the seed for this work.
Without her light, this work would not be possible.
This book represents her legacy.
I also dedicate this book to all those
Southern Black queer ancestors who had to exist
and snap beans in silence.
This is your story.*

Snapping Beans Poem

green beans. shell peas. snap
lima beans. black eyed peas. snap.
pinto. butter. bean. snap.
snapping beans. snap.

—Jayme and Eboni Canty-Williams

Contents

Acknowledgments	ix
Description and List of Interlocutor Pseudonyms	xxiii
Preface: "Oh Yeah, You Southern": Reflections from a Southern Black Queer Lesbian Woman	xxvii
Introduction: "It Is a Part of Southern Life": Snapping Beans with SBQLWP Uncovers a Racialized Sexual Queer Geography	1
"I Was Silent, But My Brain Was Loud": The Silent South	43
"The Church Is Not the Building; It's the People": The Shameful and Condemning South	65
"The World Is Set Up for Straight Folks": The Judgmental South and the Southern Black Personality	101
"I Am Standing in My Truth": The Authentic and Reconciled South	137
The Black Queer Lesbian South	167
Epilogue: We Continue to Carry On	187
Notes	189
Works Cited	199
Index	203

Acknowledgments

I tend to be long-winded when it comes to giving thanks and acknowledgment, so bear with me as I thank all the folks who helped me on this book writing journey. I've never written a book before, so I have several people to acknowledge and thank. I am also a Southern Black woman who believes in giving folks their roses while they can smell them.

"Life Is a Journey, Not a Destination"

I do not know who originally said, "Life is a journey, not a destination," but I hear India.Arie sing it to me every morning as my daily alarm clock. It seems fitting to start by acknowledging the journey of this book. I never thought the day would come when I would be writing an acknowledgments page for a book that I wrote. But here I am, reflecting on this writing journey and passing out the roses to those individuals who aided this journey. Writing this book was certainly not an easy journey. It started with a few random notes and thoughts I typed up on my MacBook while living in Las Vegas, Nevada. While locked down during the COVID-19 pandemic, those notes became sentences and paragraphs. During the pandemic, I had the time to chat with my interlocutors online and by phone. These individuals trusted me to chronicle their coming out narratives. I cried and laughed with them. I took on their pain and joy. We built community. From their interviews, those sentences became chapter outlines and eventually a full manuscript. While writing, I was eager to get the book completed. However, it was the journey from the computer note to the full book that transformed my life. This book gave me my life's purpose. The journey of writing helped me emotionally, spiritually, and academically mature. For that, I'm thankful for the rollercoaster of writing.

"I'd Like to Give an Honor to God"

First, I have to thank God, the Holy Spirit, and all my ancestors known and unknown for guiding me through this journey. As they say in the Christian Black Church: "I'd like to give an honor to God," for all the ways I've been blessed to complete this work. During this writing journey, I would often sit with the pictures of my Southern Black female ancestors and pray for their guidance. These Southern Black female ancestors of mine paved the way for me to do this work: Janie Canty, Martha Ann Carrington, Marie (Riri) Houston, and Dr. Josephine Boyd Bradley. I prayed for this book every day. I prayed that it would do what it was intended to do. I prayed that the stories and narratives were clear and authentic. I prayed in moments when I did not know what to say. I prayed when I felt overwhelmed. To be honest, sometimes I prayed that somebody else would do the work so I did not have to. God and the ancestors didn't answer that prayer. I am thankful to God, the Holy Spirit, and the ancestors for whispering to me, providing me words to put on the page, sections to consider, quotes to highlight, and giving me words of affirmation during times I doubted the value of my work. These spiritual guides ultimately transformed this book into what it is today.

"Look It Up"

I am so thankful to have the support and love of my wife, Eboni C. Canty-Williams, who has been considerably patient with me as I wrote. Unlike my family, colleagues, mentors, or friends who only heard of what I was doing occasionally, she has been listening to me talk about this work almost daily since 2019. She is as close to this work as I am. She had to deal with me during my writing season, which was not easy. I can get crazy during that time. But she continued to be loving and patient with me as I interviewed, wrote, edited, and edited some more. She acted as my thinking partner through this journey. She allowed me to share my thoughts on interviews, reassured me, helped solidify topics I wanted to discuss, and indulged in my random rants about the book and my frustration with the writing process. Because she's so churchy, she even helped me understand Church policies better. She helped me edit some sentences on my first page when I was stuck. When I did a presentation of my work at Virginia Commonwealth University, she made sure my presentation was correct and provided me with some feedback. Even when I don't ask for feedback, she provides it. That can be a blessing and a curse. But what I love most about her is that she reminds me of my humanity, that I am a whole person outside of the academy, with family, friends, and separate dreams. While I was writing, she would remind me to take a break and continue to enjoy life. I'm so blessed to have a supportive partner. For that, she will always be my rock.

I must thank my parents, James and Marilyn Canty, who have taught me to be authentic in all that I do. They always encouraged me to never be afraid to use my voice and speak up. They never allowed me to shy away from how I felt. They taught me accountability, discipline, and determination; all these skills and lessons laid the foundation for this book. My parents always encouraged me to take my education seriously. I was the "why" child, always asking my mom and dad questions I did not know the answer to. I am sure I drove them crazy because I always asked questions about the world around me. Every time I asked a question, my mom would always tell me to "look it up." She directed me to look up information before the age of Google. That meant going to the library and reading a book or grabbing an encyclopedia or dictionary. Whether or not she realized it, she planted the seed for me to be a scholar and researcher. I am thankful that my parents did not try to silence me but allowed me to explore my inquiries. I often joke that I was always in the classroom, literally sitting in my mother's womb while she finished her degree at Fayetteville State University. Even from the womb, I never left the classroom. My parents are also my loudest cheerleaders. From the time I started graduate school until now, my parents have been always loving and supportive. I am sure they do not know why it took me so long to write my dissertation, get my doctorate, and write this book. But they still supported me each step of the way. I know I was not an easy child to raise, but they were always patient and understanding and showered me with unconditional love (even some tough love at times). I'm blessed to have parents who provide me with an emotional, financial, and spiritual safety net. I honestly have the best parents.

I thank my brother, Jay Canty, whose influence on this book was greater than I had originally anticipated. We are very different in the way we approach life and the world around us. But our differences helped this work. I needed someone with a different perspective to help me get to the heart of my work. My brother has always been very smart. He was never the type of person who had to read all night and write notecards to understand concepts. I used to envy how he was able to quickly compute information. I believe because he is so smart, he was able to provide me with the question(s) I needed for this book. I appreciate him for asking me those questions. I am sure he did not intend for the question to be so profound. I'm quite sure he does not even remember the questions he asked. But his questions guided this work. Even though he had no idea why I'd take a life of minimal wealth, he always supported my work. Thanks, big bro!

I acknowledge my grandma and 'em who supported me in this journey. I am blessed to be surrounded by many Southern Black women in my family. My Southernness is rooted in what they taught me. I thank my grandma Mary Ford, whose story as a Southern Black woman became the foundation for this work. She unapologetically lived her life her way. If I asked her about something she did or said, she would respond with: "Well yes, I did, baby!" With an eighth-grade education, she raised five children in Columbus, Ohio. Her strength and determination to give her children a better life will always be an inspiration to me. As she always tells me, "I *am* a Southern woman from a farm in Richmond, Virginia." Though she moved to Ohio, she always reminds us that she was still a Southern woman. Her authority to hold on to that identity is what inspires my work. I believe that spirit is within me as well, where I unapologetically live my life the way I want while maintaining my Southernness.

I am blessed to be surrounded by exceptional Southern Black aunties. Growing up, I laid at their feet, soaking up their wisdom and affirmations. My mother is the eldest daughter with two sisters, and my dad is the only male sibling with five sisters. My aunts paved the way for the next generation to do the work we do. They showed me what it meant to be an educated Black woman who never forgot their roots. My aunts were my role models. I wanted to be like them: educated, strong, spiritual, family-oriented, smart, sassy, witty, and grounded. They always reminded me of what it meant for a Southern Black woman to have joy, always laughing. They taught me what it meant to be a Black woman, while always nurturing and supporting me. Sometimes that support came in the form of a text: "When are you going to be done with that book?" or "I can't wait to read the book!" I knew I had to finish this book before my aunts thought I wasn't doing anything with my doctorate. I must thank all of them, individually and collectively, for being my support system. I thank them for always reiterating the lessons my dad and mother instilled in me. Thanks to all the aunties on my dad's side: Auntie Lena Richardson (the matriarch and boss), Auntie Janie Canty-Mitchell (the doctor of nursing and reverend), Auntie Esther Canty-Barnes (the advocate, lawyer, and voice of reason), Auntie Loretta Tann (the fashion diva and gardener), and Auntie Siclinda Canty-Elliot (the advocate, educator, and dancer). Thanks to all the aunts on my mom's side: Auntie Rita Hale (the enforcer who will keep it real) and Aunt Yolanda Ford (the comedian who always brings laughter and joy). I'm thankful that each one of them poured into my life and aided me in this journey. Because of the ways they all poured into me, I know that I can do anything.

"Remember to Breathe"

Now that I thanked the people in my intimate circle, I must thank those colleagues and mentors who have brought me to this point. First, I thank the infamous Dr. Stephanie Y. Evans, who has always pushed my work to the next level. She can see the greater vision that we cannot see as junior scholars. What I appreciate about Dr. Evans is that she does not keep that knowledge to herself; she willingly shares her experience and expertise with others. I know I was not the easiest graduate or junior faculty mentee to deal with, but she always grounds me and reminds me to breathe.

This book came to life while sitting in her office one day. I came to her in January 2020, venting to her about my frustrations. I did not know what I was going to do. I had a new research position at Virginia Commonwealth University, but as I told her, I had no idea what I wanted to do. She gave me space to vent, but only for a moment. Dr. Evans looked at me and simply said: "Looks like you need to be writing the book." I replied, "Oh no, I'm not ready to write a whole book." She asked me, "If you could write a book about Southern Black queer women, what would it be?" She followed that with, "What Southern element or dish reminds you of Southern Black queer women?" She did not even entertain my comment about not writing the book. She simply carried on as if to say, "You are writing the book." Even though I did not think I was ready to write the book, I remembered those notes I wrote on my laptop while teaching in Las Vegas. After some conversation sitting in her office, thinking of those notes, I said, "If I wrote a book, I'd call it *Snapping Beans*." That moment in her office saying the title out loud breathed life into this journey. I added more to my notes app on my phone, and the journey started. She saw the vision that I couldn't see, and I thank her for tending and fostering that vision. I thank her for always seeing my potential. More important, I'm thankful for her reminder: "Remember to breathe." While I was writing the book, her reminder to breathe always calmed my anxiety and helped me refocus. At times I feel overwhelmed I hear Dr. Evans reminding me to breathe.

"I Know You Are Here to Teach, But Do Not Forget that You Have Your Research to Do"

I have to give a special shout-out to my University of Nevada at Las Vegas (UNLV) Interdisciplinary, Gender, and Ethnic Studies family! Even though I was a Southern transplant, nervous about living so far away from my family and partner, they immediately embraced me as family. I felt seen, inspired, motivated, and affirmed as a colleague. Being in Las Vegas inspired this work (especially the ways my colleagues reminded me of my Southernness). Javon Johnson always kept it real with me. When we had coffee during my first week in Vegas, he reminded me to continue working on my research. Even though I was hired as a visiting professor and lecturer, he encouraged me to write. I remember him telling me: "I know you are here to teach, but do not forget that you have your research to do." He even gave me a formula that should have helped me write this book sooner. I realize now that that formula only works for him because he's a lyrical and writing genius. Even after I left, Javon made sure I was still working on my research and reviewed my book proposal for me. I appreciate him for seeing my potential as a researcher and looking out for my best interests as a scholar.

I thank Mark Padoongpatt, my Taiwanese brother, who was always available to provide me with writing mentorship and emotional support. I'm sure it was not a good idea to have our offices next to each other. If we were both in the office, everyone in our hall would hear us talk about all sorts of things (music of the 1990s and 2000s, Spice Adams, food, culture, and a little bit of academic discussions). I appreciate him inviting me into his home for authentic panang curry. Even to this day, I haven't had better curry. When I returned to Atlanta, he was also willing to support my work, reviewing my book proposal before submitting it. Mark is not only my colleague but a dear friend. He helped make Vegas home.

I thank Constancio Arnaldo for embracing me with open arms, providing words of affirmation, and allowing me to stay at his house when I visited Vegas for my faculty talk. At times I wondered whether my work had any value, and he would encourage me to keep going because someone needed to hear it. I'm grateful to Danielle Roth-Johnson, who was probably the only person outside of my dissertation committee who read my entire dissertation. She provided me with some great opportunities to further my research and challenged me to reconsider my work in new ways. She always greeted me with a hug and smile. I felt comfort in her presence.

Thanks to Mujer Fiera for being a constant support for me while I was in Vegas, reminding me to always show up as a queer faculty of color. Thank you for being a representation of the possibilities of what a queer faculty of color can do for their institution and students. When I was on the job market, getting several rejection letters, Mujer's affirmation to me was: "It is not that you aren't qualified. Sometimes you are overqualified. Sometimes it's more about the fit than your ability." Those words were kind and realistic. I appreciated that so much.

Erika Abad, thank you for being my sounding board. When I had questions about pedagogy or research, you were willing to listen and talk things out. We had talks about all things QTPOC. Erika made me a stronger professor and scholar! At UNLV my research and confidence came to light. Thank the department for being so great to me! Being with them in Las Vegas reminded me of who I am.

"You Have to Do the Work Your Way, in a Way That Is Meaningful to You"

After leaving UNLV, I found two families at Virginia Commonwealth University (VCU): the Department of Gender, Sexuality, and Women's Studies (GSWS) and the Institute for Inclusion, Inquiry, and Innovation (iCubed) program (namely, the Intersection of the Lives of LGBTQIA+ persons core). This unique position allowed me the opportunity to engage with community-based work with LGBTQIA+ organizations in the greater Richmond area. VCU was the first place I was treated as a researcher first and a professor second. Thanks to Aashir Nasim for providing space in the academy for junior faculty of color to connect their work to the communities they intend to serve. He took a chance on a fellow graduate of a historically black college and university (HBCU) to show the academy what we are capable of when provided the opportunity to fully work on our research. The time and resources from VCU and the iCubed program made this book possible. Because of iCubed, I received the support needed to fully dedicate my research on Southern Black queer lesbian persons.

The community partners that help with LGBTQIA+ populations in the greater Richmond area have also been an inspiration to me, as I learned more from community partners than I ever could in a classroom. Their work and sacrifice for LGBTQIA+ communities are invaluable and will always have a legacy in the Richmond community. The GSWS Department at VCU molded me into a true gender studies scholar/researcher. In previous departments, I was still considered a professor/lecturer. However, everyone in the GSWS Department nurtured me as a scholar and researcher. Coming in as a visiting scholar in 2019, I did not know what direction my work would go in. Once I decided to focus on this book, I received so much support from my colleagues in the GSWS Department. I want to thank my chairs, Kathy Ingram and Liz Canfield, who helped me with the resources needed to make the book possible. I knew I could email either one of them for some level of support and they would find a way to make it happen. I'm thankful for department chairs who not only say they support your work but show you how they support the work you do.

Several specific colleagues at VCU showed up for me as writing mentors during this process. I recall having several tough love sessions with Archana Pathak. She reminded me several times to get it together. If I needed a clear reality check, I knew Archana would be that person. I knew her reality checks came from a place of love, pushing me to reach for excellence. I loved that she always took a holistic approach to her mentorship, allowing me to incorporate my humanity into my research. She is ultimately the one who led me to take an autoethnographic approach to my research. I remember her telling me one day during one of our lunch meetings: "You have to do the work your way, in a way that is meaningful to you." Something in my mind and spirit aligned that day. At that moment I knew I had to do this work my way. Because of her, this manuscript is not simply an academic piece but a personal one. Because of Archana, I was able to connect with the infamous Kimberly Brown, whom I've always wanted to meet and work with. She invited me to her home and took me under her wing. What started as a mentorship transformed into a friendship that I truly cherish. She provided me with professional development tools and read my book proposal and email message. When I felt I didn't have a community in Richmond, she became that safe place for me. She saw me as a fellow Black woman and a human being, not just an academic colleague. She helped me make sense of the publication process. She was a model of what it meant to be a Black woman in higher education. I thank her for being a friend when I needed one the most.

I thank my fellow iCubed scholar cohorts, Maurice Gattis and Julian Kevon Glover, who were lifelines for me. It is an honor and privilege to be working alongside two amazing Black queer scholars. Both helped me become a stronger scholar. Thanks to Maurice for sending me a model book proposal. Based on his proposal, I knew what I needed to submit. Maurice also reminded me to "close my door and write." Julian provided a light for me, even in times when I did not believe in myself. Julian provided me with peace and joy. Not to mention that she is a brilliant scholar! With Maurice and Julian, I know we make an amazing team. I also thank Chris Cyn, who provided space to speak to students about my research methodology and encouraged me as I made progress with the writing. Chris has been instrumental in assisting me as I navigate the institution as a research junior faculty. Although she is no longer with us, Matilde ("Mati") Moros saw me as a whole person. She was my safe place. After I presented my work, she said, "Remember the spiritual element that can derive from snapping beans." That was Mati, reminding me not to forget the humanity of my work. Thanks to my sister colleague Dawn Johnson, who read the first chapter and provided me excellent feedback. She is my work bestie, the person I can genuinely talk to and bounce ideas off of. It makes sense that we quickly became so connected, as she is a fellow Virgo. After our first virtual coffee meeting, I knew I found another sister colleague and support network. She is a brilliant Black feminist scholar whose work is going to change the world! I am blessed to have her as a colleague and friend.

"I Taught You Everything You Need to Know"

I'll never forget the last thing Dr. Josephine Boyd Bradley told me the weekend before she passed away. While working on my dissertation, I reached out to her to discuss my potential theory. She remained quiet as I blabbed on about my work, not realizing she was in physical pain. At the end of my rant, she simply said, "I taught you everything you need to know." I responded, "Well yeah, but what do you think about the theory?" I laughed it off at the time, not realizing that those would be the last words of affirmation she would give me in her earthly existence. While I am grateful for all the spaces I have entered and all the people I have encountered on this journey, I must pay respect to the people and the institutions that molded me and taught me everything I know. They laid the foundation for me so that I may exist in the Ivory Tower with pride. It is not easy being a Black woman in higher education, and it's even harder being an openly Black queer woman. However, I recognize the ways my educational foundations at HBCUs provided me the fortitude to enter higher education, knowing that I have the tools and determination needed to succeed. The individuals at these institutions saw something in me I did not even see in myself. They nurtured my potential, giving me affirmation and a place for my talents to shine.

While attending North Carolina A&T State University (Aggie Pride!), I took classes with some spectacular Black political scientists: Dr. James Steele, Dr. Claude Barnes, Dr. Samuel Moseley, and Professor Derick Smith. While taking their classes, they saw something in me. They would call me "little Ms. Angela Davis." I was considered woke before *woke* was even a term. Even though I could be a little extra, with my afro and all, they took my passion seriously. While everyone was applying to law school, they encouraged me to apply to Clark Atlanta University for graduate school in the Africana Women's Studies program. I had no idea why they thought I would even want to go to graduate school, but when Dr. Barnes introduced me to Shelby Lewis, the creator of the Africana Women's Studies Department at Clark Atlanta, I knew I found an academic home. I thank Cathy Kea, who called me "Doctor Canty" before I even realized that wanted to attend graduate school. She manifested the future. Working with her changed my perspective on what was possible. Dr. Kea is a one-of-a-kind educational scholar who expects her students to be excellent. We wanted Dr. Kea to be proud of us, so we made sure we did our job well. She planted the seed of excellence that I continued after graduating from A&T.

During my enrollment at Clark Atlanta University, I had the honor and privilege to meet civil rights pioneer Dr. Josephine Boyd Bradley, who took me under her wing. She was small in stature but exemplified extraordinary strength and might. I distinctly recalled our first meeting, when she shared the book list for the semester. I asked, "This is all in one semester?" Her reply was simply: "Welcome to graduate school." I knew at that moment that this woman would change my life. After that, I did all that I could to gain as much knowledge from her. I laid at her feet. She taught me everything I knew from 2008 until her passing in 2015. I dedicate this work to her because she laid the foundation for me to write this book. She taught me about all the theoretical frameworks that guide my research, how to organize my research and write questions for interviews, and the importance of using oral history to uncover the lives of Black women. She reminded me that my research was never for self-serving purposes but to shed light on experiences that are often overlooked. As she told me, "Your work should never be about making yourself look better. If it is, you are doing the work for the wrong reason." While I was working on this book, her lessons remained in my heart and mind. I would often look at a picture of her, remembering all the words of wisdom she gave me. I think I wanted to hear her voice one last time, offering me practical research advice. Any time I had a question related to this book or uncovered a quote I had never considered including, I knew it was her guiding me from the ancestral side. There are times when a thought, phrase, or idea would come to me out of nowhere. I know that was Dr. Bradley asking me, "Did you consider this?" or "Did you think about that?" Although she is not here in the earthly form to make my work stronger, I know that she was with me as I wrote every word. Without her, there wouldn't be a Dr. Canty. That's why she deserved space in my acknowledgments and that is why this book is dedicated to her. I hope and pray that I've made her proud.

Two extraordinary men at Clark Atlanta contributed to what Dr. Bradley started. It is like she passed the baton to them to finish the job of helping me complete my dissertation and prepare me for the academy. Those men were Viktor Osinubi and Rico Chapman, both former program directors of the Humanities Ph.D. Program at Clark Atlanta University. When I first met Dr. Osinubi, we clicked right away. He helped me develop my dissertation into a document I could be proud of. While I'm sure he was not personally interested in anything related to Black queer lesbians, he helped me tailor my passion into a serious research project. He always told me, "You will be good, Jayme, don't you worry." He taught me how to integrate my work as part of a humanistic inquiry. I was often in his office, asking questions, probing for advice, or simply gossiping about the latest campus drama. He gave me the confidence to know I could work independently. I remember asking him one day why he does not direct me the same way he assists others in their dissertation process. I was frustrated because I thought he was too hard on me, making me figure too much on my own. He smiled and said, "You can do more than you think. I don't have to worry about you because I know you got it." Many times, I didn't feel that way. But as I was writing, I would remember: "You can do more than you think."

After Dr. Osinubi left, Dr. Rico Chapman arrived, a fellow HBCU graduate from Jackson State and Howard University. I never met another person who got all their degrees from HBCUs like me. I had no idea that Dr. Chapman, a relatively young man in the academy, would be such a lifeline for me. Dr. Chapman helped me make sense of the job market and the academy in general. Shout-out to Rico Chapman for the several letters of recommendation he sent on my behalf (which was no easy job because I applied to several institutions). He taught me the politics of higher education and the publishing process. Any time I would want to vent to him about all the stress I was encountering, he would calmly state, "Yeah, it's crazy. But this is what you do." I don't think I ever heard Dr. Chapman yell or raise his voice. My colleagues and I always joke about how he has the same tone, no matter what is happening. We would yell, cuss, and carry on while he calmly responded, "Yeah, I know." I know we drove him crazy, but he looked out for us. Dr. Chapman also introduced me to the realm of Africana digital humanities, sparking an idea for my next research project. He opened new research possibilities for us. Because of Dr. Chapman, I was equipped with all I needed to be successful in the Ivory Tower. I already miss our lunch and happy hour conversations, but I know he'll do great things as a dean at Jackson State.

I thankful to a special group of women, my sister colleagues, whose support provided me the energy to continue this journey. While my mentors provided guidance, my sister colleagues gave me the encouragement I needed when I thought this book would never see the light of day. I've known these women for years, through our master's and doctoral programs. No matter where we find ourselves inside or outside the academy, we create space for us to celebrate and affirm one another. Every Black woman in the academy needs a community of supporters as I have with my sister colleagues. Thank you to Drs. La'Neice Littleton (HistorianBae), Courtney Terry (the witty hip-hop extraordinaire), Joyce White (the calm English scholar), Michelle Meggs (the ratchet womanist philosopher and theologian), Ebony Perro (the raging English scholar), and Alicia Fontnette (the scholar-activist for the National Council for Black Studies). I also thank the future Drs. Donielle Pace (the famous spoken word artist) and Euphemia Shelton (the best Black Spanish scholar I know and my fellow crime show watcher), who I know will earn their degrees and transform their fields of study.

"What Do You Want People to Get from This Work?"

My editors were out of this world! I remember the first thing Keri Nash asked me after I shared my proposal and first chapter with her. She asked in her high-pitched Caribbean voice: "Now, Jayme, is the South first or last?" At that point, I knew that I had a lot of work to do. Keri would ask me questions that would stop me in my tracks:

"Why didn't you use this quote for silence?"

"So I need you to drop the mic, what would Pauli Murray say?"

"What do you want people to get from this work?"

"Where is your story in all this?"

"How is snapping beans a site and place of resistance?"

These questions had me rewriting and reshaping my work. Every time she asked a question, it made my writing stronger. It is a blessing to have an editor who is also a student of Black women's works. She knows what book to grab because it is usually on her bookcase. As she tells me when we are talking, "Yeah, I'm looking at this book now." Her edits, comments, and questions added the spit shine I needed to make my work better.

I thank Jordan Gonzales, another editor who assisted me in building my prospectus and read the entire manuscript three (maybe even four) times for edits and revisions. We often had to chat at random times because he lives in California. But he means it when he says he's the academic mechanic, as he did a lot of tuning and maintenance on my manuscript. Shout out to folks like Jordan who would do the tedious formatting, copyediting, and organization. Because we both liked politics, we chatted about more than the book. He started as a great editor and is now a great friend.

Many thanks to Makala Fields for the fantastic book cover! When we met for brunch one day, I knew I wanted my cover art to come from a Black artist who understood the complexities of the work. When I told her what the book was about, she sent me a mockup that was exactly what I wanted: a collage of complex images that convey so many messages. The collage was truly a replication of what this book is all about. Thank you so much.

The most important acknowledgment must be given to the manuscript interlocutors. I wish I could name all of them, but I must legally protect their anonymity. But they know who they are. They provided the meat for the book. I had a blueprint, but the interlocutors filled in blanks, gaps, and addressed questions I did not consider. They are all brilliant. In the academy, we often think we have all the answers to every question about our work. I was humble enough to admit that I did not know everything coming into this research journey. While I knew my story, I did not know if other stories were like mine. My interlocutors provided knowledge, teaching me so much. The only thing I had to do was report on what they said. As Dr. Bradley always told me, "If you want to know more about something, ask the persons who live that life." I'm so glad I followed that advice, letting the interlocutors guide the work. They told me what they wanted me to say. I thank them for trusting me to share the most vulnerable moments of their lives. I know it was not easy to talk about some of these realities and memories. But I am so very grateful for all thirty-nine conversations and the countless hours of tears, smiles, and laughter. I am truly honored for the opportunity to meet with all my interlocutors so that I may chronicle their stories, our story. We are family now, and nothing can change that.

If I forgot to mention anyone in this acknowledgment, charge it to my head and not my heart. While this acknowledgment was long, we have lost too many people that we never had a chance to publicly thank, so I am always intentional about letting my people know how grateful I am for them. As a Southern Black woman, I would be a disgrace to my Southernness to not thank my people. I am adamant about extending my gratitude.

Thanks to everyone who saw something in this awkward Southern Black queer lesbian girl who had a dream of writing a book and actually did it.

Description and List of Interlocutor Pseudonyms

In most qualitative research, human subjects are considered "participants," aligning with the vernacular of social science research establishing the role of investigator versus subject. For this particular work, I consider these human subjects "interlocutors" because these were people with whom I was in conversation with, not a one-sided interview. Unlike a formal interview where the researcher is gathering information and data, this discussion became an exchange of information between the interlocutor and me.

The interlocutors for this work were self-identified Black queer lesbian women and gender-nonconforming people living in or from the American South. While there were some variations in sexual identity (same gender loving, bisexual, femme attracting, or lesbian in public), 55 percent of interlocutors identified as lesbian, and 20 percent of the interlocutors identified as queer. In terms of gender identity, 80 percent of interlocutors identified themselves as woman or female, and 20 percent identified as gender nonconforming. To include those individuals who are gender nonconforming or gender nonbinary, I include "gender-nonconforming persons" in my description of this population. To clarify some additional generational demographics, these interlocutors were between the ages of twenty-four and fifty-six at the time of their participation. This demographic is significant to note because they may have harsher experiences with sexual and gender differences in the South due in part to the generations they represent. When talking to these interlocutors about their harsh relationships with the Church, family, and the Southern community, age and generation played pivotal roles in the trauma experienced.

In terms of location, interlocutors fit into three categories: (1) born and raised in the South and currently reside in the South; (2) born outside of the South but have lived in the South for at least ten years; or (3) born and raised in the South but currently live in another US region. The majority were originally from the American South (81 percent). More than half of them (57 percent) had never left the South, having multiple Southern residencies. These interlocutors were more likely to self-identify as Southern.

Individuals were interviewed anonymously for this manuscript. To add some life to the Black queer lesbian South, they either provided a pseudonym or I gave them one. Table 1 details these pseudonyms, where the interlocutor were born and/or raised, and where the interlocutor resided at the time of the interview.

Table 1. Interlocutors

Name	Original Location(s)	Location at Time of Interview
Allison Chase	Born in Decatur, GA; Lived in Texas, California, Tennessee, and Florida	Atlanta, GA
Andy	Born in Oklahoma; lived in Tuscaloosa, AL	Michigan
Angel	Born in Queens, NY; lived in East Orange, NJ, and Washington, DC	Port Royal, VA
Ari	Born and raised in Lincolnton, NC; lived in Greensboro and Cherryville, NC	Lincolnton, NC
Bree	Born and raised in Hampton, VA	Richmond, VA
Brooksley Smith	Born in Atlanta, GA; raised in Chattanooga, TN; lived in Washington, DC; Atlanta, GA; Charlotte, NC	Atlanta, GA
Byanca	Born and raised in Hartford, Vernon, and Rockville, CT; lived in Atlanta, GA	Smyrna, GA (suburb of Atlanta)
Bynta	Born and raised in New Orleans, LA; Washington state, Washington, DC, Georgia, and Oregon	Northern California
Cassie	Born and raised in Birmingham, AL; lived in Jacksonville, FL	Atlanta, GA
Cayce	Born and raised in Winona, MS; lived in Starkville and Columbus, MS, and Orlando, FL	Druid Hills, GA (suburb of Atlanta)

Name	Original Location(s)	Location at Time of Interview
Endesha	Born and raised in Macon, GA	Atlanta, GA
Fatima	Born in Pinebluff, AR, and raised in Youngstown, OH; lived in Atlanta, GA	Atlanta, GA
Jae	Born in Brunswick, GA, raised in Albany, GA; lived in Baton Rouge, LA	Atlanta, GA
Janessa	Born and raised in Atlanta, GA; lived in Baton Rouge, LA	New Orleans, LA
June	Born in Port Arthur, TX; lived in Austin, TX; Houston, TX; and Baton Rouge, LA	Atlanta, GA
Kea	Born in Sumter, SC; lived in Texas, North Carolina, and Washington	Orlando, FL
Kendra	Born and raised in Marietta, GA	Powder Springs, GA (suburb of Atlanta)
Kris	Born and raised in Lincolnton, NC; lived in Salisbury, NC, Charlotte, NC, Atlanta, GA, Decatur, GA	Atlanta, GA
LaDawn	Originally from La Grange, GA, and Greenville, GA; lived in Indiana and Portageville, MO	Boston, MA
Leah	Born and raised in Waterville, MN; lived in Hutchinson, KS; Simsbury, CT; and Minneapolis, MN	Smyrna, GA (suburb of Atlanta)
Leila	Born and raised in Lincolnton, NC	Lincolnton, NC
Maezah	Born in New Orleans, LA; lived in Huntsville, AL, and Charlotte, Fayetteville, and Raleigh, NC	Denver, CO
Makeda	Born and raised in Atlanta, GA; lived in Ohio, Arizona, Oregon, and Maryland	Atlanta, GA
Marie Dylan	Born in Bronx, NY; lived in Atlanta, GA, and Miami, FL	Atlanta, GA
Neile	Born and raised in Rome, GA; lived in Kennesaw, GA	Atlanta, GA

Name	Original Location(s)	Location at Time of Interview
Nyx	Born and raised in Pineville, GA; lived in Columbus, GA, California, and Washington state	Pineville, GA
Onika Rose	Born and raised in Atlanta, GA; lived in Stone Mountain, GA (Decatur), and Los Angeles, CA	Atlanta, GA
Paulette	Born in Dolton, AL; lived in Germany, Louisiana, Texas, South Carolina, and Georgia	Pineville, GA
Reign	Born in Columbia, MD; lived in Marietta and Kennesaw, GA	Atlanta, GA
Remi	Born and raised in Fayetteville, NC	New Orleans, LA
Shay	Born in Freeport, NY, with family roots in South Carolina; lived in Maryland and Washington, DC	Knoxville, TN
Star	Born in Arkansas; lived in West Palm Beach, FL, and Hinesville, GA	Atlanta, GA
Sunshine Honeysuckle	Born and raised in Birmingham, AL; lived in South Carolina, Wisconsin, Texas, Georgia, Colorado, Florida, and Michigan	Northern California
Sweet	Born in Minnesota; lived in Texas, Massachusetts, Maryland, and Minnesota	Los Angeles, CA
Tené	Born in northwest Florida; lived in Fayetteville, NC	Richmond, VA
Tisha	Born and raised in Nashville, TN	Smyrna, GA (suburb of Atlanta)
Toni	Born and raised in Dayton, OH; lived in Bowling Green, OH and Kennesaw, GA	Atlanta, GA
Torrey	Born in Bronx, NY; lived in West Chester, NY; family from Sumter, SC	Atlanta, GA
Vanessa	Born in Bronx, NY; lived in Maryland	Knoxville, TN

Preface

"Oh Yeah, You Southern":
Reflections from a Southern Black Queer Lesbian Woman

Growing up, I was often asked whether I was actually from the South because my accent was so subtle. When I told my fellow Southerners that I was from the South, they often responded with a look of confusion, followed by "That can't be, you don't sound Southern." I am ashamed to say that for a long time, I carried that with pride. I could have told my Southern brother or sister that my accent is there if they paid better attention. Perhaps I should have explained that my parents enrolled me in speech classes at a young age, and that they were hearing my trained speech. But I would not say any of that, instead just smile or laugh it off as a joke. Deep down, I was thankful that I did not sound Southern. I was afraid that sounding Southern would somehow make me appear less capable, intellectual, valuable, and most of all, visible. Foolishly, I often took advantage of sounding different, intentionally using my voice and speech to gain some level of respect (and perhaps exercise some level of superiority) among my Southern peers. I thought that minimizing my Southern accent and diction would allow me to blend into predominantly white spaces. I thought I was able to disconnect from my Southern identity and community.

However, coming out as a queer lesbian woman reunited me with my Southern self.[1] As Alice Walker's physical return to her grandma's garden helped her understand her scholarly work, I too returned to the South to ground me while I navigated my sexual identity. After some time away from my homeplace, I found that the South and my sexuality were inevitably linked. The American South, as a place and space, was the origin of my journey to queerness. The actualization of my lesbian and queer identity allowed me to eventually acknowledge, articulate, and embrace my Southernness. The South became an integral variable in my queerness, one that had little to do with whether I sounded Southern.

I am using two definitions to capture this Southernness. First, in his book *Sweet Tea: Black Gay Men of the South*, E. Patrick Johnson describes Southernness as a performance of "politeness, coded speech, religiosity" specific to the region.[2] I also use the term the same way, addressing the ways Southern folks use politeness and coded language taught to us by the Southern Christian Church and our families. Southernness represents a moral value system that starts with God and family and ends with eating good Southern food. Southernness is filled with religious doctrines, Southern hospitality, and a bit of passive aggression. We do not yell or honk in traffic. We smile and wave at our neighbors. We stop our cars and turn off our music when we see a funeral procession. We live life at a slower pace. We are not even that vulgar. We say phrases like "bless their heart," "carryin' on," or "finna/reckon to," all with double meanings.

Second, I use the term *Southernness* to show how the South becomes part of who we are, not just the manifestation of certain sensibilities but a mode of existence based on the ways the South socialized us and shaped our worldviews. I am conscious of how I embody the South through my language, mannerisms, and how I engage the world. It is integral to the way I show up in the world and relate to people. It helps me recognize the significance of tradition and community. I realized that my Southernness has nothing to do with whether I sound Southern, but how the South is essential to who I am and central to my ontological self.

Two experiences further brought my Southernness to the forefront of my consciousness and helped me identify the ways my Southernness is inevitably connected to my identity and queerness. In 2016, I presented my research at the Southeastern Women's Studies Association conference (now Women's, Gender, and Sexuality Studies South) at Winthrop University in Rock Hill, South Carolina. Since I am from the neighboring state of North Carolina, my immediate family decided to attend, along with my partner. We made an entire weekend out of the visit. During my session, my family came and sat on the first row. I spoke at many conferences about my preliminary research, but the idea of speaking about the experiences of Southern Black queer lesbian women in front of my family caused some anxiety for me. At this point, my family knew I was lesbian and had met my partner. But we did not speak about what that meant. We only spoke about the fact that I was not heterosexual. Pushing my nerves aside, I started to talk through my paper. I was critical of the South and its impact on Black queer women. I discussed heterosexism in the South, its relation to Black queer women, and why these multifaceted realities contributed to their health challenges. I used the South as an indirect variable in these findings. While this location influenced their experiences, it was not central to my preliminary research.

During the question and comment time, my brother raised his hand. I panicked and started to sweat. I felt my heart jump into my throat. I had no clue what he was going to ask me in front of a room full of academics. He asked a simple, yet profound question: "If these women feel so oppressed in the American South, then why do they stay?" To be honest, the question stumped me. Why *did* Southern Black queer women decide to stay in or move to the South? Given all of my data and findings, why would these women and gender-nonconforming persons decide to stay in the South? Why not relocate? Why haven't I relocated to another area of the United States or abroad? I responded: "Well, why would they leave a place that is essential to their identity?" I shocked myself with my response. While my preliminary research did not center on the South, I realized at that moment that speaking to *Southern* Black queer women for my research ultimately made the South central to my preliminary research work. My brother's question helped me recognize how the South intimately connected us to our Southernness regardless of our sexual and queer identities.

After that conference, I continued to ask myself myriad questions inspired by my brother's question. How could I minimize the impact of geographic location? How can the American South act as an oppressive and significant variable to queer actualization? How can one's location affect their identity formation? How can living as a Black queer lesbian woman in the American South help Southerners understand the American South more? How do I define the South? How do Southerners define the South? How does queerness play a role in one's Southernness? Because the population I researched mirrored my identity, I had to answer these questions for myself as well. These questions reconnected me to the significance of my own Southern identity. I cannot separate myself from the location that I was raised in, nor do I want to. My Southern roots made me who I am. After all, I knew I was Southern before I knew I was queer. Living in the South helped me understand my queer identity as much as it helped me understand my experiences as a Black woman. However, I was unclear on whether this narrative applied to other Southern Black queer women. This work intends to answer my brother's question, several years later, about the glue that connects Black queer lesbian women to the South and what cultural elements reaffirm our Southernness and queerness.

The second experience occurred after finishing my graduate degree, when I was offered my first full-time teaching position at an institution in Las Vegas, Nevada. While I was genuinely embraced by my department, I felt out of place in Las Vegas, and I could not pinpoint why. It was not until my first class that I realized how my Southernness was so distinct. Every semester starts with an introductory class where professors review the syllabus and class expectations for students. One student asked a question about the syllabus. To be honest, I cannot recall their question or concern, but my response was, "Oh, okay. Bless yo' heart." In my mind, I did not sound Southern. After all, I had learned to minimize my diction. But this student, recognizing the deep Southern vernacular, smiled and responded with, "Oh yeah, you Southern." I am unsure whether the student was trying to connect with me or insult me. Either way, they pinpointed my difference: my Southern Black identity. That moment in the classroom helped me see why I felt out of place in Las Vegas.

While I thought I was able to disassociate from my Southern self, at that moment I realized my embodiment of the South cannot (and should not) be denied. Being born and raised in the South would not allow me to fully dismiss how this location created me, socializing me to be who I am. No matter how many degrees I earned or how many white spaces I entered, the South still lives within me. Whether or not I wanted to embrace my Southernness, the South had a hold on me. During my time in Las Vegas, I finally saw myself as a *Southern* Black queer lesbian woman. Instead of feeling embarrassed by my Southernness, I was surprisingly brimming with pride.

Physically leaving the South for that short time helped me realize how my Southern identity played an important role in shaping my Blackness, womanhood, queerness, and lesbianism. From that revelation, this research was born. Formulating this work helped me gain a deeper understanding of what it means to be a Southern Black queer lesbian woman. Now when I think of my identity, the American South comes first. Southern Black. Southern Black woman. Southern lesbian. Southern queer. Southern Black queer lesbian woman. Being Southern is primary, the permanent backdrop of my racial, gender, and sexual identity. It is hard to visualize what it means to be a Black queer lesbian without the backdrop of the South. In this book, I tell the stories of women like me, stories of the racially and sexually marginalized living in or from the South. Living and existing in the South is not a monolithic experience, and it varies based on other identity markers. As the Black lesbian prophetess Audre Lorde states, we do not live single-issue lives; therefore, there is no single-issue Southern narrative.

The purpose of *Snapping Beans* is to chronicle the coming-out narratives of Southern Black queer lesbian women and gender-nonconforming persons by centering the South as a main character in this narrative. I uncover how the intersections of race, gender, gender fluidity, and sexuality create a distinct but polyphonic Southern narrative. This work paints a new Southern landscape that integrates stories of hurt, healing, and reconciliation. It serves as the Southern kitchen or front porch, documenting the process from regional trauma to wholeness and reconciliation rooted in a Southern practice. This work provides a trajectory of how the silent Southern Black queer lesbian girl snapping beans in her grandma's kitchen establishes a Black queer lesbian South for her to exist and thrive in. That Southern Black queer lesbian girl has a story about the South. This work adopts the practice of snapping beans with grandma and 'em as an opportunity to slow down and hear a new Southern narrative.

This work uncovers the silent South, the shameful and condemning South, the judgmental South (where we encounter what I call the Southern Black personality), the authentic and reconciled South, and ultimately the Black queer lesbian South filled with Southern Black queer lesbian personalities. All these vantage points of the South are rooted in the hurtful cultural realities of the South and integrates how Southern Black queer women and gender-nonconforming persons make sense of our Southernness. While Southern Black queer lesbian women and gender-nonconforming persons (SBQLWP[3]) encounter several institutions in the South, this work uncovers how the overarching realities of the Southern Christian Black Church (hereafter referred to as the Church) create this silent, shameful, condemning, and judgmental South. But the pain and trauma are not the end of our story. As we say in the Church: after the storm comes joy. We find wholeness in finding authenticity, liberation, and reconciliation. From this wholeness, we establish the Black queer lesbian South, a place and space SBQLWP find joy and reconcile with our Southern queer selves.

Snapping Beans challenges the one-dimensional Southern Black female narrative. In her groundbreaking text, *A Voice from the South*, Black feminist scholar Anna Julia Cooper expands this monolithic Southern Black identity to include how Southern Black women exist in racial spaces.[4] Cooper's work was a foundational piece that integrated discussions of race and gender, sharing the ways Southern Black women have a gender consciousness. Ultimately, Cooper provides a new vantage point of the South that is inclusive of Southern Black women. *Snapping Beans* extends this tradition by uncovering new perspectives of the South from the voices of SBQLWP. Like Cooper's *A Voice from the South*, this book confirms that SBQLWP exist in this Southern landscape and the ways we also have a gender and sexual consciousness within Southern Black spaces. Cooper opened the door for readers to redefine and reimagine what it means to be a Southern Black woman, uncovering how Southern Black women do not live single-issue lives. My work intentionally centers a new voice of the South, exposing the ways Southern Black women do not have a monolithic experience, but one that varies based on sexuality and gender identity. Similar to *A Voice from the South*, this book allows Southern folks to reimagine what it means to be a Southern Black woman from the voices of SBQLWP. Southerners are introduced to a distinct Southern vantage point that integrates gender, race, and sexuality. Including the voices of SBQLWP, Southerners can witness how the South has additional heteronormative dimensions that influence one's sexual and queer actualization.

This research employs an autoethnographic method, uncovering how the experiences heard by other SBQLWP mirror my own. In the academy, we are often guilty of trying to research a subject that is outside of our home to appear objective and, therefore, validate our research. Yet I find that many humanities scholars, specifically in gender and ethnic studies, often research a topic close to us to make sense of our experiences. We understand that the personal is political. Whatever personal challenges or questions that arise in our lives or communities often represent larger systems of oppression. How can we study those external factors without first making sense of what took place at home? Our spark for a subject or theory is often rooted in trying to find answers to problems or questions we have in our own lives. We are trying to make sense of our own experiences and connect to our communities. When I speak of SBQLWP, I am speaking on behalf of the community that I also represent and my position as a Black queer lesbian woman, born and raised in the American South, socialized by the Southern Christian Black Church. This work examines the "I" and "we" simultaneously as I chronicle our journey to actualization and reconciliation. By uncovering their stories of what it means for us to reach wholeness, I am also sharing my journey. I chronicle our collective narrative, piecing together and documenting the stories of hurt and joy that we have with the South.

Previous scholars who studied Southern Black queer women or queer persons used an ethnographic approach. Specifically, in E. Patrick Johnson's work *Southern. Black. Queer. Women*, he is conscious of his outsider position as a Southern Black gay man as he discusses the experiences of Southern Black queer women. He shares some identities with his interlocutors, namely, his Black queerness and Southernness, but there are gender and class positions that he does not share with them.[5] He recognizes his positionality in the work—as an outsider—and the perceived power dynamics of conducting oral history and ethnographic research. Johnson's ethnographic approach allows these stories to "stand as quotidian forms of theorizing."[6] I understand the significance of my position as a member of the Southern Black queer lesbian community. I am not an outsider reporting what is happening inside this community. Instead, I use an autoethnographic lens to document the lives of Black queer lesbian persons. Like my interlocutors, I sat in church while the Black male preacher spoke about what it meant to be a "suitable wife" and heard Southerners say, "hate the sin, love the sinner." This autoethnographic analysis allows me to validate the experiences of these interlocutors. These are not just my stories but also my interlocutor's narratives.

This autoethnographic lens provides a perspective that is intimate and personal. Qiana Cutts states how it is easier to discuss sensitive and taboo topics with someone who is part of that community.[7] In my conversations with interlocutors, certain vernacular used during our conversations did not need to be explained because I, too, am part of the community. SBQLWP informed me how they felt comfortable sharing with someone who is part of the community. At the end of each conversation, we felt rejuvenated to share our stories. I found that being a part of the community allowed for the stories to easily flow. My interlocutors and I shared our experiences through laughter and tears. We confided in one another and found commonality from our experiences. We spoke of our trials and triumphs like two Southern Black women talking on the front porch while snapping beans. These interlocutors trusted me—virtually a stranger—with intimate, personal moments in their lives. Using the autoethnographic approach authorized me to remove my position as an academic researcher, where my interlocutors and I became family.

I was surprised by the level of authenticity and vulnerability as they divulged how the South acts as a traumatic place as well as a space of healing. As we processed our thoughts, emotions, and concerns together, I recognized this mutuality of learning, where I learned from them as much as they learned from me. The mutuality provided a space of intimacy, where the stories organically flowed, and a relationship was built with little effort. After each conversation, I was filled with the narratives of hurt and healing. In their stories, I found my story. I uncovered our story, our collective narrative. This collective narrative does not suggest that we all experience our journey of pain and reconciliation the same way. This autoethnographic study exposes stories of hurt, trauma, and wholeness that we experience in the South. The Southern Christian Black Church became central to many of our narratives of pain and joy, which is why it is central to this book.

As I reflect on the narratives from SBQLWP, I also reflect on my own life. I heard my story as a Southern Black queer lesbian woman. I felt a sense of excitement and joy that I was able to hear myself through them. We have been silenced long enough. I was determined to provide a new Southern narrative and vantage point rarely found in public discourse. Ultimately, I wanted to see myself within the scholarship. I wanted to see stories like mine uncovered, deconstructed, and analyzed. This book chronicles a counternarrative about the American South. When I moved to Las Vegas, I reconnected with my Southernness and made it part of my future work. Now when I look back at my time in Vegas, feeling like an outsider, I can be proud of the fact that I never meant to fit in. I was supposed to stand out because the truth is, I am Southern. Even with all the perceived drama of the South related to difference, the South is a large part of who I am. After all, like that student told me, I am certainly Southern. The South anchors my race, gender, sexuality, and queer identity. These dimensions make up who I am. This journey of snapping beans is to discover what the South means for us as a place of both pain and comfort. While often rendered silent, SBQLWP have a chance to speak to the collective narrative of trauma and healing to help Southerners discover a new Southern geography often unheard. It is time to sit down on our Southern porches with our colander of green beans and listen to these stories.

I am a dawta of the South.[8] I left, but I always returned home to the sound of snapping beans. When I walk through the store or a farmers' market and see a bundle of green beans, I'm transported back to my Carolina roots, which fills me with memories of both pain and nostalgia. I hope this book helps all of us return home, to our Southern roots, where we negotiate with these complex Southern narratives. This work is my love letter and reflection of the South, full of accountability and vulnerability.

Introduction

"It Is a Part of Southern Life": Snapping Beans with SBQLWP Uncovers a Racialized Sexual Queer Geography

In the American South, the kitchen fed our bodies and souls, planting the seed for our Southernness. The kitchen acted as our first classroom, an intergenerational space for us to learn from grandma and 'em. We heard stories about our families, communities, and ancestors. Preparing food gave us a chance to bond with our families while acting as the medium for transmitting knowledge from one generation to the next. Similar to other methods of food preparation, snapping green beans (what Southern folks call snap beans) established dedicated time for granddaughters to sit with and learn from grandma and 'em as we prepared for an intimate family meal or family feast. Snapping green beans with grandma and 'em reconnect us to a Southern place and space, where we would engage in a Southern activity and hear grandma's narrative of the South.

As E. Patrick Johnson states, Southern Black queer folks are reared in the same country kitchens and on the same front porches as our heterosexual siblings, cousins, and extended family.[1] Black queer lesbians raised in the South, and even those who visited the South, are part of that Southern practice of snapping beans. We, too, are fixtures in these Southern kitchens and front porches. In those moments, we were not outsiders but integral parts of a process to feed our families. Discussions of snapping beans uncover this multifaceted Southern reality for SBQLWP. We always existed in grandma's kitchen, soaking up the same lessons as our heterosexual cousins. While we are snapping beans with grandma and 'em, we are snapping in silence, engaging in the Southern culture of silence, and hiding our truth. Discussions of snapping beans uncover the shame and condemnation rooted in the religiosity that permeates the South. The chore of snapping beans conjures up the trauma of being judged by the Southern Black community. Memories of snapping beans also became a space of acceptance and belonging, where the act of snapping beans reconnected us to a Southern practice that bypasses any level of difference. While snapping beans, we felt like we were a part of Southern life, culture, and community. In this communal practice, we have a chance to be Southern and reconnect our Southern roots. Snapping beans reminds us that the South provides a sense of nostalgia and peace while also reminding us of the trauma experienced in the region. This act affirms our regional identity, invoking narratives of affirmation and reclamation. Ultimately, we can take the lessons learned while snapping beans and apply them to our Black queer communities.

There were only a few moments that I recall snapping beans with my paternal grandmother. But the moments I did so, we were sitting on her screened-in back porch, which protected us from the bugs and other outside elements. She passed away before I officially came out as a queer lesbian woman, but I always felt like she would still embrace me and maybe even have me snap beans with her to talk about it. I believe she would use the snapping beans as an opportunity for me to feel safe and heard as a queer lesbian woman. That is what snapping beans is about for us Southern Black queer lesbian women—an opportunity to feel like we belonged in the South and our existence validated. While my paternal grandma was a church-going woman, heavily involved in our family church in Sumter, South Carolina, her love for her family surpassed any form of phobia. She had a way of validating her daughters and granddaughters while also making sure we kept God and family first in our lives. She encouraged all of us to be independent, whether through thought or action. She encouraged us to pave our path. I believe that would have been true even in terms of one's sexuality.

While I conceptualized snapping beans in a theoretical way, I asked interlocutors to recall their memories and experiences of snapping beans. The practice became the entryway to discuss the South and all its complexities. Snapping beans may seem like a simple chore, but it consists of so much more for us: the actual growing and picking of the green bean, cooking the green bean, and canning the green bean. These responses prove that snapping beans was a systemic process, including practices before and after the beans were snapped. Additional discussions focused on the ways snapping beans established a significant racial and gendered practice of trust, intimacy, and vulnerability. Through this process, I recognized how snapping beans has always acted as an oral history method to capture the experiences of Southern Black women and SBQLWP. With that in mind, the practice of snapping beans relates to SBQLWP in three ways. The activity of snapping green beans (1) reconnects us to the South itself, (2) uncovers the significance of establishing a safe space for us to connect with other Southern Black women, and (3) represents a qualitative method of collecting oral narratives from SBQLWP.

Snapping Beans Reconnects SBQLWP to the South

Snapping beans is as simple as it is intricate. It helps us understand the complex backdrop of the South. Discussions of snapping beans became an entry point to discuss the South and lead to conversations about how SBQLWP define the South. Even if the interlocutor did not snap beans or have memories of doing so, they agreed that the practice represented the various dimensions of Southern life. The act of snapping beans is wrapped up in the fabric of the South, representing a Southern way of living. As Maezah mentioned, it is part of life in the South. The green bean itself is more than a vegetable in the South. It connects to the agriculture and rurality of the South and represents a sense of belonging for Southern Black persons. Ultimately, it connects us to the root of who we are, reminding us of a historical and cultural continuum that exists in this region. Snapping beans cultivates Southern identity and exemplifies the best of Southern life. It returns us to our Southern selves and reminds us of Southern life.

Snapping beans is part of a Southern practice and tradition that no one truly questions as Southern. It becomes part of a Southern tradition that connects everyone to the South, regardless of race, gender, class, or sexuality. No matter whom I spoke to about snapping beans, persons in or from the South would tell me stories of the times they snapped, cooked, and stored green beans with a maternal figure. Memories of snapping beans brings up fond memories of the South that extend beyond the narrative of hurt and trauma based on difference. In typical conversations with Southern Black folks about the South, there are usually narratives of slavery, lynching, Jim and Jane Crow, and other methods of dehumanization exclusive to the South. But snapping beans transforms us into a Southern space that connects us to a Southern life that is not connected to that regional racialized trauma. The memories of snapping beans reconnect us to our Southern identities and connect Southern folks to a sense of homeplace and belonging, regardless of difference.

One of the liveliest conversations I had was with Cassie, an interlocutor from Birmingham, Alabama. While all the conversations with my interlocutors were powerful, Cassie kept me laughing. She had the charm and wit of a Southern Black woman, with a strong Southern accent that made all her words pour slow and steady like honey. Although she did not recall snapping beans with anyone, she recognized it as a unique Southern cultural practice. As Cassie stated during our conversation, "I don't hear folks up North talkin' about snapping beans!" Whether or not interlocutors participated in the activity of snapping beans, it is the consensus that snapping green beans and the method of cooking the beans are uniquely Southern. While green beans are not distinct to the South, we cultivate and cook them differently. In other American regions, green beans may be microwaved or sautéed, but Southern folks incorporate additional steps to make green beans a savory side dish with variations of pork and chicken stock that creates a stew-like flavoring that espouses comfort. And it tastes amazing with homemade skillet cornbread.

SBQLWP agree that snapping beans neither starts nor ends at the colander of green beans. Cooking or preparing any meal in the South consists of a process that occurs well before they get in the bowl and long after they have been snapped, beginning with the growth of the green bean and ending with them either canned, frozen, or cooked. Similar to making homemade biscuits or pound cake, there are lengthy steps to snapping beans. Even though SBQLWP mentioned picking the green bean or knowing where to find it, a process precedes the picking of the bean. Many stories of snapping beans transport us to the rural South. Sticking true to Southern tradition, the process of snapping green beans includes a brief discussion of how the green beans are grown. Green beans (or snap beans) can grow from a bush or a pole that has longer, more mature beans with a vine in the middle that comes out at the top. SBQLWP discussed picking green beans from both a pole and a bush. Pole green beans "climb" as they grow, becoming a vine and requiring support in the form of a wooden pole. Pole beans require more attention and maintenance than bush beans. Pole beans should be set up either by trellises or cattle panels to allow the beans to climb as they grow,[2] which provides stability, making the beans easier to pick. In contrast, bush green beans are more compact, grow closer to the ground, and do not require support. Unlike other pole beans such as navy bean, pinto, or kidney beans, green beans continue producing even after picking them. Farmers would encourage people to remove the green bean once it has matured to allow other beans to grow. Once the bean is removed, that stem creates the energy to produce more pods.[3] This vine is the part that connects the bean to the host pole or bush from which it grew.

The practice of snapping beans reminded SBQLWP of a rural Southern landscape attached to our families and communities. Cayce discussed a family friend who had a garden where they would pick the green beans. Angel's father grew green beans in Port Royal, Virginia. Later in her life when she moved to this rural Virginia town to take care of her elderly family, she mentioned how her grandfather had a farm in Maryland where they would pick the green beans to prepare to cook or store for future use. Janessa connected the snapping of green beans to her grandmother's community in rural Georgia. She traced the growing of green beans to her grandmother's garden in Meriweather, Georgia, where they grew on a bush in her yard. While she grew up in Atlanta, Georgia, an urban Southern location, she recalled memories of her grandmother also getting green beans from her uncle's farm in Monticello, Georgia, about fifty miles southeast of Atlanta. She mentioned how her family in Atlanta got many of their vegetables from the family farmland in Monticello. Alice Walker would be pleased to hear of how these interlocutors connected snapping beans—and their Southern identities—to their family's garden.

Subsequently, there is a process of how a person snaps the green bean. When snapping beans, we are removing a vine that connects the bean to the pole or bush and snapping the beans in half for faster cooking. The name "snap beans" was derived from the snap sound the bean makes when removing the tip and snapping it in half. The strength and maturity of the green bean is determined by the distinctiveness of the snap. The snap typically indicates the freshness of the bean—I know I have a fresh, strong bean based on how loud the snap is. The rhythm of snapping the green beans becomes a spiritual meditation. We let the snap of the beans speak to us. Once snapped, the beans are cooked in a stew-like side dish with certain essential ingredients, such as chicken stock, pork, and onions. Southern Black folks know that green beans must have some meat to be a legitimate side dish. Pork adds flavor to the green beans, whether it is in the form of ham hocks, bacon, fatback, ham bone, or streak o' lean.[4] The addition of meat to green beans has deep historical significance, stemming from the scarce access Blacks had to certain parts of meat during enslavement. Because of the legacy of enslavement, we learned how to create beauty from the scraps. We always created so much out of a little.

Perhaps the most shocking part of my conversation with interlocutors was discussing the process of canning and storing green beans. I remember pressing more about it when Angel mentioned it. While visiting her father's family in Port Royal, Virginia, during the summer, she recalled the process of canning beans outside. After that conversation, I made sure to ask interlocutors about the canning process. Cayce mentioned the process of storing the green beans after cooking them, whether freezing them in a freezer bag or canning them for future use. Sunshine discussed canning the beans with smoked pork to maintain the flavor. The salt from the pork also functions as a natural preservative. My mouth watered just thinking of that. When I originally envisioned the notion of snapping beans as a project, I limited it to the process of growing and snapping the bean for the purposes of cooking only. I did not consider the methods for preserving the green bean. But when interlocutors mentioned it, I realized that finding methods of storing or canning vegetables is essential to Southern life and needs to be discussed in the context of snapping green beans.

In discussions of snapping beans, SBQLWP brought up the complexities of defining the South, uncovering the ways snapping beans connect us to both a rural and urban South. Memories of snapping beans helps us diversify the Southern landscape. It introduces a multifaceted Southern landscape and identity that sits within this juxtaposition of an rural and urban South. Many SBQLWP discussed their connection to snapping beans as part of their realities when visiting rural Southern areas. SBQLWP who knew about snapping beans would speak of it in the context of rural or agricultural spaces. In visiting these rural Southern spaces, we learn that our Southern identity has both urban and rural components. Southern Black folks in urban areas or towns would return to rural spaces as a reminder of our Southern and Southern Black roots. Thinking of this project, I was transported to the rural landscape of South Carolina, where life was slower than where my family lived. But my understanding of the South was shaped by both these landscapes. Snapping beans connects us to a racialized rurality that may get lost in Southern metropolitan spaces. Snapping beans uncovers our complex Southern and Southern Black identities that are not limited to a single landscape. SBQLWP made it clear that the green bean connects us to our multifaceted identities and homeplace.

As some explained, snapping beans was what "country folks" did. Some SBQLWP referred to themselves as "city girls," which seems like the opposite of what is considered Southern. This statement of perceived Southern rurality, interlocutors made it clear that the South represents myriad landscapes outside of what is considered rural or "country." This discussion reminds others, namely those who do not live in the South, that the South is more than a landscape of rurality and backwardness. These comments align with Christopher Stapel's concept of "metropolitan imaginaries,"[5] where we often juxtapose a seemingly normal landscape based on the presence of urbanization and modernization as "normal," while the rural spaces are considered "backward." This perceived backwardness exists in the cultural norms and the method of economic production. Geographic locations are considered normal based on how close they are to a modernized, urban society. In this case, urban spaces are equated to industrialization and thought of as a better location to live than rural, agricultural societies. In our discussion of snapping beans, SBQLWP reiterate metropolitan imaginaries, exposing the South as a multidimensional place and space. They contend that the South is more than just a landscape of backwardness and rurality. Discussions of snapping beans dispelled the myth that rurality is representative of all Southern life.

This comment about snapping beans being a "country thing" makes it clear that the South represents both urban and rural spaces. Metrocentrism dispels the myth that the South is a monolith. In the discussion of snapping beans, SBQLWP uncover how the South is a complex space outside of rurality. The SBQLWP I spoke to also made sure I understood that simply because they were Southern did not mean they were "backward." After all, there are rural, agricultural, country areas throughout America. The South does not necessarily have a monopoly on rurality. However, based on this metropolitan imagination, the South is typically perceived as synonymous with rurality and backwardness, disregarding the fact that the region has several urban spaces. SBQLWP spoke of an urban South, such as Atlanta, Georgia; Richmond, Virginia; Orlando, Florida; Charlotte, North Carolina; Baton Rouge, Louisiana; and New Orleans, Louisiana. These urban spaces are uniquely situated in the South and provide distinctive affirming spaces for Southern Black queer folks. There is a level of freedom provided to us in these urban spaces. SBQLWP dispelled this metropolitan imagination that the South is backward, sharing that the South contains queer and Black queer-affirming spaces. This does not mean that SBQLWP do not bring this practice into their Southern urban spaces or that they no longer snap beans once they leave the South. I know I still snap beans in my Southern urban location. Snapping beans reminds us of the multifaced landscape that encompasses the South.

Snapping Beans Creates a Safe Space for SBQLWP

During my conversations with interlocutors, I would ask where they would snap green beans in the house. SBQLWP mentioned snapping beans in the kitchen, porch (front and back porches), carports, and living rooms. Endesha mentioned how the women sat in a semi-circle, snapping beans in the carport. All of these spaces are intimate for Southern Black women, away from the watchful eyes of others. While not luxurious (Endesha mentions with the hot carport), these locations are private, culturally designated for Southern Black women. These physical spaces in the Southern home offer intimacy—and therefore a sense of vulnerability—for Southern Black women. Yet this memory of safety becomes complex for SBQLWP. In the context of our race and gender, these spaces provided the freedom for us to be our authentic selves. There was a racialized safety, where we were safe as Southern Black women. Although these spaces were not perceived as queer affirming, SBQLWP were introduced to the importance of establishing safe spaces in the South. When actualizing our queer lesbian identities, we attempt to emulate this model of safety in the South.

The practice of snapping beans represents this feminine power disguised in a seemingly mundane chore. Snapping beans represent a feminine, spiritual Southern practice for Southern Black women, creating a safe space for vulnerability and intimacy. We often connect intimacy in the context of romantic relationships. But for Southern Black women, it is more than that. Intimacy is a vulnerability in practice. Our first lessons of intimacy took place with grandma and 'em. The act of snapping beans establishes this intimacy with other women. Even if done in silence, this practice establishes a safe space to be vulnerable. Intimacy is not always derived from vulnerability in conversation but also from moments of stillness and quiet, an opportunity for reflection and pause. Janessa recalls the silence as a form of this intimacy. She remembered snapping beans on her grandma's porch, with no music or talking, simply the sound of street noise and the beans snapping. Even though no conversation took place, the intimacy with her grandma on that porch still resonates with her. When Southern Black women gathered to complete the chore of snapping beans, there is a feminine communal power that is intergenerational and shifts our consciousness. The activity of snapping beans ignites this power when Southern Black women congregate over a bowl of green beans. Southern Black women create that space to share their stories and opinions, establishing this trust circle and feminine communal power. This vulnerability shows a level of trust we have with other Southern Black women. SBQLWP incorporate this reality when we actualize and conceptualize our sexualities in the South. SBQLWP adopt the trust and feminine communal power gained while snapping beans to create safe spaces for us to articulate our stories of harm and reconciliation.

The act of snapping beans introduced SBQLWP to a safe space where we can be intimate, articulate, and actualize our queer lesbian identities.

These moments snapping beans gave SBQLWP our first lesson of authenticity. Because snapping beans is a slow, time-consuming process, we hear church and neighborhood gossip, family secrets, and other personal accounts from our maternal figures. Some discussions are trivial, but they expose how our maternal figures conceptualized the world around them. In this space, grandma and 'em were free to express themselves, we witnessed them share their authentic selves. SBQLWP desire to go back to this authentic Southern space, where we felt safe, even if we were silent about our sexual identities. Creating and establishing a safe, authentic space is significant for SBQLWP. For us, coming out as queer is an exercise of authenticity that we recognized as significant during our snapping beans sessions with grandma and 'em. Existing in spaces where our presence is not considered a problem, the process of building and maintaining safe, authentic spaces ensure the protection of queer persons. In some cases, having these safe spaces to be authentic is the difference between life and death. Snapping beans with grandma and 'em introduced us to the potential of creating these safe authentic spaces for SBQLWP to be intimate and vulnerable and a chance for us to share our lives and exist. Whether grandma and 'em realized it or not, they were ultimately engaged in the Black feminist and womanist practice of life sharing and the vernacular.

Black feminist and womanist scholars recognize the importance of sharing intimate stories about our lives as the epitome of identity politics, the idea that the personal was deeply and undeniably political. They highlight that their intersectional identities—namely, being Black and woman—fueled their desire to place these personal experiences into public discord. Snapping beans is connected to the identity politics of Southern Black women, fitting in the context of the Combahee River Collective process of "life sharing,"[6] and Layli Phillips's notion of the "vernacular."[7] These Black feminist and womanist frameworks describe what happens when Southern Black women and SBQLWP are snapping beans. Both life sharing and the vernacular were intended to represent one's identity consciousness and reveal larger systems of oppression that affect their daily lives. Discussions of snapping beans with grandma and 'em transport us to moments of life sharing and engaging in the vernacular, discovering how their daily lives uncover the patriarchy, sexism, and heterosexism in the South. Sharing these seemingly personal, daily experiences while snapping beans represents a Black feminist and womanist process.

The Combahee River Collective (CRC) theory of life sharing is the epitome of Black women's identity politics, a conscious-building exercise introduced by Black lesbian socialist women. The CRC's life-sharing practice integrates a consciousness-raising activity rooted in the seemingly personal life experiences of Black women: "In the process of consciousness-raising, actually life sharing, we began to recognize the commonality of our experiences, and, from the sharing and growing consciousness, to build a politics that will change our lives and inevitably end our oppression."[8] In sharing these experiences, Black women found themselves in the stories of others. While they had these experiences dealing with interlocking systems of oppressions, they claimed they had "no way of conceptualizing what was so apparent to us, what we knew was really happening."[9] They recognized the significance of Black women sharing their experiences with sexual, racial, and gender marginalization to raise individual and collective consciousness and uncover how these experiences represent racial, gender, class, and sexual oppressive realities. The practice of snapping beans engages in what the CRC defines as life sharing and, in turn, a level of consciousness raising for SBQLWP. In addition, this life sharing aided us in gaining a deeper understanding of what it means to be a Black queer lesbian in the South. The processes of life sharing and consciousness raising were ultimately at work during my conversations with interlocutors, we were metaphorically snapping beans together.

Phillips uses several tenets in defining womanism, which she identifies as the "everyday—everyday people and everyday life."[10] She discusses how the soul of womanism focuses on the masses and the betterment of all humanity. In this context, she contends that this relates to the "unifying reality that all people have 'everyday' lives and that elite status is something that cloaks this reality more than supplants it."[11] Incorporating the vernacular was an essential component to womanism because it evaluates the seemingly personal experiences of the layperson, regardless of education or societal status. It focuses less on a consciousness-raising effort of the elite and formally educated and unveils the daily struggles of the masses. In the vernacular, we center the experiences of grandma and 'em, who may not have the academic or professional vernacular, but understand how systemic oppressions affect their lives. The vernacular of the masses may sound like the Southern grandma with a fourth-grade education or the Southern Black auntie who could not attend college. The language may be grammatically broken with a thick Southern drawl. They may not have had the educational language to articulate their experiences, but they are able to speak about their racial and gendered experiences with the South in the Southern vernacular of the masses.

The process of life sharing and adopting a vernacular framing is not just a personal experience shared while snapping beans but a chance to create a safe space for SBQLWP. Life sharing and vernacular allow SBQLWP the opportunity to name the significance of these personal experiences. Interlocutors in this work spoke of their lives, in a vernacular of the masses, to address this intraracial conflict, where their daily experiences shed light on the tension that exists between themselves and Southern Black heterosexual persons. The act of snapping beans helps us make sense of and articulate our Southern experiences.

Snapping Beans Establishes an Oral History Method and an African/Black Feminist Epistemology

Initially, when thinking of the method I would use to capture these stories, I entertained the idea of actually sitting down and snapping beans with interlocutors. However, during the time I planned to interview interlocutors, the realities of COVID-19 suddenly halted all human interactions. The pandemic hindered me from physically snapping beans with interlocutors. But when I started talking about snapping beans with interlocutors, our conversations acted as that communal moment. I was able to retrieve oral histories from them. We were engaging in the same practice of transmitting and obtaining oral histories without the actual bowl of green beans to snap. With that in mind, I realized that the act of snapping beans became a qualitative research method to gain oral narratives from Southern individuals. Snapping beans is a Southern qualitative method because the practice is essential for transmitting oral histories. Southerners know that when green beans are being snapped, oral histories are being shared. Discussions of snapping beans often triggered vulnerable and intimate conversations, providing authentic oral histories. Using this method does not require real green beans but an opportunity to obtain oral histories using memories of a Southern practice. With that in mind, this method does require interlocutors to connect to a specific place and space. After all, these narratives are provided while metaphorically snapping beans, a deeply Southern practice. Snapping beans became a research method to expose the lived experiences of SBQLWP.

Grandma and 'em could have easily trimmed the green beans with a knife. But grabbing the basket and sitting at the kitchen table or back porch provides an opportunity to transmit knowledge to the next generation. This transmission of knowledge acts as a Southern Black epistemology, where Southern persons learn lessons of resistance and resilience. In this epistemology, we gain ways of knowing of how to navigate in the South. The process of snapping beans is a chance for us to gain an understanding of how grandma and 'em fought against the intersectional oppressions they experienced in the South. From these oral narratives, SBQLWP also obtain methods of resilience that they can employ as they find ways to exist and thrive in the South. These lessons provided SBQLWP the methods and lessons of resistance to combat sexism, heterosexism, and homophobia in the South. SBQLWP learned how the oral narratives of resistance from grandma and 'em laid the foundation for us to find ways to exist and thrive in what we would later call the Black queer lesbian South.

With that in mind, the process of snapping beans establishes that learning space where we learn about oppressions in the South as well as methods of resistance and resilience our maternal figures used. SBQLWP take these lessons as we negotiate our queer and lesbian actuality. For many of us, these oral narratives provided the footprint for how to exist and even thrive in a contentious region. We gain lessons about resilience and the importance of establishing a community. The act of snapping beans helped me appreciate the lessons from my maternal figures. I assumed that appreciation came from growing older, but it was a result of actualizing my queer lesbian identity. While snapping beans, these maternal figures used this Southern Black epistemology to teach resilience and strength. While they may not have provided lessons on how to survive as a Southern Black queer lesbian woman, their oral histories allowed the opportunity for us to find methods of resistance and resilience that can be applied as we actualize our queerness in the South. If my fraternal grandma can raise six children in the rural, segregated South, then surely I can survive as a Black queer lesbian woman in the South. I could adopt the lessons of resilience from my maternal grandma, who found a way to raise five children after leaving an abusive, alcoholic husband. The oral narratives from my maternal figures taught me lessons of authenticity, tenacity, and fortitude that helped me actualize my queerness in the South. While grandma and 'em may not be able to provide much information about how to navigate sexual differences in the South, snapping beans creates an opportunity for transmitting knowledge of resistance and liberation. The oral tradition of passing down information about resilience and resistance for future generations is essential to our survival.

In this context, snapping beans and the oral history method that exist in this Southern kitchen represent what Patricia Hill Collins calls the African/Black feminist epistemology. Because Black women exist within a racial and gender standpoint, they have a unique epistemological standard that reflects their African/Black selves and their gender identities. One of these practices of the African/Black feminist epistemology includes wisdom from maternal figures, who are viewed as epistemological agents, not simply persons with anecdotal information. African/Black feminist epistemology understands the ways that oral transmission of knowledge has epistemological value. This epistemology relies on lived experiences and acts as a criterion of meaning, the use of dialogue, the ethic of personal accountability, and the ethic of care.[12] These elements are employed while snapping beans. When snapping beans with grandma and 'em, we are engaging in dialogue, establishing community through accountability and care. Ultimately, this dialogue has epistemological elements that SBQLWP employ as we navigate our lives.

Snapping beans represent a practice of knowledge formation rooted in the experiences of Southern Black women. It reiterates the ways Southern Black women act as epistemological agents, a manifestation of an African/Black feminist epistemology. Epistemology is traditionally viewed as the process of creating and disseminating new knowledge. The Afrocentric approach places the history of African persons throughout the diaspora at the center of analysis. The feminist approach places women/gender construction at the center of all analysis. In this context, Southern Black women are those knowledge creators, as they center both a diasporic/Black and gender perspective to their understanding of Southern life. As Collins discussed, this knowledge from grandma and 'em is frequently taken for granted, often dismissed as solely anecdotal with no real foundation in epistemological practices. In traditional academic epistemology, what Collins notes as the Eurocentric knowledge validation process, knowledge must be evaluated by a group of subjective experts and must have some level of academic credibility to be epistemological agents. In the South, however, Southerners know that grandma's wisdom is knowledge. Southern Black women do not disregard those small moments with grandma and 'em in the kitchen, on the back porch, or in family communal spaces because these individuals shift our lives somehow, even in subtle ways. For Southern Black women, the kitchen and snapping beans is a Black feminist epistemological space. Snapping beans establishes this epistemology and a Southern gender politic used to transmit knowledge to Southern Black women and SBQLWP.

According to Collins, this African/Black feminist epistemology makes Black women agents of knowledge formation through truth telling. She notes, "The existence of a self-defined Black women's standpoint using Black feminist epistemology calls into question the content of what currently passes as truth and simultaneously challenges the process of arriving at that truth."[13] This truth telling is a representation of this Black feminist epistemology. Snapping beans uses this African/Black feminist epistemology to engage in truth telling. This truth telling does not mean that grandma and 'em were always telling us the truth, but she questioned what is considered truth. Although we may have not considered the gossip while snapping beans to be a process of inquiry, grandma and 'em questioned the validity of certain statements, questions, and realities in their worlds. They may ask, "How do we know . . ." or "What makes you think . . ." as an opportunity to arrive at some level of truth and challenge traditional assumptions. Ironically, that is what queerness is all about. While queerness represents the embodiment of gender and sexual fluidity, it also challenges individuals to question the world around them. Snapping beans was an opportunity for grandma and 'em to question Southern life. This process of inquiry laid the foundation for Southern Black queerness that we carry with us as we reconcile with our truths. Even when coming out, SBQLWP do not use the terminology "coming out" but say phrases such as "I'm living in my truth," or "Standing in my truth." Snapping beans was an opportunity for grandma and 'em to both prepare a meal and speak their truth. SBQLWP carry on this tradition as we actualize our queer identities. We continue the practice of speaking our truth, applying it to our queer lesbian selves.

While SBQLWP recollect snapping beans, we see a process of sharing intimate stories and witness the power of vulnerability. This intimacy allows for us to be vulnerable in sharing experiences often hidden and untold. The goal of snapping beans is to break that silence like we break that bean. This vulnerability from SBQLWP allows other Southerners to have a better understanding of the South. Each snap of a bean invokes a memory of hurt and a shift in consciousness. Each snap provides additional context to the Church hurt. Each snap unlocks another level of vulnerability, uncovering a new Southern narrative. By the time we get to the end of the basket of beans, we learn more about the South as a sociocultural space and discover a new geography rooted in racialized, sexual, and queer realities. In employing the African/Black feminist epistemology, we gain a new truth. This is why we snap beans—to uncover our experiences in this racialized sexual queer geography.

Uncovering Southern Complexities and a Racialized Sexual Queer Geography

When discussing the role that the South plays in our lives, several questions arise about how I conceptualize the South. At the beginning of this research work, I made certain assumptions when defining the American South. Originally, I rigidly defined the American South in conjunction with the US Census.[14] While I attempted to give a basic definition of the American South based on parameters from US Census data, I recognized that defining the region has some intricate components. What is considered Southern has some distinct social, economic, and political realities. Over time, I learned to narrow down what "South" I was referring to in this work. Reta Ugena Whitlock deconstructs the South as a complex space of identity formation that cannot be explained by census data alone: "The South is a place with multiple, variable, and interlocking stratifications. It is a site where race, class, gender, religion, and sexuality interact continually and comprehensively, having implications that play out in a range of public arenas—politics, media, organized religion, social activism, and arts."[15] This discussion fits in a body of literature that focuses on the South as a sociocultural space.

Making Southern and South a proper noun signifies a certain type of American experience related to a specific cultural reality. Unlike phrases like the "US South," the "American South" represents a specific cultural geographic experience that fits in the context of what we broadly define as American. The US South is political, referring to a restrictive boundary, established and reinforced by enslavement, the American Civil War, political representation, and methods of economic production. Shifting from the US South to the American South compels Southern scholars to rethink the sociocultural context in defining the location. Defining the South as a cultural space is timeless and not restricted by rigid geographic boundaries. Including "America" helps Southern scholars and researchers alike reconsider what it means to be American and who has the authority to dictate what is—and what is not—American. Although framing the American South as a sociocultural discussion can be subjective—rooted in the individual experiences that people have in the region—it is also defined by what individuals consider American and how the South differs from and aligns with their version of America. The American South is framed in the context to which Southerners reconcile with our version(s) of America, which, according to James T. Sears, is a defined history and culture.[16] Or, as W. Fitzhugh Brundage articulates, this memory and history provide Southern folks, regardless of race and gender, a sense of self and articulation for the region they call home.[17] For Sears and Brundage, the American South contains several complex histories that influences the region's social and cultural realities. This perspective also dictates how Southerners conceptualize their versions of America.

In addition, Southern history becomes "woven into Southern life and institutions."[18] Even in a sociocultural context, the South represents *several* histories, cultures, cuisines, and moralities related to what is American while uncovering the sociocultural realities of what it means to be Southern. The more I explored the social context, the more I realized that defining the South raises more questions than answers. The central question is how those individuals historically marginalized by race, gender, and sexuality conceptualize the South. What does this South mean for those who exist in multiple margins in the South? How do our stories help us understand what is considered American and Southern? Moreover, I questioned how growing up or living in the South directly affects how SBQLWP actualize our queer lesbian selves. Simply put, in what ways does one's location influence their queer actualization? To gain answers to these questions, this work centers the American South as a central character. To do that, I must define the South in a sociocultural place and space.

This work uses Katherine McKittrick's framework of Black and Black women's geography, which signals an alternative pattern that works alongside and across traditional geographies.[19] McKittrick notes that traditional geography is often rooted in a white, patriarchal, Eurocentric, heterosexual, and classed vantage point.[20] She argues that this traditional framework is limited by physical landscapes, infrastructures, and imaginations. The traditional geography does not signal a cultural reality or the ways historically marginalized persons find space to exist in a location. This traditional geography aligns precisely with what the US Census would define as the US South, using sterile, nonimaginative markers for determining variations in location. In this context, the US South is a result of this traditional geography, which also focuses on the physicality of the South, adopting a white, patriarchal, Eurocentric, heteronormative framework in defining the American South. In this traditional geography, the South nods to the memory and legacy of the Confederacy as the primary basis for defining the South, rooted in the capitalist framework of (re)claiming land. The capitalist nature of this traditional Southern geography disregards the cultural context of the South, silencing those who do not benefit from this capitalist geography.

Consequently, incorporating historical racial realities challenges the traditional Southern geography. McKittrick contends that Black people in the diaspora represent a "geographic story that is, at least in part, a story of material and conceptual placements and displacements, segregations, and integrations, margins and centers, migrations and settlements."[21] Studying the experiences of Black folks in a specific location means exposing particular racial histories and realities there. Challenging this traditional geography makes Black folks "geographic beings who have a stake in the production of space."[22] The legacy of enslavement challenges this traditional Southern geography, as Southern Black folks historically did not directly benefit from Southern capitalism. For Southern Black persons, this means uncovering how they are Southern cultural agents, even with the oppressive legacies of enslavement. Southern Black folks recognize the South as a racially situated space and how they found tools needed to survive and even thrive amid the backdrop of Southern capitalism in this Southern traditional geography. These methods of survival uncover a Southern narrative that directly challenges this limited Southern geography. These methods of resistance are evident in how Southern Black folks found ways to navigate in sundown towns,[23] created a sense of unity and community through establishing kinships, and used the Southern Christian Black Church as a spiritual and communal space to incorporate their African practices. SBQLWP are descendants of this historic memory, also existing in this racialized geographic space. By including a Black queer lesbian perspective of this Southern traditional landscape, we must extend this Southern traditional geography to include the roles gender and sexuality play in this racially situated space.

McKittrick's geographic framework extends to Black women, specifically the ways overlapping realities of gender and race manifest themselves differently based on location and space. According to McKittrick, the history of Black women in transatlantic slavery history illustrates how Black women are both shaped by and challenge traditional geographic arrangements. She states that the classification of Black women aligns with historically present racial-sexual categories. The historical realities that Southern Black women experienced with sexual violence is a result of their placement in the domestic sphere—during and after enslavement. This reality provide new ways for us to understand the racialized sexual realities in the South. Tera W. Hunter nods to these experiences as well, establishing how Southern Black women's labor is often tied to certain assumptions rooted in gender and sexual exploitation. Hunter's piece exposes this racialized sexual historical reality rooted in both urban and rural Southern spaces after the antebellum South that ultimately "set the stage for renegotiations of labor and social relations for many years to come."[24] Because of these racialized sexual realities, Black women in the South have their own historical geographies. Centering the experiences of Black women in this region can create visibility and alternative modes of understanding geographic phenomena.[25] According to LaToya Eaves, Black women are necessary for creating productive knowledge in support of Black geographies.[26]

How does queerness show up in this racialized sexualized geography? Black queerness and queer embodiment expands this racialized sexual history of the South. Because of our Black queer identities, SBQLWP create historical geographies in the South that may align with and vary from these racialized sexual historical geographies. In these discussions about differences in the South, SBQLWP expose a new cultural landscape that does not rely on a heteronormative narrative. We exist in myriad Southern experiences with distinct racial, queer, and sexual components. Because of these overlapping identities, we define the South from various vantage points rooted in a queer, racialized, gendered, and sexualized geography.

SBQLWP expands on this Southern traditional geography to include a potentially new cultural geographic landscape, a racialized sexual queer geography that is inclusive of sexuality and queerness. The racialized sexual queer geography (1) represents the ways queerness and queer embodiment manifests in a specific geography and (2) provides an intersectional framework that directly challenges this Southern traditional geography. Discussions of a racialized sexual queer geography uses an intersectional lens to the South and uncovers how queerness and sexual fluidity exists in this racialized sexual geography. This geography creates a new way to discuss the South, exploring the ways queerness and lesbianism exist in the Southern sociocultural landscape. Using this framework demonstrates how the South shapes Black female sexuality, queerness, and gender fluidity. This framework dares to uncover how the South has queer and sexual dimensions. Regardless of racial, sexual, and gender identities, this racialized sexual queer geography allows all Southerners to make sense of their heteronormative gender and sexual identities. Although this discussion focuses on the South, this geography can be used in various locations to determine how certain sociocultural realities affect how one's intersectional identities are actualized.

The racialized sexual queer geography directly challenges the heteronormative and heterosexual foundation of traditional geography. It explores the heteronormativity that exists in the Southern traditional geography and its disregard for sexual and gender fluidity. Regardless of race, this traditional geography amplifies the voices of heterosexual Southern folks and silences those who do not exist in this traditional heteronormative geography. In the South, the Christian Church reiterates and further justifies the heteronormative sexual hegemonies. This racialized sexual queer geography also uncovers the glaring ways homophobia and queerphobia exist in this region. This racialized sexual queer geography also reveals how these dimensions of heteronormativity can exist in Southern Black spaces as well, perpetuated in the ways Southern Black heterosexual persons maintain this Southern sexual hegemony and heteronormative traditional geography, using the Christian Black Church as justification for this marginalization. The Southern sexual hegemony and heteronormativity in this traditional geography are evident in this collective narrative. Discussion with SBQLWP helped me further conceptualize the South as complex racialized sexual queer geography. Before long, we start muddling into some complex geographic analysis. As geographic scholars mentioned earlier, physical place (geography) and culture (space) are inevitably connected. The responses from SBQLWP shed light on how the South acts as a physical place and sociocultural space. For example, SBQLWP born in other regions of America and currently residing in the South define themselves as Southern. How can someone born outside the South define themselves as Southern? SBQLWP born outside of the South understood that their Southern identity had little to do with where they were born. They connected to the sociocultural landscape of the South, where the South acts as a place and space of ancestral comfort. In some instances, interlocutors had family members who were from the South, bridging their connections to the South. The South connected SBQLWP to their ancestral lineage, where they honored the homeplace of their African/Black ancestry. Regardless of whether SBQLWP were born in the South, the South acts as that homeplace for them.

The majority of SBQLWP in this study distinguished themselves as Southern, but 37 percent of SBQLWP did not. These individuals were either born and raised in the South or born and raised in other American regions. How can someone be from the South and not consider themselves Southern? Their responses challenge traditional notions of geographic location and space. Defining oneself as Southern is not limited to being born in the South but uncovers a sociocultural connection to the region, namely, the infamous Southern and/or slave mentality. When these particular SBQLWP framed what is considered the South or Southern, they were considering whether they were products of this Southern and/or slave mentality. Many interlocutors used the key terms when describing the Southern mentality or slave mentality: oppressive, slow, conservative, racist, rural, agricultural, and, of course, slavery. More discussions of the Southern or slave mentalities will appear later. However, those interlocutors who did not define themselves as Southern applied these key terms to how they conceptualize what they consider Southern. Their connection to the South is not tied to a specific location but a perceived cultural reality, mentality, and way of living. While they do not identify as Southern, they were able to provide an accurate picture of the South. These SBQLWP recognize the sociocultural dimensions of the South.

Racialized Sexual Geography and Notions of Homeplace

Fitting in this racialized sexual geography SBQLWP view the South as a Southern Black woman and/or a Southern Black mother. This metaphor of the South as a Southern Black mother exposes how we define the complexities of the South. The South becomes the personification of "she" or "her" who raised, nurtured, and provided a safe space for us. She gave us the tools needed to survive and established a legacy for us to be grounded in. She has church hats in every color, cooks homemade food, and is the embodiment of Southern hospitality. When anyone walks into her home, it is filled with pictures of Black Jesus, Rev. Dr. Martin Luther King Jr., and various family members both alive and deceased. They would also see a large red and brown well-worn Bible with several obituaries tucked inside. She may have gospel music playing in the background. While she is my homeplace, I admit that at one point in my life, I was embarrassed by her. She appeared backward, less progressive, too churchy, too Black, too Southern. She reminded me of all the things that I tried to minimize to fit into white-centered spaces. It was not until my queer lesbian journey, with all its complexities, that I reunited with her and found the beauty in who she was. I am no longer embarrassed by her. However, like my interlocutors, I am also critical of her.

  Like any mother–daughter relationship, SBQLWP have a beautiful and distinct relationship to the South. The South reminds us of the pain and healing that can only occur between a Black mother and her daughter. Like that Southern Black mother, they birthed us, molded us, and shaped our worldview. These Southern Black grandmas and mothers taught us Southern ways, gave us a coded language, and a thick Southern dialect. Grandma and 'em educated us about the values, morals, and practices integral to Southern Black womanhood. Ultimately, these Southern Black mothers planted the seeds for our Southernness. When I hear SBQLWP conceptualize the South, I hear the lessons from our Southern grandmas and mothers. Those who were not born in the South attempt to connect and return to that Southern Black mother. That pull to the South can only be from a Southern Black mother or grandma who asks, "Dawta, when do you plan to come home?" No matter where we find ourselves, the South is that Southern Black mother who anchors us to who we are.

These Southern Black mothers and grandmas may have pure intentions, but it does not always translate to growth. Sometimes the seeds they plant are potted in unfertile ground, where growth is stunted or tarnished by faulty soil. Perhaps the soil is damaged by the trauma that these foremothers experienced. After all, they experienced the pain of being a Black woman in the South and encountered the interlocking oppressions of race and gender that can exist there. Grandma and 'em are direct descendants of this historical racialized and sexual oppression. As suggested by the racialized sexual geography, these Southern mothers and grandmas experienced the trauma of being a Southern Black woman. They may pass that hurt and trauma down to their Black queer lesbian daughters like a banana pudding recipe. Unfortunately, this is all our foremothers knew. With that in mind, the South as a Southern Black woman is multifaceted, operating as both a spiritual anchor and a location of trauma. The South as the personification of her represents the Southern Black woman's pain, suffering, joy, spirit, and love.

Because the this, we recognize the South as home. When asked why interlocutors defined themselves as Southern, they would often respond with, "The South is home." Even for those who no longer reside in the South, the South remains that homeplace. For those SBQLWP who moved to the South, the South became home, a place of comfort. How can a contentious region be considered "home" for SBQLWP? Home represents a physical place, signifying a specific location with certain foundational roots, including family, church, and childhood friends. Home holds memories of an ancestral past. Even in the trauma that can exist in this region, the South is that place that anchors us. But SBQLWP discuss how this homeplace exists in contradiction. It is filled with joy, trauma, fulfillment, disappointment, hurting, and healing. But it is still our home. We are walking on the soil of those ancestors who came before us. We know that the South runs in our veins. The South as home inevitably links us to a sense of identity. We can heavily critique the South as being racist, slow, and homophobic, yet it is still home. It is our homeplace, the place that reminds us of grandma and 'em.

In *Yearning: Race, Gender, and Cultural Politics*, bell hooks discusses the complexities that make home place an epistemological space and a site of resistance and safety for Black women. The creation of the homeplace is an attempt for Black women to find ways to keep something for their own in an oppressive society.[27] Because it is an autonomous place of safety, the homeplace becomes a space of healing for Black women. hooks asserts that using the homeplace narrative is a method to use a feminism formed for Black women's specific needs and concerns.[28] But this homeplace is not without critique, and SBQLWP have plenty to critique. This Black feminist framing of homeplace evaluates how the South acts as a complex home place for SBQLWP that is safe and traumatic. This homeplace ultimately represents this racialized sexual geography, where we can actualize our racial and gender identities in a place and space.

In this racialized sexual geography, the South as a home place represents a place of socialization. Similar to discussions from hooks, the South becomes a learning space that shapes the way Southerners operate and see the world. It is foundational to what we describe as our Southernness. This socialization becomes an epistemology, a way for us to conceptualize what the South means for us. However, we are critical of this socialization in this racialized sexual geography. Existing in the margins of this homeplace gives a unique perspective to this homeplace. Home is a place where we can rest our heads, but it is also a space that causes internal conflict. We reconcile with this homeplace, finding healing and wholeness while simultaneously critiquing it. SBQLWP uncover the complexities of this homeplace, forcing us to critically analyze the realities that exist in this racialized sexual geography.

Naming and Renaming in This Racialized Sexual Queer Geography

This racialized sexual queer geography creates a fascinating dimension to sexual and gender identity, particularly the way interlocutors named and defined their sexual and queer identities. Many SBQLWP were more likely to describe themselves as lesbian over queer (55 percent identified as lesbian while 20 percent identified as queer). With that in mind, naming and renaming becomes an essential component that arises from this racialized sexual queer geography. This racialized sexual queer geography is an opportunity for Southern and queer studies scholars alike to comprehend how geographic location challenges traditional notions of naming. While academics (me included) would quickly label folks outside the heteronormativity as "queer," we must consider how geographic location challenges that notion. The premature practice of labeling SBQLWP under the umbrella of queer often dismisses how race and geographic location alter one's identity. Black feminist and womanist frameworks suggest that Black women's identity includes the attempt to redefine their experiences. This self-naming and self-defining as lesbian or queer allow us to regain a sense of humanity and redefine notions of Black womanhood, lesbianism, and queerness in the Southern landscape. Our practice of self-naming and redefining challenge myths and limitations associated with Black sexuality in the South. For SBQLWP, defining oneself as a lesbian becomes a way of resisting the gender and sexual norms and expectations placed on Southern Black women. Naming and renaming rejects assumptions associated with lesbianism and queerness for SBQLWP to make sense of our realities in this racialized sexual queer geography.

The practice of self-naming and redefining stems from a Black feminist and womanist theoretical framework. According to Collins, self-defining is a method Black women utilize to humanize their experiences as Black women:

> By insisting on self-definition, Black women question not only what has been said about African-American women but the creditability and the intentions of those possessing the power to define. When Black women define ourselves, we clearly reject the assumption that those in positions granting them the authority to interpret our reality are entitled to do so. Regardless of the actual content of Black women's self-definition, the act of insisting on Black female self-definition validates Black women's power as human subjects.[29]

For Black women, SBQLWP included, self-definition allows us to question the assumptions made about our lives and reject them with new images of womanhood and humanity. As Collins further notes, "Black women's lives are a series of negotiations that aim to reconcile the contradictions separating our own internally defined images of self as African-American women with our objectification as the Other."[30] The naming and renaming becomes a reconciliation process for Black women, determining how our lives are in contradiction to our assigned names. This tradition of self-naming extends to SBQLWP as we find ways to resist heterosexist hegemonies. As Collins says, this process of self-definition "offers a powerful challenge to the externally defined, controlling images of African-American women."[31] When Black women engage in naming and renaming, they directly challenge the myths associated with the assigned names of Jezebel, mammy, and Sapphire. For SBQLWP, naming oneself as lesbian challenges the myth that Southern Black persons are inherently heterosexual or only engage in heteronormativity. Moreover, it uncovers the heteronormativity associated with these assigned names.

Clenora Hudson-Weems provides additional context for SBQLWP practices of self-definition. While Africana womanism is not queer-friendly, Hudson-Weems defines this self-definition as having "her own reality, with no particular allegiance to existing ideals."[32] Her theory of Africana womanism does provide Black (or in this case Africana) women the power to self-name and self-define their lived experiences. She aligns with the tradition of Nommo, an African cosmology that breathes new life into a being. According to Janheinz Jahn, Nommo is "a life force . . . a unity of spiritual-physical fluidity, giving life to everything, penetrating everything, causing everything."[33] Jahn describes the ways Nommo is directed by man, as he (humans) has the power in the world and directs that life force. Because man is the director of the life force, he "shares it with other beings, and so fulfills the meaning of life."[34] Hudson-Weems nods to this Nommo tradition in her understanding of self-definition, as Africana women use names to breathe new life into their present realities. Hudson-Weems understands that Africana/Black women have the power to direct that life force, where our self-definition connects the physical with the spiritual. Because of this reality, SBQLWP adopt the Nommo tradition to rename ourselves to claim a sense of agency and redefine our intersectional experiences. In naming and reclaiming ourselves as queer and/or lesbian, we are connecting to the physical with the spiritual and breathing in a new life that is inclusive of our queer lesbian identities.

This naming and redefining in this racialized queer sexual geography is connected to a Southern Black cultural reality. SBQLWP do not align with white feminist queer discourse to define or rename our lesbianism or queerness. Instead, our understanding of our queer and/or lesbian identities stem from the Southern Black community. SBQLWP were not quoting white queer scholars like Judith Butler, Eve Kosofsky Sedgwick, or Jack Halberstam. Southern Black culture helps us make sense of our lesbianism and/or queerness. In book *Loving in the War Years*, Cherríe Moraga points out the significant role cultural norms play in one's sexual naming and identity. Moraga articulates how she learned notions of her sexuality, not from the society at large but from her Chicano/Mexican culture.[35] The same dynamic applies to SBQLWP, describing how we negotiate our sexualities in a racialized Southern Black space. Our understanding of lesbianism and queerness is based on how we embody or challenge Southern gender norms.

This self-naming as lesbian over queer stems from a few Southern racial realities. The term *queer* is still seen as a derogatory term and perceived by some Southerners as an embodiment of gender fluidity over one's sexual identity. While gender studies and Black queer studies scholars recognize the interlocking elements of race, gender, and sexuality, in the South, they can be separately compartmentalized. Moreover, in the Southern Black community, the term *queer* is attached to white persons and how they engage in sexual difference, which causes some hesitation for Southern Black queer folks who do not want to be perceived as racial outsiders. Furthermore, in the Southern Black queer community, the term *lesbian* or *same-gender loving* appears easier to define for Southern folks. The terms *lesbian*, *gay*, and *same-gender loving* exist in finite ways with clearly defined sexual realities. Simply put, it is easier for us to explain to grandma and 'em that we are lesbian and prefer to date women over men. Saying that we are queer raises more questions.

The term *lesbian* appears limiting in queer and gender studies because it appears to be a definitive, binary identity in comparison to *queer*, which allows for an embodiment of fluidity. Consequently, lesbianism has often been overlooked as a method of resistance. Historically, lesbianism acted as a revolutionary identity and consciousnesses in mainstream second-wave feminist scholarship with the infamous slogan, "Lesbianism is the practice and feminism is the theory," which equated lesbianism to feminist ideologies. Black feminist lesbian women such as Audre Lorde, Barbara Smith, Cheryl Clarke, and June Jordan attached themselves to this slogan in the form of radical Black feminism, while other Black feminists and Black women made lesbianism and feminism a white female phenomenon. Clarke contends that lesbianism is a revolutionary act against "male supremacist, capitalist, misogynist, racist, homophobic, imperialist culture."[36] According to Cherry Smith, gay women decided to identify themselves as *lesbian* because the term *gay* became synonymous with cisgender gay men and connected to the HIV/AIDS epidemic.[37] Smith contends that lesbians in the 1980s felt the term *gay* rendered them invisible. Adopting the term *lesbian* distinguishes how gayness manifests differently based on gender identity. Regardless of race, self-identifying as lesbian was a method of responding to invisibility.

We redefine lesbianism outside the context of this binary sexual identity. Naming oneself as a lesbian in the South is revolutionary and becomes a method of survival and resistance against this Southern traditional heteronormative geography. Although it appears limiting, the naming of lesbian is a queer activity because it makes heteronormativity and heterosexuality an option, not a requirement, for Southern Black women. Defining oneself as lesbian fits in this racialized sexual queer geography because it challenges this Southern racial and sexual hegemony in the region. Many of us grew up feeling that we were different from our peers. The term *lesbian* was eye opening and revolutionary for some SBQLWP, whereas others found it as a step toward reaching their queer identity Regardless, self-naming as lesbian is essential to our sexual actualization process. SBQLWP attaching ourselves to the term *lesbian* does not automatically remove a queer consciousness or a fluid gender identity—it is merely the queer and Black feminist practice of self-naming and redefining our sexual identities within the Southern landscape. SBQLWP identifying as lesbian is an intentional method of resistance, as we are intentionally showing how our lives differ from our Southern heterosexual brothers and sisters. More important, our lesbian identification provides more possibilities for how all Southern Black women can exist.

SBQLWP who identified as queer adopted this identity as a worldview and consciousness-raising activity. For queer interlocutors, embodying queerness was a way to challenge all forms of gender and sexual fluidity. Gender-nonconforming interlocutors often identified themselves as queer, recognizing how their sexualities were merely the entry point for discussing how their multifaceted fluid identities can be fully recognized. When initially coming out, queer persons defined themselves as lesbian because there was no other word to describe the embodiment of their sexual and/or gender fluidity. Naming themselves as lesbian helped queer folks reconcile with that sexual difference, but it did not fully explain their fluid gender embodiment and how they want to show up in the world. Once the term *queer* became part of academic and public discourse in the 1990s, they attached to that identity over lesbian. The queer embodiment allowed them to expand how they defined themselves.

The term *queer* had its start in feminist and queer studies, referring to individuals who resist or challenge heteronormativity in social, economic, or political ways. Queerness represents an act of embodiment, an outward expression of one's internal gender and/or sexual fluidity. Queerness pushed back against heterosexist practices and notions that can exist in gay and lesbian spaces. Although many scholars have defined queerness, queer interlocutors align with both Cherry Smith's and Poet on Watch's notion of queer. Smith and Poet on Watch examine how the term *queer* is rooted in a sociocultural line of questioning while presenting some distinctions in how using the term changes based on the racial and ethnic communities and identities they also represent. Smith contends that the term *queer* "articulates a radical questioning of social and cultural norms, norms of gender, reproductive sexuality, and the family."[38] Poet on Watch describes *queer* as a "word undergoing process; a kind of questioning that creeps into the very fiber of our sexual, spiritual, political eccentric and most unconventional thoughts and behavior."[39]

Using these frameworks, we understand that queer is a continuous process of questioning what is considered normal or traditional in this racialized sexual queer space. Queer extends beyond the embodiment of a gender and/or sexual identity by questioning and redefining these narrowly defined parameters surrounding identity on any level. Queerness is the embodiment of both sexual and gender fluidity and questions and redefines traditional sociocultural constructs. Black queerness operates as a worldview and consciousness that extends beyond sexuality. As interlocutor Toni noted, queerness is nonhierarchical and nonbinary, focusing more on consciousness and providing an analysis of body politics and pleasure. Comparatively, lesbian/gay can be heteronormative and does not necessarily rely on a shift in consciousness. Toni says that *lesbian/gay* "just means you are in a same-sex relationship." With the term *queer*, queer interlocutors recognize how queerness is the pathway to discuss additional systemic oppressions and ways of being, such as questioning assumptions related to gender, race, class, sexuality, abilities, body size, and citizenship. These queer interlocutors show that they have a queer consciousness, not just a sexual identity. Like Poet on Watch's definition, SBQLWP acknowledge that queerness is an ongoing process, far from being a single-moment revelation or a linear activity. They find that queerness is a continuous process of reconciliation with how one decides to show up in the world. This work documents that journey.

The "Outsider Within" and Insider/Outsider Positionality in This Racialized Sexual Queer Geography

In this racialized sexual queer geography, SBQLWP exist as insiders and outsiders, representing our outsider within positionality. We exist in the South and the Southern Black community while simultaneously rendered invisible and silent in these spaces. Collins describes this peculiar societal position based on the standpoint of Black female domestic workers in a postbellum America. These Black female domestic workers existed inside these white intimate spaces while operating as an outsider because they could never actually belong to these white families.[40] Operating as an outsider within, these Black women provided their families and communities the knowledge needed to exist in a racist society. Because they worked in the homes of upper-class white people, Black women gained knowledge of the intimate workings of dominant persons. According to Collins, "working for Whites offers domestic workers a view from the inside and exposes them to ideas and resources that might aid in their children's upward mobility."[41] For Black female domestic workers with children, these firsthand experiences gave them insight into the kind of tools needed to gain social mobility for their children and grandchildren. In the context of this racialized sexual queer geography, SBQLWP also occupy this position of the outsider within.

In aligning with Collins's notion, Carlos Dews describes gay, lesbian, and queer Southerners as insiders/outsiders of Southern families and Southern communities, but these positions provide a sense of survival strategies for gay, lesbian, and queer Southerners: "The queer southerner's position relative to the South is split—insider/outsider—thus creating a double or triple vision of the world, a position from which one may both participate in Southern culture yet remain apart from it. Like the double consciousness of African Americans that W. E. B. Du Bois described, the double vision of Southern queers, inside/outside members of Southern families and Southern communities, becomes a survival strategy in a world simultaneously nurturing and hostile toward its queer children."[42] This outsider within or insider/outsider position establishes a survival strategy and perspective to this racialized sexual queer geography. In the South, gayness and queerness create a double or triple vision of the world.[43]

Using this racialized sexual queer geography as a theoretical foundation enhances our understanding of how this position applies to SBQLWP, particularly in how this population exists outside and inside multiple communities. We are outsiders in the Southern LGBTQIA+ communities because of our race and outsiders in Southern Black heterosexual communities because of our sexuality and gender identities. This outsider within status creates an invisibility and polarity in both communities. Further, this position of the outsider within informs our understanding and knowledge about racism, heterosexism, homophobia, sexism, and patriarchy in the South. This complex position affects who we are in the Southern Black community. We operate in this peculiar position, exposing the realities that exist in this racialized sexual queer geography. This position benefits us, allowing us to gain the knowledge needed to survive in this region with certain dominant forces in the South, namely the Church and the Southern community. We learn how to survive in this heteronormative South. Similar to the critique of the traditional Southern geography, the position of the outsider within shows how heteronormativity exists in traditional and even racialized sexual geographies.

However, SBQLWP extend on this outsider within and insider/outsider position by incorporating how this position operates as an intraracial position. SBQLWP speak of this position in our racial communities. This peculiar position means existing inside and outside a dominant and subordinate space. Yet this racialized sexual queer geography shows how we exist as outsiders within subordinate spaces. While Collins refers to the opportunity to understand the mindset of dominant wealthy white spaces, we use this position to learn about Southern Black heteronormativity and heteropatriarchy. Unlike Black female domestic workers who will never be a part of their white families, we are still regarded as members of the Southern Black community. We are considered those wayward distant cousins who bring family members shame, but there is still an undeniable connection to their Southern families. We are fixtures in our Southern families, even as outsiders. This unique position causes us more anguish because we are marginalized within our community and family. This racialized sexual queer geography tracks how that this position affects the trauma and hurt we experience as well as determines how we make sense of our social positioning.

Discussions of "Quare" in This Racialized Sexual Queer Geography

Johnson's theory of "quare" establishes queerness in the Southern Black community. The naming of quare represents this racialized sexual queer geography as it situates queerness in a Southern racialized space. Johnson drew from the words of his grandmother to define *quare* as a theoretical lens for understanding how queerness manifests in the Southern Black community. His grandmother asked him whether he was quare, a Southern Black vernacular for "queer." By making the term *quare* both a noun and an adjective, Johnson adopts a similar format to Alice Walker's definition of womanism. According to Johnson, *quare* is a noun, describing a person who is "odd or slightly off-kilter: from the African American vernacular for queer; sometimes homophobic in usage, but always denotes excess incapable of being contained within conventional categories of being."[44] *Quare* is also an individual whose sexual and gender identities always intersect with racial subjectivity.[45] The quare person embodies several intersectional identities in the South—as an adjective, the term describes a "lesbian, gay, bisexual, or transgendered person of color who loves other men or women sexually and/or nonsexually and appreciates black culture and community."[46] Although queer people throughout the world are defined by similar parameters, the use of *quare* denotes how this racialized sexual queer geography is significant to how one actualizes their sexuality and queerness in the South. After all, the South is where we first learn of our marginalized sexual and gender status. *Quare* becomes the epitome of this racialized sexual queer geography, pinpointing the significance of defining Southern Black queer identity in the context of a Southern landscape. Even as quare, we appreciate and represent our Southern culture and community.

Using *quare* as an example in this racialized sexual queer geography raises a significant question about why I choose to refer to interlocutors as queer instead of quare. Although this position is central in this racialized sexual queer geography, I do not call my interlocutors quare because they do not define themselves in this way. I wanted to honor the Black feminist legacy of allowing Black women to engage in the practice of self-definition, where they define themselves for themselves. Even though they identify as queer, SBQLWP engage with Johnson's notion of quare. I recognize that their understanding of queer is not based on traditional white feminist lesbian frameworks but on the ways their identities are multiple, fluid, and continuous in a Southern context. The way we embody queerness in this racialized sexual queer geography is rooted in our Southernness, uncovering our understanding of what it means to be Southern and queer. In this racialized sexual queer geography, we understand queer as quare. When SBQLWP use *queer*, it is in response to this racialized sexual queer geography, how it shaped and molded our approach to our fluid and interlocking identities. While I speak of these individuals as "queer," I also understand the ways interlocutors and I are engaged in the quare framework.

The Southern Christian Black Church as a Fixture in Southern Black Queer Reality

The Southern Christian Black Church operates as a primary social institution in the South. Regardless of race, every person living or from the American South is connected to a church in some way. In the South, the church is not simply a building where one worships on Sunday—it is the backdrop of Southern cultural realities. It shows up everywhere and is foundational to Southern culture. Even if an interlocutor did not grow up in a specific church or engage in organized religion, they felt the remnants of church indoctrination because the church has a chokehold on secular Southern life. Southerners see the church on restaurant to-go cups, pro-life billboards, or the "Heaven or Hell" billboards with a phone number to a prayer line. The South and the Church are intimately connected. Ultimately, the Church inspires and informs our Southernness.

Bernadette Barton echoes the sentiment that the Church dictates Southern living. She argues that the construction of the conservative Christian Church in the South normalized certain ideologies and valued certain ways of living. Barton uncovers how the evangelical Southern Church influences a Southerner's sexual identity. Her work primarily focuses on how the evangelical Southern Christian Church shapes and molds the lives of Southern LGBTQIA+ people. Redefining the South as the Bible Belt South and her research participants as "Bible Belt gays," she incorporates how religiosity permeates the South. In a sense, the Bible Belt acts as a social construction that develops Southern culture and represents the ideologies and ways of living in the American South. She finds that the Southern Christian Church is based on the ideologies of Christian fundamentalists, who represent a conservative Christianity that focuses on evangelicalism, which consists of three components: recognizing the authority of the Christian Bible, salvation through being "born again," and spreading the news of Christ.[47] Barton reiterates that Bible Belt Christianity in the South is not confined to religious institutions and Sunday worship but affects secular institutions, such as schools and workplaces.[48] Ultimately, churches in the South are not separate from the rest of the community but are intimately connected to Southern culture and life. For Southern people, the Church functions as the ethical and moral authority. While different denominations are included in this fundamentalist, evangelical Christianity (Baptist, Methodist, Pentecostal, Catholic, and nondenominational megachurches), they all assert that homosexuality is a sin. Barton notes the ways the conservative, fundamental Christian Church has affected the culture of the South, solidifying and maintaining the marginalization of Bible Belt gays.

The Church serves as a foundational institution for Southern Black folks. For Southern Black persons, the Church functions as the cornerstone of the Southern Black community and Southern Black life. The Southern Black Church is a spiritual and social institution that is inevitably tied to American Black culture and heritage. In their groundbreaking text, *The Black Church in the African American Experience*, C. Eric Lincoln and Lawrence H.

Mamiya explain that the Church represents the womb of Black culture and Black institutions.[49] It is the birthplace of American Blackness. For Southern Black folks, the church acts as a significant historical socialization institution, from enslavement to Black liberation movements. The Church is one of the only institutions that Southern Blacks may refer to in a possessive context because it represents a sense of autonomy and freedom. Albert J. Raboteau argues that the Christian Black Church is the social center of Black life as "an agency of social control, a source of economic cooperation, an arena for political activity, a sponsor of education, and a refuge in a hostile white world."[50] This reality is even more evident in the South, where the Church is a refuge from the Southern white gaze. From being an "invisible institution"[51] to an independent, autonomous space, the Christian Black Church acts as a safe space for Southern Black folks. Enslaved Africans did worship on the same plantations as white persons, but they created sacred spaces to worship outside the watchful eye of elite white Southerners. The essence of Southern Black Churches was born from the allotted time given by enslavers and eventually shaped into physical spaces that became the cornerstone of Southern Black life. The Southern Black Church represents the ancestral gift given to Southern Black folks.

More important, the Southern Black Church socializes many Southern Black persons, contributing to the ideologies of Southern Black folks. It is the moral and ethical compass for Southern Black folks and contributes to our understanding of gender and sexual norms and ideologies. While churches exist throughout America, Southern Black Churches are the microcosm of Southern Black culture and ideologies. SBQLWP are also socialized by these limiting gender and sexual norms; we were also members of these churches socialized by fundamentalist evangelical Christian indoctrination. This is the first place we learned of the gender performance of Southern Black womanhood. We are taught about the value of wearing modest clothing. We learn of the sin of fornication. We are indoctrinated into what it means to be a pious and virtuous wife. We absorbed lessons of domesticity and submission. Consequently, the Church acts as the first place we understand the value of cisgender heteronormativity.

The Church is a fixture in our Southern queer lesbian reality. It is the first institution where we encounter homophobic and heterosexist messages, making it difficult for us to live our authentic lives. Our coming-out stories are directly attached to our connection to the Church because coming out means being subjected to demoralizing treatment from Church members and family. Coming out challenges that significant sense of belonging for us. This treatment forces us to remain silent about our sexual and gender identities as that initial method of coping with our sexualities, queerness, and gender fluidity. Shame, condemnation, and judgment from the Church also contribute to our coming-out journey. The Church institution is foundational to the ways we negotiate and ultimately reconcile with our lesbianism and/or queerness.

Barton's text uses oral histories of gay and lesbian people who live in or from the South and how the Church doctrines related to gender and sexuality affected their journeys of self-exploration. Barton includes a few oral histories about the Southern Black Church from Southern Black queer folks, but she speaks primarily about the Southern white gay and lesbian experience. She does not fully address the cultural realities that are unique to the Southern Christian Black Church. One of her participants claimed that when it comes to the Black church, his racial identity trumps his sexual identity.[52] This book acknowledges the validity of this statement, where the Southern Christian Black Church connects to the history, heritage, family, and culture of Southern Black folks and even for Black queer persons. As a result of oppressive racial realities, Southern Blacks attempted to find safe spaces in their families, churches, and communities. When speaking to SBQLWP, and reflecting on my own experiences, I could not ignore the significant racial impact of the Southern Christian Black Church.

The existing body of literature related to homophobia and the Southern Christian Black Church reinforces this reality. Much of the existing literature about Black lesbians discusses the impact of the Christian Black Church. When uncovering previous works on SBQLWP, literature focusing on the Southern Christian Black Church uncovered the narratives of Southern queer folks. Foundational Black lesbian psychologists Beverly Greene, Vickie Mays, and Susan Cochran provide background information regarding the social, economic, and political experiences of Black lesbian women, specifically their relationships with family, lovers, friends, community members, and the Christian Black Church. Greene found that Black lesbians experience family, Church, and intimate relationships differently than their heterosexual counterparts do. She found that the Church acts as a significant socialization institution for Black lesbians that reiterates male dominance and homophobia. Based on the residual effects of the Christian Black Church, Black lesbians keep their relationships with other women hidden and invisible from their Church and family.

For some Black lesbians, the family acts as the first primary social unit, but families may not be as supportive of their homosexual lifestyle because they are perceived as deviant.[53] The SBQLWP of this work expressed how the Church is an extension of the Black family. Family and the Church are not separate social Southern institutions but two social spaces that merge. For us, the Church represents the family and family represents the Church. Many SBQLWP describe a similar reality in the South in the discussion of the "double life." This double life, what I call a duality, is defined as that time in our lives where we exist one way with Church and family and another way in gay/lesbian circles. Living in this duality was the closeted period to avoid being perceived as deviant and allowed us to maintain our sense of belonging to the Southern Black community. While the Church affects all Black lesbians, regardless of location, there are distinguishing elements of the Southern Christian Black Church that affect the coming-out narratives of SBQLWP.

James Sears's text *Growing Up Gay in the South* provides a specific example of how the Southern Christian Black Church affects the lives of Southern Black lesbians through the narrative of "Obie," a Southern Black lesbian youth from South Carolina who grew up in a two-parent Jehovah's Witness household. Sears's purpose for highlighting this story is to expose the importance of Southern Black families and their impact on Black youth's sexual exploration. Obie's story further addresses how the Southern Black families uphold traditional conservative Church values and rigid gender and sexual norms. As SBQLWP state in their stories, the ideologies from the Church often show up in their families. Even though Obie had her first same-sex sexual encounter at the age of thirteen, she remained silent about her sexuality out of fear of being separated from her family. This reality is manifested differently in the Jehovah's Witness faith, where church policies enforce disfellowship for those who commit sins against God and the Church. Being homosexual could have a congregant disfellowshipped from their Church and family. That individual cannot have any more contact with their family and Church community. Obie could not be disfellowshipped from her family because that is her only social and economic support system. However, her family and Church support system became the root of her trauma, causing her to try to end her own life and drop out of high school. Obie's story explicitly outlines the ways that the Church in the South infringes on the lives of SBQLWP, reiterating how the Church and family are inevitably connected in the coming-out narratives of SBQLWP. SBQLWP in this book who were also Jehovah's Witnesses shared similar narratives. These interlocutors speak to the Jehovah's Witness ideologies related to sexuality, how their lesbianism and queerness caused them to disfellowship from their Kingdom Hall,[54] and how that process of disfellowship influenced their coming-out narratives.

In both of Johnson's comprehensive texts,[55] he dedicates a chapter uncovering the role the Southern Christian Black Church plays in the lives of Southern Black gay and lesbian persons. He recognizes how the Black Church in the South has a "formidable presence in the struggle for racial equality"[56] but turns its back on its gay and lesbian parishioners. Due to the gender politics of the Church related to patriarchy and male dominance, Black gay men experience the Church differently than Black queer lesbians do. While the Church has certain religious morals and practices, it also teaches particular gender norms that influence how Black queer lesbians are expected to exist. For example, Black girls are pressured to use the Church as a space to find a husband and create a family, while Black boys are encouraged to be the head of that family. The Church socializes Black girls differently, causing a unique reality as we actualize our queer lesbian sexual identities. Being socialized by these rigid gender norms limits how SBQLWP can exist, causing us to experience Church hurt differently from our Southern Black gay male counterparts.

According to Johnson, the Church is complex for Black gay men. While it is homophobic, they also find comfort in the Church, as it is the first place where they feel a sense of community and belonging to find a nurturing space.[57] He also mentions rumors of same-sex behavior among Southern Black male ministers and leaders. Many Southern Blacks heard of these rumors of a Church leader having same-sex encounters with a male congregant or leader. Although they can engage in same-sex behavior, they are not necessarily labeled as gay or queer by congregants. While Southern Black folks may talk about it in their gossip circles, Black gay men are given the autonomy of a cisgender, heterosexual Black men, and allowed to engage in various sexual encounters. Southerners may say to their friends, "Chile, did you hear about Pastor/Elder/Deacon with that man . . ." But because they are male, a Black male Church parishioner or leader is given some level of sexual autonomy. As long as they maintain the Church code of silence, these Black men can engage in same-sex relations. Being born male provides them some freedom to exist as sexually autonomous beings. Moreover, according to Johnson, participation in the Church choir provides Black gay men a way to "adhere to the religiosity of southern culture but also build a sense of community within what can sometimes be a hostile space."[58] They must be silent parishioners but can also participate in the musical pageantry of the Church. For Black gay men, the Church can be a place for them to navigate their sexual identities while finding a sense of community.

For SBQLWP, there is a level of cultural shame attached to Southern Black women who do not adhere to the Church gender norms, a societal punishment for not conforming to heteronormativity. If Southern Black women do not create heteronormative families, then they are inevitably contributing to the death of heteronormative Southern Black family that the Church values. After all, Black women are the wombs of the Black community. Unlike Southern Black gay men, there is not a perceived safe space for us to exist in the Church. Although we may exist in the Church as leaders or congregants, we cannot exist as sexually autonomous beings. There cannot be a rumor of same-sex relations that simply passes as gossip. Our same-sex relations may lead to public shame for our families and ourselves. Some interlocutors did mention that their first same-sex engagement was with another Church member, but it was rarely a harmless rumor. For Cayce, it led to her disfellowship from the Jehovah's Witnesses. For Kea, it led to a potential death threat from her mother. More of their stories are discussed in chapter 2.

As Johnson mentions, the Church is no longer a place of refuge or belonging for SBQLWP. In fact, like many SBQLWP I spoke to, the interlocutors in this book tried to separate religion from spirituality, where they "sought out forms of worship that were more women-centered or turned inward to a self-discovery of a communion with a higher power."[59] We understood that making peace with the Church meant disconnecting from the institution itself and finding new ways to engage in spirituality without the Church's trauma. This book documents this complex spiritual journey of SBQLWP, exposing how we are treated differently in the Church, why we disconnect from the Church, and how we reconnect to our spiritualities. Some SBQLWP return to the Church but in other denominations that allow them to participate and/or be Church leaders as queer lesbians. While queerness and gay identity are still considered taboo by the Church, there are still variations for how we experience the Church given the limiting, overarching gender norms and expectations.

The purpose of this discussion is not to outline everything related to the Church but to frame it as a humanistic institution. This discussion is more about how the Church acts as a social institution embedded in certain cultural realities related to gender and sexuality. Because of the intersections of race, gender, and sexuality, SBQLWP can articulate how the Church represents certain gender and sexual normalcies that continue to exist in the consciousness of Southern Black persons. This discussion frames the Church as a gendered institution rooted in certain assumptions related to gender and sexuality, the way this institution molds and shapes the gender and sexual consciousness of Southern Black folks, and determines what is considered "normal" in terms of gender and sexuality. These gender realities make the Church a social institution with a history, culture, morals, ethics, and standards that Southern folks closely follow. The Church disseminates cultural norms and morals to the Southern community that ultimately affect how SBQLWP actualize our queer and/or lesbian identities.

Chapter Overview

Snapping Beans documents a journey of hurting and healing rooted in the South. It chronicles the narrative of the silent Black queer girl as she experiences pain, trauma, and reconciliation with the South. This discussion documents the sexual actualization of SBQLWP as they find wholeness and freedom. *Snapping Beans* shows the darkness and the light at the end of the tunnel. Chapter 1 defines and frames what the South means for SBQLWP and how we exist in the backdrop of the South in silence. Chapters 2 and 3 outline the shame, condemnation, and judgment faced by SBQLWP because of the Church and the Southern Black personality. Chapter 4 and 5 uncovers how coming out for SBQLWP represents a journey to wholeness through liberation, authenticity, and reconciliation that allows us to fully exist as our authentic selves in this region and ultimately establish a Black queer lesbian South.

This introduction set the stage for *Snapping Beans*. It answers some foundational questions about location and its application to this population and justifies the need to focus on the impact of the Southern Christian Black Church on SBQLWP. It provides context for the journey this silent Southern Black queer lesbian girl encounters. This introduction established why I incorporate the practice of snapping beans when speaking of this population, as it reconnects us to the Southern landscape and signifies the importance of intimacy and vulnerability. Moreover, I found that snapping beans acts as a qualitative oral history method for SBQLWP. Using the existing conversations from Southern queer scholars, I situate the South as a sociocultural place and space in what I call the racialized sexual queer geography, a geography that allows us to center the voices of SBQLWP and uncover the significance of queer and lesbian naming, experiences as an outsider within, and negotiation with the quare terminology. The first chapter provides the framing and definitions, and the remaining chapters center on quotes from SBQLWP to establish a collective narrative on what it means to be a Black queer lesbian person in the South. Each remaining chapter begins with a quote from an interlocutor that helps frame the discussion and exposes a new Southern vantage point from the lens of SBQLWP.

The first chapter, "'I Was Silent, But My Brain Was Loud': The Silent South," exposes silence as the first hurtful and traumatic experience in the South. Moreover, it focuses on the Southern cultural practice of silence and how SBQLWP exist in this culture of silence as we navigate our sexualities in the South. It first outlines how SBQLWP exist as the silent Black queer lesbian girl in the kitchen of our foremothers while snapping beans. I document how silence becomes a coping mechanism for that Black queer lesbian girl and the ways snapping beans in silence reinforces her Southernness. While she is silent, SBQLWP paint a picture of the South and depict this racialized sexual queer South. We attain a picture of the South that maintains the trauma and culture of silence.

The second chapter, "'The Church Is Not the Building; It's the People': The Shameful and Condemning South," addresses how the Southern Christian Black Church invokes the realities of shame and condemnation for SBQLWP as we actualize our identities. This chapter outlines how the toxic traits of the Church create a shameful and condemning South that limits sexual and queer embodiment. The first part of the chapter describes the limiting gender and sexual politics perpetuated by the Church. The second part discusses how these toxic practices are maintained through shame and condemnation. Finally, I outline how the culture of shame and condemnation affects the coming-out narrative for SBQLWP, uncovering what I call a duality, where we have to exist in two worlds. In this duality, this chapter documents how we experience internalized homophobia and self-hatred.

The third chapter, "'The World Is Set Up for Straight Folks': The Judgmental South and the Southern Black Personality" focuses on the ways SBQLWP encounter this massive cruelty, the judgment in the South, that describes how SBQLWP experience Southern Black heteronormativity and heteropatriarchy. I define the Southern Black personality as a personification of the heteronormativity and heteropatriarchy that exists in the infamous "Southern slave mentality." The description of this personality represents the societal judgment SBQLWP encounter as we navigate our sexual and queer identities. This chapter outlines how the Southern Black personality shows up in Southern sociocultural norms, such as the limited gender roles, heteronormativity, and Black heteropatriarchy. This chapter also addresses how Black lesbianism is considered anti-Black by the Southern Black personality and how lesbians are perceived as a threat to the Southern Black personality.

The chapter "'I Am Standing in My Truth': The Authentic and Reconciled South," addresses how SBQLWP find healing through coming out and reconciling with our Southern, sexual, and queer identities. This chapter documents the journey of how SBQLWP got out of this duality and internalized homophobia, come out, and began to live authentic lives. This chapter uncovers the ways SBQLWP equate "truth telling" to our coming-out narratives and why the language of truth is essential in this discussion. It also outlines the liberation process of SBQLWP as we come out or "find our truth." The discussion exposes the ways coming out helped SBQLWP reach a sense of reconciliation with the South, where our Southern identities are not in opposition or a hindrance to our Black queer lesbian identities. Moreover, this chapter uncovers the various ways SBQLWP reconcile with the Southern Christian Black Church and reports how reconciliation acts as a method of resistance to the traumas experienced with the culture of silence, shame, and the Southern Black personality.

The final chapter, "The Black Queer Lesbian South," uncovers a new Southern place and space that I call the Black queer lesbian South. This place and space is the epitome of this racialized sexual queer geography. SBQLWP find a place and space in this racialized sexual queer geography where we not only exist but thrive and fully live our authentic lives. Once SBQLWP come out and reconcile with the South, we establish communities in the South or among other SBQLWP to freely exist and thrive in wholeness. This chapter outlines the ways the Black queer lesbian South also acts as a method of resistance to the silent, shameful, condemning, and judgmental South, where SBQLWP attempt to carve a homeplace within a homeplace. This chapter discusses different tropes that exist in this Black queer lesbian South, such as the Southern Black femme, the Southern masculine queer embodiment, and the Southern gender-nonconforming person. The chapter ends with a description of how the practice of snapping beans can exist in this Black queer lesbian South.

Hopes for Readers

I hope that you, the reader, see this book as a testimony of love: self-love, communal love, and love for the South. But with any kind of love, there is beauty, pain, accountability, and vulnerability. With love comes truth, a truth that is often suppressed or silenced by others. I want our truths to free somebody from the shackles of silence, shame, and condemnation. I want the truths of this book to provide someone with a hug and a few words of affirmation. You do not have to come out to the world, but I hope that this book helps you find ways to authentically live in your truth, so you can be free to organically love yourself, your community, and your Southern roots. I hope the readers who find themselves in a dark place know that they are not alone. Let this book be your support and guide, affirming you that you are not alone and that your journey is not in vain.

I hope the reader receives a new narrative of the Black South, one that is filled with complexities, contradictions, joys, pain, and freedoms in a seemingly contentious region. I hope the reader realizes in this journey that the Black South does not solely belong to Southern Black heterosexual folks. I want readers to know that the Black South is diverse, with many colors and layers. There are many ways one can exist and thrive in the Black South. I want the reader to get a glimpse into a world we rarely see. This book provides visibility for Southern Black queer folks, maybe not for all the queer or LGBTQIA+ identified persons, but at least for one segment of the community that is hidden among the letters of sexual identity.

This book is for all the sons and dawtas of the South. Regardless of your personal identity markers, I hope you see yourself in this book so that you know the significance of your story of the South. No matter how far we remove ourselves from the South, I hope this book reminds you that the South is woven into your being. Instead of carrying it with shame, let it be a marker of pride. For those who encounter this complex Black South daily, I hope also you find part of your story in this book. For my Southern sistas both queer/lesbian and straight,[60] I hope that this work helps you realize that we all deal with the same societal oppressions, even if they manifest differently for Southern Black queer lesbians. In our lives, we had to unlearn some toxic gender norms that kept us suppressed for generations. For my Southern brothas,[61] both queer/gay or straight, I hope you gain some perspective about how these toxic gender norms we value in the South also affect you. I hope these words help you unlearn some generational norms related to masculinity. I hope it breaks your chains. While I am using the words of Southern Black queer lesbians, I know that their words are also your words. This book is a glimpse into Southern humanity and nuances that bring Southerners together while shedding light on the silent voices of the Southern landscape.

This book is not intended to speak to the experience of all Southern Black queer lesbian folks. The text is not intended to water down the Southern Black queer lesbian experience as a monolithic experience. However, this book shares some common threads that exist in many of our lives. The collective narrative is not the only narrative, nor is it the end of uncovering the lives of Southern Black queer lesbians. This book is merely the beginning of sharing our many voices.

This book is for all those SBQLWP who had to remain silent about who they were. This book is for those Southern Black queer ancestors who did not or could not exist in their truth out of fear of being silenced by violence, shame, condemnation, and heteronormativity. This book is dedicated to the women and people who could not speak or live in their truths. I know Southern Black queer ancestors existed long before I even considered writing this book. Black queer folks have always lived in the South and found ways to thrive. But our stories were overlooked and silenced. With this book, folks get a glimpse into our world. I invite you all to sit down at the kitchen table, snap beans with us, and listen to our journey to wholeness.

"I Was Silent, But My Brain Was Loud"
The Silent South

What are the words you do not yet have? What do you need to say? What are the tyrannies you swallow day by day and attempt to make your own, until you will sicken and die of them, still in silence?[1]

Many Southern Black women have a story about our grandma's kitchen. We recognize the beauty that exists in grandma's kitchen. Stories are told. Recipes are shared. Laughter permeates the air. We may hear grandma scolding somebody. These moments shift our lives somehow in the most subtle ways. Fatima still feels the presence of her grandma there even after she died: "Grandma still speaks to me in the kitchen." The kitchen acts as the birthplace of our Southernness, foundational in our understanding of what it means to be a Southern Black woman. For Southern Black women, the kitchen is a communal space. I vividly remember the communal interactions in my grandma's kitchen in Sumter, South Carolina. I recall the smell of her house and the way it gave me comfort. I would sit at the kitchen table as conversations happened around me. I am not sure what I was looking for. But I knew that if I sat at that table long enough, I would receive a gem from my grandma or aunties talking over each other. In my family, pleasant conversations were often loud—the louder, the better. Sometimes it was hard for me to keep up with the conversation happening around me. As I sipped my drink, the loud conversations coupled with extensive laughter comforted me. My grandma's laugh came from a place deep down in her soul. The laughter in the kitchen while preparing meals still rings in my memory. Even today, my family laughs because my grandma always laughed. It is a way to keep her legacy alive. The Southern kitchen represented that space where I saw my grandma in her element. Sitting in the kitchen with my aunties and grandma was the first time I recognized the powerful feminine spirit that manifests when Black women commune together. Those sounds from my grandma's kitchen became a source of inspiration for my scholarly work and reminds me of my Southern roots.

Even during the comfortable chaos, I was silent. I knew that I was what Southern folks would call "different," or as E. Patrick Johnson's grandmother would say, "slightly off kilter."[2] While my aunties and grandma were in the kitchen preparing meals, talking about men and relationships, I said very little. I would laugh along with the stories and lessons, trying to figure out how they related to my life. Like many SBQLWP, I became a silent Black queer lesbian girl in my grandma's kitchen. I laid at the feet of my grandma and aunts trying to catch a gem I could use to help me with this inner turmoil and unknown space I felt regarding my sexual fluidity. I waited for words of wisdom and comfort to quiet the questions and confusion I silently dealt with. Maybe while cutting sweet potatoes, making dough, or snapping beans with my aunts and grandma, someone would drop a nugget that I could use. But it never came. I remained silent about my truth, thinking my foremothers would never understand. Like many silent Black queer girls growing up in the South, we laughed with grandma and 'em to maintain our silence. The laughter becomes a mask, muting us. This torment may have caused some Southern Black queer lesbian girls to remain silent for years. Some for an entire lifetime.

The cultural practice of silence is as a significant aspect of our collective narrative. Byanca discussed this practice as a pivotal component of our coming out, connected to the act of snapping beans. She recalled having conversations with her grandma while snapping beans. She recognizes that as a Black queer lesbian girl, she was uncomfortable in that intimate space. She noted during our conversation, "I was silent, but my brain was loud." She noted conversations that occurred with her maternal figure were more often superficial small talk and that there was a lot she did not share with her. Byanca states: "There's a huge piece of me that I did not discuss." She feared that speaking of her sexuality would cause her to encounter some religious-based chastisement. Even during my time with my grandma and aunts, I silenced myself. While they would talk with me, I realized that there was a part of myself I did not share with them. Like Byanca, there was a lot I did not discuss with my grandma. I realized that fear was the root of my silence. While snapping beans is meant to be an opportunity to share, SBQLWP may have seen it as the time we were silent and did not share all of ourselves with grandma and 'em. While grandma and 'em felt safe and could be vulnerable, we were silent. We engaged in that Southern cultural practice of silence. Even in those spaces that should foster community and conversation among Black women, Southern Black queer lesbian girls remained silent about our inner turmoil. As we sit with these maternal figures snapping beans, our brains are loud, even in our silence. While our minds and souls were at war, we remained silent.

Audre Lorde depicts a similar silence in her work when she asks her audience whether there are words not yet spoken or tyrannies that are swallowed day by day.[3] Many SBQLWP discussed knowing they were "different," even before they had a name for it. They recognized this difference but remained silent about the tyranny, swallowing it daily. Previous generations of Southern Black gay, lesbian, and queer persons remained silent about their lives to survive in the South. This silence becomes a generational curse in the South. As Lorde posits, we swallow this tyranny day by day, an internal battle of defining who we are and how we can exist in the South. The silence created internal tyranny because we were encountering the unknown.

The silent Black queer lesbian girl fears the ramifications that come from being different in the South. She has valid reasons to remain silent, as there is fear associated with being visibly different. Lorde nods to this fear: "In the cause of silence, each of us draws the face of her own fear—the fear of contempt, of censure, or some judgment, or recognition, of challenge, of annihilation. But most of all, I think, we fear the visibility without which we cannot truly live."[4] Imagine how this fear of visibility manifests in the South. That Southern Black queer lesbian girl fears her queer lesbian visibility will lead to contempt, censure, judgment, recognition, challenge, and annihilation in the South. She fears contempt and judgment from the Southern Christian Black Church, family, and community. She is quiet while the pastor speaks of homosexuality as an abomination and when family members spew homophobic comments. She fears being censured and silenced by those who do not understand this inner turmoil. In public gatherings, she does not speak of her love life out of fear of judgment from others. She fears her annihilation in the form of physical violence. After all, if we are openly queer in public Southern spaces, what kind of violence may we encounter? The fears mute us. While the South silences us, we also silence ourselves. As Lorde says, the fear is within the transformation of silence into action, because it is a method of self-revelation that is fraught with danger.[5] The potential danger of being queer in the South stifles us into silence. Because of these realities, silence becomes the first part of our collective narrative as we actualize our queer lesbian identities in the South. The cultural practice of silence is an extension of a Southern cultural reality that SBQLWP are familiar with. After all, many Southern Black persons are silent about the painful and unknown.

The South creates beauty, but it also can cause the tyranny of silence. Southern folks recognize this contradiction as a regional reality. In the South, it is normal practice to not speak of certain realities. As Marie Dylan discussed, it is a Southern cultural norm to not speak about certain harsh realities. She further notes, "You learn to keep things quiet" as a means of safety and respect. Silent represents a certain morality in the South, where not speaking of trauma, hurt, or pain is a sign of respect. Southern folks are silent because speaking about the reality may cause pain and suffering. The perception is that silence prevents trauma and becomes a coping mechanism. Speaking about a certain painful reality causes that pain to live. Silence kills it. We believe that if we simply do not speak of something, then it fails to exist. There are stories in our families that we never hear about because the memory is too painful. Silence becomes a method of holding onto pain and hurt, the tyranny that we swallow each day. Although silence is essential to our survival, it also damages our ability to communicate harm. This Southern cultural practice of silence mistakes silence for comfort. It is a false sense of comfort, wrapped in a survival tactic, rooted in fear. That silent Black lesbian girl in grandma's kitchen is merely emulating the Southern cultural practice of silence for her protection and safety.

The damaging silence is an essential component to SBQLWP's Southern narrative. Before learning about our sexuality and gender fluidity, we learn about the cultural practice of silence. From an early age, we are socialized to adopt silence as a survival method. Even as we experience this inner turmoil, we do not speak about it. We assume that if we do not speak about it, then somehow it will cease to exist. If we do not speak of our sexualities and/or gender identities out loud, then somehow, we are killing that part of ourselves. If we remain silent and perform as a heterosexual youth, somehow the inner turmoil will stop. As Lorde points out, our silence will never save us.[6] It may provide us comfort for a moment but will never help us find wholeness.

Silence permeates the Southern air as one snaps and cooks beans. Janessa notes the silence, namely, how she and her grandmother would sit on her front porch in Atlanta and "listen to the street" while snapping beans in silence. Her grandmother indirectly taught her about the Southern cultural legacy of silence. The cultural silence is oppressive as it is therapeutic. In the silence, we can hear the snap of the beans that reminds us of our Southernness. Some conversations happen while snapping beans, but there are also moments of silence. That Black queer lesbian girl may be comforted by that silence as she sits with the colander of fresh beans. The snap of the green beans is a Southern rhythm that penetrates the silence. In the rhythm of snapping beans in silence, she engages in a complex simplicity—one is silent while also making noise. It is not coincidental that through the silence of snapping beans, we learn more about the South or, rather, because we were silent, we hear more about the South. The silent Black queer lesbian girl can hear and witnesses the complexity of these Southern realities. Even in our silence, we help Southerners recognize the racialized sexual queer elements of the South.

"It Has Its Ups and Downs": The Silent Southern Black Queer Lesbian Girl Exposes a Multidimensional South

The Southern Black queer lesbian girl sits in silence, giving Southerners a distinct vantage point of the South. Our multifaceted positionality helps uncover the components of this racialized sexual queer geography. SBQLWP exist in what Katherine McKittrick calls "knowable, unknowing, and expendable: she is seemingly in place by being out of place."[7] We expose what is known and unknown about the South, as well as who is expendable. The racialized sexual queer geography places SBQLWP as the outsider within, a distinct position that allows us to define the South as a complex place with certain elements that affirm our Southernness while also exposing trauma. We represent a geography where we are simultaneously in and out of place. Yet similar to Patricia Hill Collins's outsider within assessment, this positionality provides other Southerners a new vantage point of the South inclusive of racial, gender, sexual, and queer components. Our distinct position in multiple margins allows us to define and challenge what is traditionally understood as Southern. We can distinguish what it means to be Southern and critique this place we call home. For example, the South is known for its hospitality, but SBQLWP uncover some negative realities associated with it as we actualize our queer lesbian identities. Our intricate position allows us to paint a picture of the South, one that includes both positive and negative realities. From our vantage point, we can articulate what is known and unknown about Southern life.

The South is complicated for many SBQLWP, as it is defined by many contradictions. As I was reviewing the notes from conversations with interlocutors, I uncovered a multifaceted South that is both clear and complex. Even with the complexities of the South, the region is considered home. Andy stated that the "South is all I've known. It's home." Ironically, even while in silence, we see the South as a comfortable and familiar place and space. Although it is the first place that silenced them, it is still considered a homeplace for them. As Kea noted, we have a love/hate relationship with the South: we love the culture, hospitality, and everything else related to Southernness and hate the conservative upbringing that silenced our queer and sexual identities. Cassie provided a simple explanation of this multidimensional South: "It has its ups and downs." The "up" is the way the South represents a homeplace for her, providing a sense of belonging and connection to all things Southern and Black. Jae discussed the South as a place of comfort because she would "feel out of place in other areas." I experienced a similar sentiment, as I felt out of place when I moved to Las Vegas. Like Jae, we felt out of place because we were away from our homeplace, which gives comfort and connection to our Southernness. When I returned to Atlanta after my time in Vegas, I felt a sense of ease because I was returning to my homeplace. While I was free to express my queerness in Vegas, there was a part of me that yearned to return home. Coming back to the South was like going back to my grandma's kitchen where I felt comfortable to express my Southernness.

For many SBQLWP, the South represented a place and space where they felt a sense of belonging and connection as Southern Black persons. We understand our Blackness in the context of the South, where we are connected to other Southern Black folks with similar upbringings and worldviews. Andy directly stated, "I can see people who look like me." Sunshine noted that while living in the South, there is a sense of belonging among Southern Black people, where they "see you." Southern Black folks believe in establishing community, where we acknowledge and validate one another. Andy and Sunshine recognized that Southernness is attached to a racialized place, where they are likely to connect with Black folks who share similar experiences of growing up and living in the South. There are certain realities that only Southern Black folks understand. We know what it means to be outside in the Southern heat, going to Church weekly, and having Sunday dinner with grandma and 'em. As Tisha noted, "The South is like Sunday every day," where Southerners are surrounded by community, Church, family, and some good cooking.

SBQLWP recognize the significance of our complex Southern identity. There are a few responses from SBQLWP that allude to this sense of Southern Black socialization and further proof of the South as an identity marker:

Jae: "The South molded so much into who I am,"

Janessa: "It [the South] is part of my identity,"

Kris: "I am all South,"

Marie Dylan: "It [the South] is imprinted on me,"

Fatima: "The South is the root of who I am."

This Southern identity is not lost in our queer lesbian identity. Our queerness and lesbianism do not disconnect us from those elements that make us Southern and Black. We see the South as a foundational identity marker. Even in our queerness and lesbianism, our identities are also inevitably connected to a racialized South. This connection to the South is the "up" of Southern Black life, even if we previously existed in silence.

Consequently, we experience some negative realities in this Southern Black life, such as racially hostile experiences, the infamous Southern mentality, realities of community judgment, and Southern Church trauma. Some SBQLWP connected the South with racism, where there are still certain places where Black folks cannot visit or live. Ari noted that the west side of her small town is still considered racist. There are certain places and spaces still designated to Southern Black folks, a kind of racial containment. While not explicitly, Ari is leaning into discussions of a Southern Black memory, where Southern Black folks are always dealing with this racially contentious history and legacy. Her discussion of this racial containment highlights the "down" that exists in the Southern Black memory, exposing the "where" of race in America.

Location is significant for how Southern Blacks understand how race and Blackness are actualized. McKittrick would call this the "where" of race,[8] rooted in a certain geographic location and reinforced by historical and cultural realities. Because of this, SBQLWP can pinpoint the "where" of race in the South, where race has a significant component in conceptualizing and defining the South. For us, the South represents the "where" of our Blackness. For SBQLWP, the South represents a racialized space and place.

We cannot conceptualize the South without including the backdrop of race and the historical ramifications of racism. We contend that the South is connected to Black culture, centered on Black traditions and legacies rooted in certain historical realities related to racial difference. With the legacy of enslavement, Jim Crow laws, and lynching, Southern Black folks found methods of survival and birthed a distinct Southern Black culture. Establishing Blackness with the legacy of enslavement helps Black Southerners understand how some of these historical realities created Black culture and identity. As McKittrick discusses, this connection to enslavement is part of our "historical geographies and the ways in which we make and know space now are connected."[9] Enslavement helps us make sense of the South and the creation of our Southernness rooted in this memory and identity. Bynta noted that this Southern Black memory is tied to plantation life, slavery, and the lynching of Southern Black persons: "When I think of the South, there's a lot of strange fruit and pain." Bynta and Nina Simone both recognize the strange fruit of racism that exists in the South.

Even with the backdrop of horrific racial historical realities, Southern Black folks developed and sustained a recognizable culture. The central theme of the South is the ways Blacks resisted white presence in Southern public spaces[10]—this resistance has become the foundation for the ways we define and uncover the South as a Black space. The South prides itself on being the rebel, but Southern Black folks were the real rebels, attempting to claim autonomous space in the South. This reality is uncovered by my interlocutors as they define the South as a Black—and even an African diasporic space—similar to the discussion outlined by Paul Gilroy in *The Black Atlantic*. SBQLWP recognize how the South connects us to our Black and even African selves. Interlocutors recognize that the South has a closer connection to Black history and identity. SBQLWP contend that the South is the literal and metaphorical birthplace of Black culture in America. As June stated: "We Black, Black down here." According to SBQLWP, Blackness has its roots in the South. In this context, the South is the embodiment of American Blackness. So if we are Black and live in the South, we are closer to that embodiment of race. We Black, Black.

SBQLWP born and raised outside of the South found their way to the Black South. Moving to the South allows for SBQLWP to connect to that Black history, culture, and life. Leah from Minnesota reflected, "I just wanted to learn more about Black history and culture." Toni from Ohio felt drawn to the South, specifically Atlanta, because of the legacy of Rev. Dr. Martin Luther King Jr. and his social justic work. From this pull to the

South, Toni connected her family lineage to the South by way of Opelika, Alabama, and Atlanta. Even though she was raised in Ohio, she reiterates how she has roots in the South. For folks outside of the South, there is a pull to the South rooted in the desire to connect to the origin of what is considered Black. It is a magnetic energy. Regardless of where they were born, there is a consensus among **SBQLWP** that the South is directly related to our Black identities. Even in our queerness, we recognize the South as a racial identifier that resonates with us. This observation represents a racialized sexual queer geography, where our racial identities remain prevalent alongside our sexual identities. We uncover what is known, unknown, and hindering about the South.

SBQLWP seek to attach themselves to the "ups" of the South without having to deal with the "downs." The South creates a duality for us, where we recognize the region as sacred and problematic. June stated, "I want the community without the homophobia." Marie Dylan claims there is "an erasure and danger to Black queer people in the South." Bynta agrees, noting that this erasure assumes that all Southerners are cisgender and straight. While we feel connected to Southern Black life, we may feel silenced by the Southern Black community. As long as we remain silent about our queer lesbian identities, we are affirmed by Southern Black folks. We want to feel affirmed by the Southern Black community, where we do not have to exist in silence. The South as a homeplace is connected to the Southernness that we want to align with, without the oppressions of silence. Even in our silence, we identify this location as safe and contentious. For us, the South is a distinct location filled with complexities and contradictions.

This racialized sexual queer geography helps us recognize how one's perspective on location can be multifaceted and complex. This geography is certainly the case with **SBQLWP** who have a unique vantage point of the South. In our silence, **SBQLWP** recollect the racial and sexual components of the South that they experience as a Southern Black person and as a Southern Black woman. They hold on to the legacies of Blackness in the South and its connection to the legacy of Southern Black womanhood gained from maternal figures. However, in this racialized sexual queer geography, they recognize what traumas silenced them. This geography helps us see how the South has complex elements as it relates to sexual and gender differences. Furthermore, this geography helps other Southerners understand how we can exist in silence. Existing in silence allows us to uncover both positive and negative realities elements of the South and the known and unknown elements of Southern life that we encounter differently than our cisgender heterosexual brothers and sisters. Some of these elements are the discussions of what is known and unknown about Southern hospitality, the Southern Black family, and the infamous Southern and slave mentality. Each element ultimately silences us. Southern hospitality silences us with the societal "don't ask, don't tell," policy. Southern Black families silence us and encourage us remain silent to maintain our family legacy. We are silent when encountering this Southern and slave mentality to survive and exist in the region. These elements uncover how SBQLWP remain silent in our queer actualization.

"Hospitality Thrives in the South": Silence in Southern Hospitality

When asked to describe what the South means to them, SBQLWP pointed to Southern hospitality, which consists of certain unspoken sensibilities and social norms of how one should exist in the South. We do not honk our horns at others, we do not cuss in front of elders, we say "ma'am" and "sir" to others, we apologize if we bump into you at the store, we offer food or drink to guests when they come over, and we fix plates for new guests. Southern women do not discuss gender or sexual matters in "mixed company," and we are taught not to be crude and loud in public. Southern folks believe in being hospitable; it is as sacred as the Christian Bible. Due to this perception, Southern hospitality is a type of moral system in the South and serves as a litmus test of respect. Hospitality flows smoothly from a Southerner. Southern hospitality is a service to others, making everyone feel like family. As Remi pointed out, "hospitality thrives in the South" because it not only exists, it is also a significant component of our Southernness that we take with us regardless of where we are geographically located. Alison Chase recognized her Southern hospitality as an aspect of her Southernness even during her brief stay in Los Angeles, California. Her invited guests walked into a Southern portal where they were embraced with Southern hospitality. No matter where the Southerner resides in America, we take Southern hospitality with us because it is an essential part of our Southernness. However, Southern hospitality is an external exercise, established to make others comfortable.

SBQLWP continue this tradition of service by making others comfortable, even if we are silent. Southern hospitality is often gendered and leads our silence. Southern women are socialized to be hospitable. We are trained to ask a guest, especially male guests, if they want something to drink or to fix their plate. Southern hospitality forces women to serve others. Southern hospitality thrives because women are socialized to carry on the tradition of serving others and making them feel comfortable. It is no surprise that SBQLWP, socialized to be hospitable, continue to maintain Southern hospitality amidst our silence. Southern hospitality is one of those elements of Southernness we are indoctrinated with that ultimately causes our silence. When we invite people over for dinner, we still want to serve them. Even in our queerness and gender-nonconforming identities, we use the binary "ma'am" and "sir" as a form of respect. We want to ensure others are comfortable, even if we are not. Southern hospitality causes us to minimize our queerness when with our families. Masculine-embodied queer lesbian women may try to perform some level of femininity in public spaces to make others comfortable with their presence. We may not disclose our sexualities at work to make others comfortable. Southern hospitality socializes us to follow the tradition of serving others over ourselves and prioritizing others' comfort over our own.

This Southern hospitality leads to our silence and stifles our voices. As SBQLWP, we often are silent as a way of "showing respect." Because of Southern hospitality, queerness and lesbianism became synonymous with that loud, crude, disrespectful person that Southern folks despise. Our unapologetic queerness becomes the antithesis of Southern hospitality. We are approached as outsiders, even though we are from the South. Southern hospitality is inevitably linked to our Southernness, but we also are suppressed by it. When we describe the South, this notion of Southern hospitality is raised because it represents how we exist in silence.

In the South, the "don't ask, don't tell" (DADT) social policy is an extension of this Southern hospitality that keep SBQLWP silent. The idea of DADT was part of military policy signed into law by President Bill Clinton in 1994, where LGBTQIA+ military service persons were required to remain silent about their sexuality or gender identity because, supposedly, having openly LGBTQIA+ persons in the military would somehow taint morality, order, and discipline. This absurd policy was rooted in the assumption that LGBTQIA+ persons invoked a disturbance that could hinder the cohesiveness of a military unit. The policy ultimately silenced LGBTQIA+ persons who were enlisted and those who wanted to serve in the military. Consequently, this policy shows up in Southern culture. The South deals with sexual and gender differences by keeping our sexual or gender differences secret. The secrecy allows Southerners to maintain the "normal" societal order in the South. The moment the secret is out, it disrupts Southern normalcy. Like the military policy, it is assumed that the expression of one's gender and sexual fluidity may hinder the cohesiveness of the Southern Black community. DADT as a social policy normalizes and accepts the suppression of those with any kind of sexual or gender difference. Southern Black folks may recognize someone who is lesbian, gay, or queer but do not speak of that difference. They do not dare to ask about, and no one tells. DADT allows for queer and sexual realities to exist in silence. As Makeda stated, this Southern social norm allows Black queer folks to hide in plain sight.

The reason Southerners do not hear much about the experiences of SBQLWP is partly a result of this DADT social policy. Southern Black elders would often say that children should be seen and not heard. SBQLWP are the epitome of this: we are seen but not heard. The DADT social policy allows for our existence but not our visibility. We may be accepted, but not necessarily affirmed. Acceptance means that one is simply allowed to exist; affirmation means that someone validates our existence and makes space to ensure that we can thrive. Andy contends that affirmation asserts one's humanity, making the person whole. The DADT social policy makes sexuality or gender fluidity a topic of gossip, not intended to affirm one's humanity. The DADT exists in the whispers of "Have you heard so-and-so likes girls?" Many SBQLWP referred to the gay male choir director whose sexuality may be a "known fact," but no one dares to talk about it. This reality is understood, but not explained. He is visible and exists as a fixture in the Church, but no one talks about his lived experiences. No one affirms him as he negotiates his sexuality and gender fluidity. As long as no one asks, no one tells. Southern hospitality is an attempt to accept queer lesbian folks and make them feel some sense of comfort, even if that means not focusing on them as queer lesbian people. Marie Dylan mentioned that her coworkers ask about her children but never her partner. The overshadowing of gender and sexual differences by focusing on the kids is also a way of being hospitable by establishing conversation about anything other than the evident gender or sexual difference. Southern folks ask about the elements of our lives that are adjacent to heteronormativity. A Southern person will be hospitable, even to a fault. DADT contributes to this normalcy of silence.

Southern folks do not speak of a person's sexuality to extend a level of respect to those individuals. Southern hospitality means that folks do not discuss anyone's queerness in public. Calling out someone's gender and sexual fluidity is considered rude and a direct insult to their personhood. There is little worse than labeling someone else gay, lesbian, or queer. Also, in true Southern hospitality, no one openly talks about someone's sexuality without appropriate evidence. This reality explains how SBQLWP can exist in the South, even when silenced by the DADT and Southern hospitality. SBQLWP folks exist while hiding in plain sight. Ironically for some SBQLWP, this DADT and Southern hospitality can provide a level of safety. As Cayce put it, "Thanks to Southern hospitality, folks simply don't ask. And I do not tell because it's not their business." Because of Southern hospitality and DADT, we do not have to talk about our lives. This reality does not mean that this silence is liberating, but it allows some of us to remain safe and comfortable in the South. It also allows us to participate in the Southern Black community without fear.

The silence from the DADT and Southern hospitality provides a level of survival, comfort, and discomfort for us. Some SBQLWP may adhere to this social policy as a survival method, as it allows them to exist in this region, even if they are muted. The DADT and practices of Southern hospitality provide some comfort because it appears that no one is paying close attention or asking about personal lives. While the DADT social policy is problematic, there is a level of comfort that exists when no one asks about your sexuality. Allison Chase and Cayce, both of whom were educators at the time of our interview, were not openly queer or lesbian at work because of these social policies. Although they are not closeted lesbians, they compartmentalize their personal and professional lives. They can live their lives as queer lesbian women while also working in public school education. Although it is not the story of many SBQLWP, it shows how they use the DADT social policy to their advantage. Simultaneously, DADT causes some discomfort for those who are constantly watching how they present themselves in the South. This contradiction of comfort and discomfort is what Bernadette Barton refers to as the "Bible Belt panopticon and social surveillance."[11] She defines it as how Bible Belt gays police themselves in social spaces due to being socially watched by others. It seems like a contradiction that one can find comfort and discomfort in a space, but that represents our experience in the South: a walking contradiction.

"Who Yo' People?": Southern Black Families Silence SBQLWP

Southern Black families and communities are a significant part of our Southern identity. In the South, family and community are intertwined, as one's family may not be limited to biological relatives. Families in the South include kinfolk, a tradition based on our desire to maintain families during enslavement. Kinfolk may include your mom's best friend whom you may call "auntie" or your cousin's childhood friend who you may also call "cousin." Or, as we say in the South, "yo' cousin and 'em." In the South, Southern Blackness represents how Southern Black folks create a sense of family, regardless of whether one is blood related. In the Black South, we all family. In one conversation, LaDawn and I laughed at the phrase/question that Southern folks often ask one another: "Who yo' people?" This question drips with Southern vernacular to distinguish one's racial identity and ancestral roots. This question seems simple, but it forces a Southern Black person to connect and trace their identity to a specific family or community. "Who yo' people?" establishes our Southern roots and may vary based on who asks the question. This question solidifies one's legacy to a specific Southern location, answering the question of who one is "kin to." If I am in Sumter, South Carolina, I may respond by stating how I am kin to the Canty, Geter, and Mitchell families. It is not about me, but whose family I represent. I trace the legacy of my father's family. This question is also a way for those asking to establish one's value and character. Southern Black folks do not operate as individuals but as a part of a larger family and legacy. SBQLWP exist in this space, representing our family legacies.

Southern Black families (both biological and kinfolk) were established as a method of resistance to combat the harsh realities of enslavement and the overt racism in the South. The maintenance of family and community in the South had utilitarian purposes, essential for our survival. As outlined by Angela Davis, Black women maintaining biological families and fictitious families during enslavement established "strong personal bonds between immediate family members which oftentimes persistent despite coerced separation bore witness to the remarkable capacity of black people for resisting the disorder so violently imposed on their lives."[12] Families and kinfolk became the life force in the South to sustain Southern Black folks as they faced racial marginalization. Southern families act as the foundation that ties Southern Black people to a unit of support and a homeplace. Moreover, the creation and maintenance of the Southern Black family humanizes us. We are more than oppressed persons, connected to the life force of our families. For Southern Black folks, our families connect us to the South.

Memories of snapping beans also represents the significance of the Black family and community in the South. Many of us remember snapping beans with family members, where the process acts as a family activity. Snapping beans is a Southern Black communal practice because you must sit down—often in the company of other family members—and go through the process of snapping and/or canning the beans. This communal, collective chore is an essential component to eating for Southern Black folks. As LaDawn said, when snapping beans, it was "all hands on deck." If you had a bowl in front of you, then you were snapping the green beans. LaDawn mentioned that this communal effort that is essential to Southern cooking: "If you want to eat, come snap these beans." This statement shows the communal practice of Southern cooking, where we cook with family. No one was rushing to make a meal because it was more about the fellowship with family. Family members were encouraged to participate in either growing the food, buying the food, preparing the food, or cleaning up after the meal. Snapping beans is simply a part of the Southern Black communal process often done with family. The process of snapping beans could not happen without the backdrop of the Southern family. We need our cousins and 'em to snap beans.

On the other hand, Southern Black families can lead to the silencing of SBQLWP. Existing openly as a Black queer person in the South could ultimately result in bringing shame to one's family. This fear of bringing shame to our families causes us to be silent because we do not seek to embarrass our family or community. We do not operate as autonomous beings but as extensions of our family. This lack of autonomy makes it difficult for us to actualize our queer lesbian identities without bringing our family into it. Some of our family members may be respected members of the community. We are daughters of preachers, bishops, teachers, and community leaders. For example, because Jae's father was a well-known school principal in a small Georgia town, she remained silent about her fluid gender and sexual identities. This reality caused some tension in her coming out as a masculine-embodied queer lesbian, and she did not reach the fullness of her queer lesbian identity until she left her small town. Coming out ultimately causes some level of shame to your family name and legacy. Collins mentions how Black queer folks appear to hinder Black liberation and drain the progress Black folks have made.[13] In this case, being openly lesbian or queer in the South is perceived as hindering one's family legacy and draining the social, economic, and political progress the family has made. Somehow, a queer lesbian daughter will crumble all that hard work a family has made toward social mobility and status in the South. God forbid.

Although it may be connected to economic status, Southern Black folks recognize societal status as a symbol of Southern Black progression. For example, a Southern Black educator may have societal and moral status, not necessarily economic status. This progression is also tied to how closely they imitate their prominent white counterparts. Having a queer lesbian Southern Black family member somehow hinders that progress and social status. If a family member is openly queer, that somehow reflects on the whole family. If the family has some level of societal prestige or is connected to a well-known church, then the perception of the family diminishes. To avoid this pressure, we remain silent. This question "Who yo' people?" sticks out for us because the question reminds us of our silence. While LaDawn and I laughed about this phrase, we also knew that this question established and maintained our silence to protect our families.

Once we actualize our lesbianism and queerness, we transfer that sense of belonging to our queer communities, where we create our own fictitious families to reaffirm other Southern Black queer persons. Even in our queerness, the South represents generational family connections. Whether we live in the South now or grew up there, our Southernness recognizes the South as a physical and cultural space that connects us to family and kinfolk. As Toni stated, the South is "part of who I am. I was made here." This statement is a form of affirmation, connecting to our Southern families and other kinfolk. Southern Black families provide a sense of identity for us, where we learn who we are and whom we are kin to. Southern Black families anchor us, providing us a sense of belonging to the South that seems to bypass sexuality. SBQLWP are not only connected to our biological family and kinfolk, we are also connected to our Southern queer families that provide safety against homophobia and heterosexism. Our Blackness and queerness help us understand the significance of creating and maintaining a sense of family to sustain our humanity and community.

SBQLWP carry on this tradition of creating fictitious queer families to combat the trauma and silence that exists in this region. The maintenance of our Southern Black queer community is part of our Southern Black identity, hence we often refer to the Southern Black queer community as "fam." Similar to biological and fictitious Southern Black families, these people are imperative for the survival of the Southern Black queer community as it continues the tradition of anchoring us and connecting us to a community. The establishment of the "fam" is a way for us to find a sense of belonging, reestablish our humanity, and helps us to actualize our identities. This fam unmutes the silent Southern Black queer lesbian girl, and she has a safe space to discuss her joys and pains that come from being a Black queer lesbian in the South. The fam combats the Southern culture of silence. In the "fam," we are establishing our connection to our Black queer kinfolk.

Similar to creating a fictitious Southern Black family, SBQLWP create kinships as a method of resistance against the culture of silence. Like our Southern Black families, these queer families are a life force. My understanding of maintaining a strong family unit was derived from the lessons learned from grandma and 'em. Replicating the Southern Black family was instilled in who we are as Southern Black women, where we maintain that Southern Black memory through the creation and sustaining of families. In this case, the fam allows us to maintain the Southern memory, applied to the sustainability of Southern Black queer lesbian folks. We extend this legacy as we recognize the necessity of establishing a shield of protection for Southern Black queer folks. This fam represents a method of resistance against the dehumanization we experience in our silence. For queer folks, the question "who yo' people?" is a way of connecting us to our Southern Black queer community, a safe space where one can speak and exist in our authentic selves, separate from the silence that exists in our biological families and homophobic kinfolk. "Who yo' people?" addresses the question of whose community or communities we are connected to.

"It's That Slave Mentality": The Infamous Southern and Slave Mentality Silence SBQLWP

When describing the South, SBQLWP noted the Southern mentality that caused their silence. When SBQLWP think of the South, we think of that mentality and the ways Southern folks are "simply stuck in their ways." This Southern mentality represents a person, place, or thing that does not like or affirm anything or anyone considered different. Regardless of race, class, or gender, this mentality contributes to a conservative worldview. Marie Dylan went into detail as to what this mentality entails: the limited ways people internalize the significance and value of heteronormative marriage, sexual purity, and toxic masculinity. Moreover, this mentality has sexist and patriarchal views of women, Black people, and trans persons. Many SBQLWP first noted this mentality rooted in the infamous phrase "Hate the sin, love the sinner." This quotation became the epitome of the Southern mentality because it represents a tolerance of Southern Black queer persons. We have permission to exist but we are not embraced. This Southern mentality upholds conservative Christianity and morality that limits how Black queer folks can exist in public spaces.

This Southern mentality is not necessarily limited to Black folks in the South, but SBQLWP encounter it more in Black spaces. As Torrey said, the Southern mentality is synonymous with the "slave mentality," which is connected to race dynamics in the South. Torrey provides examples of how this mentality manifests in the way Southern Black folks engage with

Southern white persons. She describes how silence becomes a way for Southern Black folks to exist among Southern white people. For example, Southern Black folks code-switch in front of Southern white people, address Southern white folks as "ma'am" or "sir," and whisper about white domestic terrorism in public. The slave mentality is not to say that enslaved Africans were less intelligent or backward. In fact, enslaved Africans were geniuses. However, the slave mentality gives a sense of what the enslaved person may have internalized as "normal" sexual and gender identity. This normalcy was dictated by white, cisgender heteronormative oppressors, who established a hegemonic caste system of sexuality in the South. As a result of chattel slavery, the South established a gender and sexual hierarchy that categorized Southern Black folks as sexually deviant. Collins notes how chattel slavery "marked the emergence of a hegemonic white masculinity rooted in a dual relationship of the White gentleman/White lady so celebrated in Southern folklore, and in a racialized master/slave relationship."[14] The Southern mentality honors toxic cisgender heteronormative white masculinity and femininity, considering them the model for other Southerners to follow. In the South, if one can emulate the Southern gentleman or the Southern belle, they will gain respect.

The slave mentality is transferred to the ways Southern Black cisgender, heterosexual folks view normal gender and sexuality. The slave mentality represents a consciousness that cannot see representations of Blackness outside of cisgender heteronormativity. It judges other Southern Black folks who challenge this gender and sexual hegemony. Those with this mentality internalize the consciousness of their oppressors, understanding sexuality and gender only in the context of this hegemonic white masculinity. Kea described this slave mentality as someone who "thinks inside the box about what it means to be Black." From her perspective, the slave mentality judges whether one is Southern enough or Black enough. This mentality has a limited understanding of Blackness and Southern Blackness. It dictates acceptable embodiments of Southern Black womanhood as well, determining how Southern Black women and persons should embody their gender and sexual identities. In this mentality, Southern Black women need to emulate the Southern belle, exemplifying purity, submissiveness, piety, and domesticity. The slave mentality contends that Southern Black women should operate in this gender binary, existing as either a pure, asexual mammy or the hypersexual heterosexual Jezebel. A Southern Black woman is either a saint or a sinner.

The Southern and slave mentalities are rooted in the Church. For Black people in America and in the South specifically, the Church is the cultural womb of the Black community.[15] The Church determines one's social value, using Southern and slave mentalities as enforcers. SBQLWP cite the ways the Church reinforces these mentalities. Even if a person does not attend Church regularly, a Black Southerner recognizes how the institution establishes certain Southern norms. Even heathens know Church politics and ideologies. In Robin Boylorn's depiction of the town of Sweetwater, she acknowledges that everyone believes in God and has a church home even if they do not attend services regularly.[16] The Southern and slave mentalities begin in the Church and permeate into the greater Southern Black community.

The overly religious and conservative ideologies fuel the Southern and slave mentalities, questioning any sign of gender and sexual difference through the lens of evangelical Christianity. Homophobia, sexism, and heterosexism are problems that exist throughout America, but the Southern Church informs how Southern folks should deal with sexual and gender differences. The Southern and slave mentalities consider sexual and gender differences to be an embarrassment because they are considered sinful in the eyes of the Church. Cisgender, heterosexual persons in the South with monogamous, heteronormative families have social status because they maintain the Southern evangelical Christian value system. Those outside of this image are considered socially deviant and should be silenced. Because of the Southern and slave mentality, SBQLWP are silenced. SBQLWP note that these Southern and slave mentalities hindered us from reaching our authentic selves and explains why the South silenced us.

The Southern and slave mentalities resonate with us because they are the first Southern reality that silences our queerness. They act as the antithesis to all things different as well as a method of social surveillance to ensure that Southern Blacks align with this hegemonic model of heteronormativity. This surveillance makes it difficult for us to actualize our sexualities and queerness. Southern Black queer folks feel like we are under constant surveillance, which is not far-fetched in a technological world. In public spaces, we must watch our backs from the societal surveillance of folks who internalize the Southern and slave mentalities. While we love our people, we recognize the homophobia, heterosexism, patriarchy, and sexism in these mentalities. These oppressive ideas and principles become deeply ingrained in the consciousness of Southern Black folks. The Southern and slave mentalities even manifest in our families. These mentalities may rear their ugly heads while talking to a homophobic uncle or heterosexist mother. These mentalities represent the darker side of this Southernness. We cannot escape it; it suffocates and engulfs us like the humid air. SBQLWP find that the best method to exist in the South amidst these mentalities is to remain silent about our queerness or lesbianism. We swallow the tyranny daily to simply exist in the South alongside these mentalities.

The perception of the South as slow and backward does not mean that it is devoid of intellectualism. This "backwardness" relates to economic production and the perceived limited urbanization. The backwardness of the South relates to a metrocentric lens, where Christopher Stapel (along with some SBQLWP) contend that urbanization is often connected to an increased intellectualism. However, Stapel and SBQLWP find the South as a location, Southern rurality, and possibly the Southern mentality have something to contribute to intellectual discourse. While the Southern and slave mentalities appear to make the South devoid of intellectual consciousness, we express concerns with the racism, patriarchy, and heteronormativity in the South. The South and these mentalities have limitations regarding difference, but this discussion does not suggest that Southern folks are not smart or have intellectual thoughts. The South is a complex intellectual space, even with some limitations related to gender and sexual hegemonies.

Silence of SBQLWP Sharpens Their Image of the South

Silence is the first part of the trauma SBQLWP experience in the South. Our queerness and lesbianism are silenced due to certain regional cultural realities. That culture of silence stifled us from fully exploring our queerness. While SBQLWP were silent about different realities, the culture of silence represents the first step to actualizing our queer lesbian identities. In our queerness, we participate in the culture of silence to save ourselves from contempt, censure, judgment, and annihilation. Because we fear being targets of oppression, we use certain Southern cultural realities of silence to our advantage. We found that the DADT in Southern hospitality provided an opportunity for us to remain silent. Our Southern Black family lineages force us to minimize our queerness and lesbianism. As long as we remained silent about our queerness and lesbianism, we could maintain our connection to our Southern Black families and lineages. Finally, we remain silent to avoid judgment from Southern and slave mentalities. We find ways to use these elements to exist in silence. Sometimes this silence saves us. But many times, the tyranny we swallow day after day chokes us.

Even in silence, SQLWP can define the complexities of the South and observe a geography that has beauty and tension. Our silence helps us to see how the South is a multifaceted place and space. From our position in silence, we have a stronger understanding of the South, which sharpens our image of the region. Even in her silence, a Southern Black queer lesbian girl in her grandma's kitchen can paint an accurate picture of the South. She knows that this homeplace exists in a contradiction, not always filled with comfort or nostalgia. She may be choked in her silence, but this silence acts as a space to build knowledge. As an outsider within, this silent Black queer lesbian girl can conceptualize what queer and gender elements exist in this notion of Southernness. From her standpoint, she can pinpoint all these contradictions. She can capture the hurt and wholeness the South provides for SBQLWP. However, because of the presence of the Southern Christian Black Church, the trauma is ongoing. The silence transforms into shame and condemnation, weapons used by the Church against SBQLWP.

"The Church Is Not the Building; It's the People"

The Shameful and Condemning South

"Their own receive them not," a paraphrase from John's Gospel, recognizes that African American lesbians and gays have endured a history of misunderstanding, pain, sorrow, and rejection by their own people.[1]

It starts with the fire-and-brimstone Church sermon with phrases like "homosexuality is an abomination to God," or "hate the sin, love the sinner." We get warm, clam up, and start sweating. We look around to ensure that no one is looking at us. We almost forgot to breathe. We feel like we have been punched in the stomach and want to disappear. Instead of the Church acting as a space of spiritual refuge, it becomes a space of shame and condemnation for SBQLWP. Because of the Southern Christian Black Church,[2] the silent Southern Black queer lesbian girl encounters shame and condemnation. That silent Southern Black queer lesbian girl hears words of hate in an institution she frequently encounters. As she is coming out (to herself or to the world), she is met with words of shame and condemnation rooted in conservative Christian doctrines and ideologies. The Church's rigid gender and sexual cultural norms create shame and eventually condemnation for us.

We are told that we are abominations, that our lives are unworthy in the eyes of God. That silent girl hears that she will never prosper in life as a queer lesbian. These weapons of shame wielded by Church folks are methods of dehumanization, causing her to see her queer lesbian self as a problem, as less than human. We directly encounter shame and hate in a place that is supposed to represent love. Many SBQLWP noted that the Church is foundational in our queer lesbian actualization. Cassie joked how the Church represented the "meat and potatoes" of how we explore our sexual identity. I used a similar language in future conversations with interlocutors when we were getting ready to talk about the Church. At that point in our conversations, they knew the heavy conversations were coming. The shame and condemnation from the Church is foundational to what we experience as we actualize our sexual and queer identities. While Black folks often speak of Church hurt, the SBQLWP experience Church trauma through shame and condemnation.

"The People Make Up the Church": Church Trauma Wielded by Southern Black Families and Mothers

This shame and condemnation from the Church creeps into Southern life and exists in the consciousness of our communities and families, making it overt and direct. In the South, the Church is the family, and family is the Church. As Fatima said, "You know what they say, the people make up the Church. The church is not just the building, it's the people." When reminiscing about her family in South Carolina, Shay notes: "The church was family, and family was the church." The Church represents the people, and the people are the Church. Church folks, and subsequently the Southern Black community, internalize certain cisgender heteronormative ideologies and morals upheld and valued in the South. For us, Church was not always the physical building or the homophobic sermon, but how Southern folks wielded this homophobic and heterosexist rhetoric to dehumanize anyone who steps outside of this cisgender heteronormativity. Unfortunately, this dehumanization was not from some random Church congregant, but from people close to us—our family members and mothers. In the South, there is not much separation between the Church as an institution and our intimate families The shame we encountered by the Church came from the ones closest to us. We encountered homophobia and heterosexism from our own.

Families are typically safe places for Southern Black folks, but it was not always the case with Southern Black queer folks. Churches often represented family lineages to the South. The Church connects many Black Americans to their respective families. These Southern Black families act on behalf of the Church to denounce any type of sexual impropriety, especially homosexuality or gender fluidity. This church shame was worse for some SBQLWP, whose family members were also Church leaders. These family members were pastors, first ladies, deacons, missionary members, or trustees. Horace Griffin acknowledges the ways the Church is an extension of the family as he notes that the Black Church was "a place where family members and neighbors gathered weekly to renew their faith, take refuge from racism, and find hope for the future."[3] The Church existed in our families, where we would hear homophobic or sexist comments. It is one thing for a Church pastor to shame us, but it is different when the weapon of shame is wielded by a family member, someone we love. As Griffin suggests, our own receive us not. The Church causes our families to reject us. Instead of the Church acting as that space of peace and refuge, it becomes an institution that rejects its own. We hesitate coming out because we realize that our families will wield the weapon of shame against their own.

Because of the evangelical religious practices of passing along "the good news" of Jesus Christ, family members find it their Christian duty to minister to those queer lesbians who are considered lost in the deviant world of homosexuality. Family members take it upon themselves to be a Church guide. Because we are perceived to be devoid of any spiritual grounding, family members feel compelled to shame us under the guise of trying to save our souls from damnation. These individuals pride themselves on shaming us, believing that using shame to save their queer lesbian sisters from a life of turmoil and sin. These Southern Black families will still consider us family, but as those wayward members who are lost in the sinful perils of homosexuality. In sharing God's message with these wayward souls, these families members believe they are spiritually saving us. The shame wielded by our own families plants the seeds of condemnation, and we start to believe that our lives are sinful and problematic. This strife establishes the internal homophobia SBQLWP experience, a phase in our queer lesbian actualization where we hate ourselves and exist in a duality to stop the family shame.

What does it mean to shame someone? What is the root of this shame? What is considered shameful in the South? SBQLWP understand shame as an external exercise manifested by social norms. Shame becomes a social method of dehumanizing queer folks, where SBQLWP are treated as inhuman and disconnected from the Southern Black community. Shame from the Church attempts to isolate us from our Southern Black communities because we choose not to conform to preestablished gender and sexual norms valued by the Church. The Church uses homophobia and heterosexism to shame others. Homophobia and heterosexism are strategic methods of shaming anyone who threatens the integrity of the Church. They are employed to shame those who do not align themselves with the conservative sexual norms established by the Church. Ultimately, homophobia and heterosexism forces Southern Black folks to align with what is considered "normal" sexuality, namely, heterosexuality, heteronormativity, and sexual purity. The Church uses homophobia and heterosexism as a way to "protect" the Church and Black sexuality. Kelly Douglas explains that homophobia is a "misguided strategy for protecting Black lives and the integrity of Black sexuality."[4] In line with Douglas, homophobia intends to "protect" Black lives by keeping Black sexuality pure from the "devil" of homosexuality. This method of shaming infers that Southern Black people are saved by heterosexuality. Not Jesus Christ, but being straight will somehow save us. Oddly, Southern Black folks shame others to protect one another.

Because of this shame and the preconceived myth of saving the souls of Black folks, the Church does not provide a safe space for female sexual and gender fluidity. Shame also invokes a level of unworthiness. Remi (they/them) noted this: "I harbored shame for myself like I did something wrong because there was no space for me in Church." They felt "wrong" for not being heterosexual, not participating in heterosexism and patriarchy, and not adopting binary gender identities. Like Remi, the shame from homophobia and heterosexism causes many of us to think that something is wrong with us. Because our lives do not align with what is normal in the eyes of the Church, we are viewed as unworthy of God's love and blessings. Ultimately, shame is the Church's method of creating, establishing, and reiterating a sexual and gender hierarchy in the South, punishing those who choose not to exist as a heteronormative Southern Black person. SBQLWP note that these punishments ultimately lead to Church trauma, causing us to experience self-hatred as we actualize our queer lesbian identities. Shame creates a Church trauma that is ever present in our Southern narratives.

Unlike shame, condemnation represents an internal spiritual warfare, manifested by internalizing the homophobic and heterosexist ideologies from the Church. Shame is invoked by hearing the words of dehumanization; condemnation is believing those words to be true. Condemnation is rooted in the perception that one's gender and sexual identity lacks spiritual grounding. We believe that we are a sinful abomination. It is an internalized shame, where the Southern Black queer lesbian girl may hate herself or feel that she lacks spiritual anchoring. Condemnation causes the Southern Black queer lesbian girl to believe she is unworthy of God's love and blessings.

Condemnation is the process by which the external shame transfers to self, where we internalize our existence and humanity as a problem. These internal conflicts may cause some self-destructive physical behaviors, such as attempts at self-harm. Paulo Freire would refer to condemnation as a self-deprecation, where the oppressed see themselves the way the world sees them. Freire contends that the oppressed internalize the opinions of their oppressors, convinced of their own unfitness.[5] This notion of self-deprecation means that one internalizes these negative stereotypes of themselves. The oppressed (in this case SBQLWP) internalize the negative ideologies of their oppressors (conservative Black Church folks). SBQLWP believe these negative stereotypes of ourselves and our queer lesbian community. Condemnation means that we encounter a spiritual battle, where we are operating from the perceived position of spiritual deficiency. Because of Church shame, we question what we did to deserve such a terrible fate of queerness. The condemnation is the untold narrative of SBQLWP. Some of us experience this condemnation for years, some for a lifetime. We may speak of the shame from the Church but rarely discuss how it manifests internally. Condemnation uncovers how the Church's shame creates a tumultuous, internal struggle for us.

Not every interlocutor had this experience with the Church. A few mentioned that the Church did not have a significant impact on their narratives. Kendra discussed how "Church was never a priority, and I wasn't forced to attend Church." Even though she grew up in the South, the Church was not central to her life. Endesha, who grew up in a Missionary Baptist Church, did not experience this Church trauma because she came out later in her life. As she stated, she was able to "intellectually engage in queerness" as a student at Spelman College. She did not experience much of the shame and condemnation that many SBQLWP encountered. While she had tensions in her family because of Southern Black conservative upbringing, she experienced it as an adult. However, the majority of SBQLWP have a story of Church trauma. Their narratives are outlined here.

"You Know Where We Are At on Sundays in the South": SBQLWP as Fixtures in the Church

Before the shame and condemnation, the Church played a pivotal role in the lives of SBQLWP. The shame and subsequent condemnation had a harsh impact in our lives because the Church was (and still is) a major social institution for us. If you are a Black person from the South, you recall memories of going to Church. Attending Church or being active in Church was not an option but a requirement, an expectation. As Kea noted, "You know where we are at on Sundays in the South." Growing up, I did not have a choice whether I would attend Church. Sunday mornings were designated for Church, and I would be going to someone's Church. My mother woke me up every Sunday with the expectation that I would be ready for Church and any Church activities. Like other SBQLWP who grew up in the Church, we did not realize anything else could happen on Sundays. As Tisha said, "I didn't know anything else." For many SBQLWP, Church life happened to us. We were expected to participate in Church activities in some capacity. Once I learned to play an instrument, I was highly encouraged (in other words, expected) to play for our Church. During summers, I attended Vacation Bible School. While in college, I was expected to teach at Church summer day camps. Many SBQLWP mentioned that they were frequently at Church growing up, even beyond Sunday mornings. As long as the Church doors were open, we were there. The Church operated as a permanent fixture in our lives. Like our heterosexual brothers and sisters, we were inevitably connected to and existed in the Church.

Ironically enough, many of the interlocutors I spoke to were (and currently still are) active in their Church. In some cases, interlocutors were significant fixtures in the Church, hidden in plain sight, working as musical directors, missionary leaders, preachers, and theologians. This reality shows that we have always existed in the Church. Some SBQLWP served in the Church's music and youth ministries, led volunteers, and were even youth regional denominational leaders. Although they left the Church, Remi previously worked as a Southern Baptist youth leader. Andy began (and continues to) work with the video and audio ministries at her Church. Though not currently connected to the Church, in the past, Maezah worked as a Church musician. Cayce and Kea worked as watchmen in the Jehovah's Witnesses hierarchy.[6] To me, it was ironic that they were considered watchmen, as they are both masculine-embodied lesbians. Kea noted, "I took a deep drink from Jehovah's Witness," as she immersed herself in the Church as a way of hiding her sexuality from herself and others. Cayce stated that before she came out and eventually was disfellowshipped from the Jehovah's Witness faith,[7] she had helped build her local Kingdom Hall. According to Cayce, building a Kingdom Hall means that you have a position of authority. Other SBQLWP noted how they were heavily involved in volunteering at the Church, even without an official title.

As Griffin mentioned, the presence of lesbians in the Church is not as clear as it is for the gay man because it is assumed that Black lesbians do not have a Church affiliation.[8] Before our sexualities were known to others (or to ourselves), queer lesbian folks were on Church staff, doing what Southern Black folks call "the work of the Lord." Like many Churches, Black women act as the backbone. This backbone included SBQLWP. Our involvement in the Church aligns with the tradition of Southern Black women acting as Church supporting staff. Our involvement relies on the assumption that Southern Black women engage in Southern hospitality in the Church, where our work for the Church is for the betterment of the congregants. While homophobic Church folks assume that our queerness and lesbianism is a selfish identity, our Church work challenges that myth. The heavy Church involvement of SBQLWP challenges the idea that we are somehow disconnected from Church. While Southern Black folks like to assume that we are hidden in the margins of society, we always exist in Church congregations, working in ministries and even as Church leaders. We were and continue to be significant fixtures of the Church. Despite what is assumed about us, we were always doing the work of the Lord, even as we experienced Church shame and condemnation.

"I Did Not Want to Embarrass My Family": Shaming Evident in Church Gender Presentation and Aesthetics

Southern Black Church folks have a historical connection to what we call our "Sunday best," the aesthetics of wearing our best outfits for Church on Sunday. I recall having certain outfits that I could only wear for Church: a particular knee-length dress or skirt with a long-sleeved blouse. Our Sunday best is how Southern Black folks closely mimic the embodiment of traditional Southern masculinity and femininity. This external presentation and aesthetics have some historical elements, where appropriate presentation allowed us to avoid some unwanted sexual confrontations. During enslavement, our Sunday best was the only outfit slaveholders granted enslaved Africans to wear to Church on Sundays. Even amid oppression, Southern white folks still believed their enslaved workers should attend Church as a method of keeping them docile. The notion of wearing our Sunday best was an opportunity for us to engage in a traditional feminine and masculine performance to regain a sense of humanity in response to harsh racial realities. These historical realities cause Southern Black Church folks to reinforce importance of external presentation and "appropriate" aesthetics. We knew that once we stepped outside our homes, we represented our families. When attending Church or engaging in any Church activity, one represents their family. After all, appropriate aesthetics and presentation in the South equate to whether the person was raised with the "proper" morals and values. For Southern Black girls, feminine presentation was proof of proper training. As the elders would say, it was proof that we were "raised right." Church aesthetics related to the Southern embodiment of femininity become a foundational tool used to shame SBQLWP. SBQLWP noted that Church folks place significant value on external presentation, especially for Black girls.

This notion of Sunday best is etched in our brains as significant both inside and outside of the Church. My godmother Marie (whom we also called Riri) took her Sunday best seriously, known by other parishioners for her fashionable Church outfits. She made sure she coordinated her hats and shoes, all of which perfectly matched her dress. But the practice of wearing our Sunday best is a daily practice in the South, where one must present themselves "properly" in public spaces. In other words, Church folks understand the significance of maintaining an aesthetic that aligns with politics of respectability. I can hear Riri, known as the Church diva, telling me "You ain't finna go outside lookin' any type of way." Southern Black Church girls are socialized to understand the significance of gender performance and aesthetics in public spaces. We were encouraged to embody a certain level of appropriate aesthetic (read: respectability) to avoid social judgment. After all, as Riri would say, "You never know who you will see." Southern feminine aesthetics and presentations were essential to our value as Southern Black women, causing us to think that we could not leave the house without looking presentable. Fatima discussed how a "good Church girl" was always expected to look presentable. Southern Black Church girls were expected to embody holiness and traditional femininity, such as knee-length skirts, blouses to cover up their arms and chest, and sensible shoes (no stiletto heels here). Our aesthetics needed to represent purity and align with Southern femininity. The purity was inherent in the performance of heteronormativity.

The silent Black queer lesbian girl understands the significance of Sunday best, negotiating what that means for her as she actualizes her queer lesbianism. The same expectations of Southern feminine aesthetics and presentation are used against SBQLWP, forcing us to adhere to a certain level of femininity in the Church. Gender-nonconforming and masculine-embodied queer lesbians are pressured to embody the Southern feminine aesthetics in Church to alleviate the shame they may cause their families. For not aligning with the traditional feminine aesthetics and presentation, masculine-embodied and gender-nonconforming SBQLWP are perceived as an embarrassment to their families and shamed for not presenting themselves within the confines of Southern femininity. Several of my interlocutors disclosed the fear of embarrassing their families when wearing traditionally masculine clothing at Church. Ari noted that she had to "put on a show" in Church, where she would engage in traditional notions and embodiment of femininity because wearing masculine clothing "seemed like a sign of disrespect" to her family. Somehow, it is disrespectful to embody gender fluidity. Out of "respect" for their families, these masculine-embodied and gender-nonconforming folks would try to blend in at Church. As a result of Church shame, embodying masculinity or gender nonconformity is perceived as form of disrespect and embarrassment. As LaDawn noted, "A queer person in Church has to be able to pass." To "pass" and avoid shame, we must present ourselves as heteronormative as possible, which means embodying aesthetics of traditional femininity. As discussed by LaDawn, SBQLWP are perceived as less of a problem if they can pass as cisgender and heteronormative. Fatima nodded at this, stating "I knew what I had to do to keep other folks happy." Even as a feminine-embodied queer lesbian who grew up Baptist and Catholic, she recognized the politics of passing as heterosexual to gain acceptance and minimize Church shame. In aligning with Bettina Love's "active coping,"[9] masculine-presenting or gender-nonconforming SBQLWP would adopt the aesthetic culture of the Church to save themselves and their families from shame, even if they are uncomfortable. According to Love, active coping represents the ways Black lesbians negotiate spaces that minimize their "outness," particularly for Black lesbian women to survive the Church. SBQLWP in this work concur that we attempt to minimize our lesbianism and queerness to cope with the Church shame we experienced.

As masculine embodied and gender nonconforming SBQLWP actualize their queer lesbian identities, they would perform as a feminine-embodied cisgender woman to avoid embarrassing their mothers. As Cayce noted, Southern Black women, regardless of sexuality, internalize our mothers saying, "Don't do anything to embarrass me." For masculine-embodied and gender-nonconforming SBQLWP, this means existing as a cisgender, heteronormative Black woman. Even as our mothers are the ones weaponizing shame against us, we still do not want to embarrass them. As Jae points out, it was less about the clothing and more about the shame she feared her mother would encounter. In her small Georgia town, she was more concerned that Church folks would shame her mother for her masculine embodiment. We would often take on the shame from Church folks to save our maternal figures. The mother becomes content with her daughter's discomfort because it allows the mother to be free from Church shame. As Kris, said, "Back in the day, I wanted to try and please my grandmother." She would indulge her by wearing more feminine clothing and even wearing makeup to Church and family events. While in a space of discomfort, we are still doing what we can to please our grandma and 'em. Perhaps this sacrifice is our way of trying to regain our mother's love and respect. If we can only please our mothers and help them avoid social shame, then somehow we will regain our mother's love and acceptance.

"When I Think of the Black Church, I Think of Mama": Shaming from Our Southern Black Mothers

For many SBQLWP, our mothers represented the Church that wielded weapons of shame against us. As many interlocutors said, "It's always those mothers." In some conversations, this statement was met with laughter. In others, it we made with a traumatic sigh. We saw our mothers as the Church. As June put it, "When I think of the Black Church, I think of mama." Similarly, Janessa said, "My mother was the Church." This conflict with our mothers is significant in our coming-out narratives. In many cases, coming out was not so harmful from the Church institution but from our mothers who used toxic, heteronormative Church doctrines to shame their daughters. Perhaps our mothers believed that shaming us would somehow ensure that we maintained a level of sexual purity and social status. Maybe these Southern Black mamas used shame as a way to shield their dawtas from judgment. Like other family members, maybe our mothers believed that shaming us would ultimately save our souls. These mothers brought us into this world and were invested in ensuring that our souls are saved from eternal damnation. Whatever their reasons, our mamas were the root cause of our Church trauma.

Regardless of our sexual identities, Black girls raised in the South see our mothers and other maternal figures as an integral component to our socialization into Southern Black womanhood. They help us understand who we are as Southern Black women, integrating us into a type of womanhood only found in the Black South. Through conversation and modeling, Black mothers provide their daughters with the tools needed to survive and thrive in America. Black mothers are essential in teaching their daughters how to fit into the sexual politics of Black womanhood.[10] These individuals are significant in raising future generations of Black women, protecting them from harm as long as possible, while teaching them independence and self-reliance so they can protect themselves.[11] While they played this role in our lives, they are also the main source of the trauma and hurt experienced by the Church. It was not just the homophobic sermon but the way our mothers shamed us as we actualized our queer lesbian identity. When it comes to queer lesbian daughters, Southern Black mothers transform from a loving individual to a significance source of pain. In many instances, this taints our relationships with our mothers during a season in our queer lesbian actualization. For some of us, the relationship was never reconciled.

Our sexualities and queer identities become permanent identity markers when we come out to our moms. As Janessa said, "I didn't come out until I came out to my mom." Coming out to her mom became the final step to actualizing her sexual identity. This dynamic with Southern Black mothers establishes a unique narrative for SBQLWP. For us, maternal figures are pivotal in our coming-out narratives. Once we come out to her, we are fully embracing our queer lesbian selves. Because our mothers are so essential to our lives, coming out to her becomes the final step in our journey. Like Janessa, I did not see myself as an openly queer lesbian woman until I came out to my mama. I told my father and brother several months before telling her. My sexual and queer identity did not become real for me until I told my mama. Coming out to our moms is like coming out to the Church community because they mark the moment we encounter the source of our Church trauma. Once we come out to our moms, we are preparing ourselves to directly encounter Church shame. Telling our mothers marks a moment of resolve for us, where we have the emotional strength to confront the source of our Church trauma.

The Church trauma from our mothers came in many forms. This maternal shame caused painful memories for SBQLWP as we actualized our queer lesbian identities. Hearing these stories brought me to tears several times, as I also know the pain and hurt of this maternal shame. When June was a teenager, coming to terms with her lesbian identity, her mother wrote Bible verses about the abomination of homosexuality on her bathroom mirror. After Janessa told her mother that she was bisexual, she described how her mother, who was a Church deaconess at the time, told their pastor to go to her college dorm room to "lay hands" on her.[12] In many cases, the laying of hands intends to heal people from their emotional and physical pain and suffering. The laying of hands often represents freedom from any ailment or sorrow. For SBQLWP, the laying of hands is an act of oppression and suppression, like putting chains on our wrists, causing additional suffering and leading to more bondage. For Janessa, the laying of hands was not meant to set her free from her queer lesbian identity but to place the chains of oppression on her.

For those SBQLWP who were formally in the Jehovah's Witness faith, disfellowship establishes shame. Once a person is guilty of certain sins, whether against an individual or Church rules, they are disfellowshipped from the Kingdom Hall. Once disfellowshipped, this person can no longer benefit from church membership and cannot participate in the Jehovah Witness faith. This disfellowship extends to family. No one in that person's family can have contact with a disfellowshipped person. Because Cayce grew up in the Jehovah's Witness faith, she was forced into disfellowship after the Church heard of her homosexual identity. She did not go into detail about how they found out, but the Church ultimately saw her behavior as a sin against the Kingdom Hall. Because she was disfellowshipped, her mother and sister were not allowed to have contact with her. However, they continued to have contact with her. After all, she was their daughter and sister. For her mom, nothing should be able to separate her from her daughter.

After some time, her mother felt conflicted about speaking with her. Cayce recalled the moments her mother would come in and out of her life. Cayce eventually cut ties with her mom and discussed how the back and forth caused her too much emotional pain. Kea, another former Jehovah's Witness, recalls her mother threatening to kill her in order to stop her from running away with a woman (ironically another Jehovah's Witness). When I asked her why her mother seemed intent on killing her, she stated that her mother would rather kill her than suffer the embarrassment or shame of having a lesbian daughter. But Kea told her mom, "You'll have to kill me if you want me to live a lie." For Kea, this maternal shame was a question of life or death. Her mother used the promise of death to shame her daughter. These mothers wielded weapons of shame against their own children. It is unfortunate that an external institution dictated how these mothers treated their queer lesbian daughters. SBQLWP experience the ways that mothers use the Church as a weapon (literally and metaphorically) to dehumanize us.

Maternal shame often perpetuates patriarchy. bell hooks provide evidence on how Church women often use shame to reiterate patriarchy: "At Church they learned that God created man to rule the world and everything in it and it was the work of women to help men perform these tasks, to obey, and to always assume subordinate role in relation to that powerful man. They were taught that God was male."[13] Our Southern Black mothers are often the practitioners of patriarchy, heteropatriarchy, and heteronormativity, perpetuating Church shame and teaching us to indoctrinate ourselves in this existing patriarchal structure. Although it is easy to assume that men are the ones who wield patriarchy, we fail to realize how women in our racial communities also weaponize patriarchy. Church women will use these weapons of patriarchy against other Church folks. Even phrases such as "boys will be boys" or "do not be so open with your sexuality" reinforce the acceptance of patriarchy as a form of sexual violence, shaming those who do not center men or align with patriarchal principles. They internalize the patriarchal mentality, thinking that will give them validation and social status, or as hooks calls it, patriarchal approval.[14] This approval is assumed to grant social status in the South, but it does not come without shaming others.

Black mothers, socialized by older generations of conservative Church ideologies, believe that existing in heteropatriarchy and heteronormativity is the godly way to exist, the only way to live a life pleasing to God. The realities of patriarchy, heteropatriarchy, and heteronormativity learned by the Church brainwash Southern Black mothers to believe that it is necessary to exist in these structures. Unlike our fathers, our mothers are charged with teaching us how to live and exist in the world. In some cases, shame is used to further ensure that we are aligning with these oppressive structures. Our mothers were possibly shamed for living or existing outside of these predetermined boxes of heteronormativity. Shaming us became a way of stopping us from being shamed as they were. This shame becomes a generational curse. Southern Black mothers believe that shaming their daughters will keep them in alignment with the same Southern and Church norms they learned. Unfortunately, these mothers do not know any other way to exist. When we come out to them, they do not know what to do with that information. So instead, they shame us to conform to Church patriarchy and heteronormativity. While our mothers were teaching and trying to protect us, this socialization translates to maternal shame.

Black mothers represent the Church because they often hold the spiritual/moral compass of the Southern Black family. Black mothers may not be Church leaders, but they are often the gatekeepers of spirituality and morality in the Southern Black family. Southern Black folks revere mothers more than the Church itself. Church folks and Southern Black families are more likely to ask an elder Black woman to pray for them (also known as the church "mothas" in Black Southern vernacular). These church mothas are unique to Black Churches, usually designated to the wife of the founder of the church or the oldest and most respected woman of the congregation.[15] There is no equivalent position in predominantly white churches.[16] Church mothas often play an advisory role, sought out when trying to make a decision related to the Church. While her position is respected, her significance is ultimately linked to her service to the pastor and clergy. This unofficial position gives the female elder a sense of authority and influence. Given their position as spiritual counselors, official or otherwise, Black mothas are more likely to carry strict Church doctrines with them. This position heavily relies on socializing Black female youth in limited gender roles and sexual expectations associated with Southern Black womanhood and motherhood. Many Southern Black mothers think of themselves as the Church mothas in their families. No matter who you are, you will listen to your mother. Southern Black mothers are the spiritual and moral barometers of their families. Because of this, they also influence the morality of future generations of Southern Black girls. Black mothers may teach their daughters about the significance of sexual purity and encourage us to continue the tradition of respectability politics. Having a queer lesbian daughter challenges this pure, spiritually connected position of Black mothers in their respective churches and families.

"My Mom Did Not See Me as Her Daughter": Separation from Mother as a Manifestation of Shame

Shame manifests as we emotionally or physically separate ourselves from our mothers. Southern Black mothers would separate from their daughters to avoid the shame of having a queer lesbian daughter. This emotional or physical separation was also a method of shaming the queer lesbian daughter, almost as a form of punishment for not aligning with Church gender norms. This physical and emotional separation is a method the mother uses to shame her daughter. This separation allows mothers to disconnect from and come to terms with their daughter's evolving gender and sexual identity. Once Janessa came out, she noted this emotional separation: "my mom did not see me as her daughter." Cayce mentioned the tension between herself and her mother was strained because of the Church trauma her mother put her through. This physical separation becomes a permanent strain on their relationship, eventually leading to an emotional separation.

Shame causes Black mothers to not see their queer daughters as their children. This queer lesbian person is no longer viewed as a daughter and child, but as a random person she does not claim as her own. Because of these toxic Church practices, it is easier to separate from their child than embrace their queer lesbian identity. This physical and emotional separation is a mourning period for these mothers. During this separation, mothers cope with the reality that all the dreams they had for their daughters ended. The images of a heteronormative marriage and family die. The separation is also a chance for Southern Black mothers to come to terms with who their daughters are. After all, these mothers were raised by the Church as well, conflicted with the ways that they too have been socialized by the Church to see lesbianism and queerness as a sin. Southern Black mothers are also victims of the patriarchal misinterpretation and misinformation from the Church about sexual purity and homosexuality. This separation, whether emotional or physical, helped the mothers disassociate themselves from the perceived immorality of their daughters and maintain their societal position in the Church and family. Having a queer daughter challenges the assumptions related to their sexual purity. The separation is not to save the queer lesbian daughter but a method for mothers to save themselves from Church and family shame.

This separation from our mothers is our way of separating from the South in general. To avoid additional shame from our mothers, we want to separate from our Southern roots. After all, our Southern Black mothers represent the South and are a reminder of our Southernness. Once we separate from them, we inevitably separate from what reminds us of the South and our Southernness. This separation causes us to be ashamed of our Southernness because we internalize that the South is ashamed of us. Southern Black mothers and the South shame us for our queer lesbian identities, so we are ashamed of them and subsequently embarrassed by them. This process of separating from our mothers is a way for us to separate from our Southern selves. We are ashamed to be associated with the toxic culture of Church shame, and we disassociate from all things Southern. The shame creates the assumption that there is no place for Southern Black queer folks in the South. The South becomes associated with all things backward and heteronormative. Due to the prevalent amount of shame, we feel the need to leave the South and/or all things Southern to make sense of our queer lesbian identities. In separating from our mothers, we separate ourselves from the South and our Southernness.

"Shame Is the Currency of the Church": Additional Manifestations of Church Shame on SBQLWP

Vanessa stated bluntly during our conversation that "shame is the currency of the Church." The currency of shame is rooted in certain Church practices related to gender and sexual fluidity. Regardless of race or gender, Southerners are socialized by specific toxic gender and sexual Church politics that affect how SBQLWP navigate our gender and sexualities. Southern women understand sex, gender, and sexuality based on limited Western evangelical Christian ideologies. Southern women, regardless of race or sexuality, must exhibit purity, piety, submission, and domesticity. We are encouraged to sit like a lady, dress as a respectable lady, and speak quietly (especially in the company of men). We learned the importance of sex after marriage and that notions of sex and sexuality are only allowed in the context of heteronormative marriage and the creation of the family unit. We are taught to suppress our sexual selves and not challenge these Church norms. If someone does not align with these limited, traditional notions of gender and sexuality, they are often shamed and silenced. The Church uses shame to keep Black folks in line with traditional politics of respectability. Southern Black Church women use politics of respectability to shame their own. According to Evelyn Higginbotham, Black Baptist women condemned what they perceived to be negative practices and attitudes among their own people.[17] They force dawtas to adhere to these politics of respectability. Not assimilating into traditional notions of womanhood and politics of respectability taught and dictated by the Church subsequently leads to social shame for Southern Black women and SBQLWP.

"Anything Outside of Heterosexuality Is an Abomination": Church Shame Related to Female Sexuality

In most conversations I had with SBQLWP about the Church, I received a similar sentiment: Church folks do not talk about sex or sexuality. The Church does not have discussions of sex and sexuality outside the context of a monogamous, heterosexual marriage. Heterosexuality was the only option for Southern Black Church women. Many SBQLWP agree that sexual fluidity is not an option in the Church. Lesbianism and queerness exist outside of that norm, making it an abomination in the eyes of the Church. As Tené noted, "anything outside of heterosexuality is an abomination." Black Church girls learn from an early age that heterosexuality is the only sexuality validated by the Church, with limited or no discussion of sexual or gender fluidity. Like many Southern women, SBQLWP are socialized to think of sexuality only in the context of heterosexuality. As Brooksley Smith stated, "If I knew a woman could be gay, I wouldn't have been with a man." The only way a Southern Black woman can be sexual, without judgment, is to be in a relationship with a cisgender, heterosexual man. She would be praised and honored even more if her husband was a Church-going man. Many SBQLWP I spoke to dated and married men because they were socialized to believe that it was the only way to exist. Marrying or dating men was their only option. Even though I was never really attracted to men, I believed that I would eventually fall in love with and marry a cisgender heterosexual man. Like other SBQLWP, I thought there was no other option. The Church shame socializes us to believe that heterosexuality is the only way to be in a romantic relationship and trains us to be a suitable wife for that future husband. We are socialized by the Church to think our existence is solely to serve others, namely, cisgender heterosexual men. We understood that being in this heteronormative lifestyle would ultimately give us God's favor and blessings.

Sex and sexuality are connected to the perceived purity of Southern Black Church women. Church folks assume that Southern Black women who attend Church do not engage in any form of sexual impropriety outside of a cisgender, heteronormative marriage and family. Church girls are not taught to see themselves as sexually autonomous beings. This idea of perceived sexual purity is what Janessa called "inherent purity," which relies on the assumption that Black Church women are inherently pure when it comes to sex and sexuality. For a Southern Black woman to be pure, she must be a cisgender, heterosexual woman who embodies limited gender and sexual expression. I found it interesting that Janessa used the term inherent in this discussion, as the wording frames purity as permanent, essential attribute. This purity is not a gift or something passed down to women but a permanent characteristic one has by simply existing as a cisgender heterosexual person. However, this inherent purity is largely based on perception, not reality. A Church girl can engage in certain sexual behaviors, such as masturbation and sexual fluidity, as long as she remains discrete about it and publicly performs within the confines of cisgender heteronormativity. Moreover, it is the expectation for Southern Black Church women to do whatever they need to do to maintain their sexual purity. Ironically, this expectation of purity is not extended to men, but it is the woman's duty to "tame" men's sexual behaviors. Southern Black women who grew up in the Church are not provided the freedom to explore their sexual selves but to publicly maintain the image of sexual purity. This imagery becomes a permanent, essential attribute of Southern Black womanhood. Sexual and gender fluidity represents the opposite of this inherent purity.

Historically, sexual purity was used as a tool to liberate Southern Black women from the perils of sexual exploitation that occurred during enslavement in America. The legacy of enslavement caused a different type of sexual norm for Black women. According to Higginbotham, respectability offered Black Baptist women a weapon in defense of their sexual identities lost during enslavement.[18] Sexual purity has traditionally been a privilege given only to white women, while Black women received sexual purity as a societal gift. Higginbotham claims that "certain respectable behavior in public would earn their people a measure of esteem from white America, where they would win black lower class's psychological allegiance to temperance, industriousness, thrift, refined manners, and Victorian sexual morals."[19] In the South, upholding politics of respectability provided Black women with a sense of value and allowed them to gain respect in Southern society. The Church provided a space for Southern Black women to reclaim some level of humanity through politics of respectability. Given the brutal realities of enslavement that made Black women into reproductive agents, respectability politics was a method Black Church women used to redefine themselves as pure and pious. The politics of respectability was then translated into the Black Club movement as a way to reclaim dignity.[20] The politics of respectability created this inherent purity for Southern Black Church women, a permanent attribute to Southern Black church women's sexuality. Sexual purity became a characteristic of Southern Black womanhood. If a Southern Black woman was connected to the Church, her purity was an essential sexual identity marker.

While sexual purity attempted to liberate Black women, it also became a tool to limit their sexuality and a weapon the used to judge other Black women. Kelly Brown Douglas cites this as sexual patriarchal dualism. While the term *patriarchal dualism* was coined by James B. Nelson, Douglas contends that this dualism often placed Black women's sexuality in a binary—they are either sexually pure or promiscuous. According to Douglas, the sexually pure woman is submissive and willing to produce children with her husband.[21] This dualism laid the foundation for demonizing women's sexuality.[22] Douglas contends that dualism limits the manifestation of Black female sexuality. Many Black women scholars cite the negative tropes and stereotypes of Black women: the Jezebel, Sapphire, mammy, and the welfare queen. According to Collins, these negative stereotypes have been fundamental in Black women's oppression.[23] These negative tropes are rooted in this sexual patriarchal dualism, also equating Black womanhood to either being sexually virtuous or tainted. The Jezebel trope, while biblically referring to a Phoenician princess, often becomes a character of sexual immorality. According to Tamura Lomax, the Jezebel trope represents "North American black patriarchy that is circulated in black religion and black culture of how to deal with black female body."[24] The Black patriarchy that exists in the Church uses the Jezebel trope as the antithesis to this inherent sexual purity. No Church-going woman wants to be labeled as a Jezebel. God forbid. On the other hand, the mammy trope renders Black women as asexual and maternal. Collins notes that the "mammy image is one of an asexual woman, a surrogate mother in blackface."[25] A Church woman's connection to motherhood establishes her image as an asexual person, devoid of any sexual desires. In the context of Southern Black church women, there is seemingly no other way to describe their sexuality. You are either inherently pure or a "worldly" woman.

The question is how queerness and lesbianism exist in this duality. Because Southern Black women's sexuality fits in this toxic patriarchal duality, SBQLWP are automatically labeled as Jezebels because our lesbianism and queerness do not allow us to benefit from this inherent sexual purity. Our sexualities are demonized by the Southern Black Church patriarchy that categorizes Black female sexuality as either moral or lewd. We are considered unholy and sinful because our lesbianism and queerness are perceived as the antithesis of inherent sexual purity. We do not benefit from inherent purity because we are now characterized as "street" or "worldly" women, not Church-going women. Only Church-going women can be perceived as pure. Moreover, our sexuality and queerness do not have patriarchal benefits. Because of this dualism, we are categorized by Southerners as the Jezebel, shamed as only sexual persons. We are not seen as whole human beings, but as sexually degrading persons. The absence of heterosexuality and cisgender identity places SBQLWP in a marginalized space riddled with shame. Because we are perceived as disconnected from the Church and the opposite of cisgender heteronormativity, we do not benefit from inherent purity. Instead, we are shamed by the same space that should protect us from societal judgment. Inherent purity cannot apply to SBQLWP, LaDawn said, because lesbians are "not good enough, not pure." June noted, "lesbian identity is not meant to be protected." Black lesbian identity is not protected because it does not fall in line with this inherent purity provided to Church women. We are shamed for challenging "normal" sexual behavior. Because of our queer lesbian identity, we are demonized and do not receive societal protection. While there is an overall shame related to Black women's sexuality by the Church, SBQLWP experience further shame for not aligning with the curriculum of respectability politics, namely, cisgender heteronormativity. We are shamed because our gender and sexual fluidity automatically challenge these limiting sexual norms.

On the other hand, many SBQLWP discussed the heterosexist permission given to cisgender men (both gay and straight) and cisgender heterosexual women. Our cisgender heterosexual sisters and brothers are granted, as Leah noted, "heterosexual permission," where a certain level of sexual fluidity is permitted as long as it is not homosexuality. SBQLWP noted this phenomenon in the hypocrisy many of them witnessed as it related to male sexuality. Many other SBQLWP recognize the sexual immunity granted to cisgender heterosexual Black men and women. A heterosexual person's proximity to the Church permits them to engage in sexual improprieties if it is heteronormative sexual behavior. If it is not such behavior, then it must be done discreetly while one publicly performs as a heterosexual person. SBQLWP highlight the Church hypocrisy and immunity of Black male Church leaders who were given heterosexual permission to do whatever they desired as long as they upheld the ideal image of Black manhood. If they played the part of an honorable Black man, they were granted social permission to participate in certain sexual behaviors. While the pastor is seen as an extension of God and the epitome of Black manhood, he is also viewed by SBQLWP as the embodiment of hypocrisy in the Church given sexual immunity. Black Church men and pastors represent Southern Black patriarchy that can bypass the expectation of sexual purity. They can do what they want because their proximity to patriarchy provides them sexual immunity.

This discussion of heterosexist permission allows for Southern Black gay queer men to have some level of sexual autonomy in the Church. Because of Church patriarchy, they benefit from the heterosexist permission provided to cisgender heterosexual Black men without being heterosexual. Southern Black cisgender queer gay men are shamed because their gayness or queerness does not align with traditional notions of Southern masculinity. However, a Southern Black gay man's shame is individual, whereas SBQLWP represent a communal shame. A cisgender Black gay man is still allowed to embody a level of sexual freedom not necessarily extended to us. He can benefit from this heterosexist permission because he can be sexually fluid as long as he performs as an honorable cisgender Southern Black man. Because of patriarchy, Southern Black gay men can take advantage of heterosexist permission.

"I Felt Different, But I Didn't Have a Name for It": Naming as a Manifestation of Shame

Once SBQLWP start to name our sexual and gender differences, there was often shame attached to the naming process. Because of the patriarchal dualism set by the Church and the limited discussions of sex and sexual identity, we experience shame in naming ourselves as lesbian and/or queer. If we could not benefit from inherent purity or gain sexual immunity through this heterosexist permission, then how do we identify ourselves? The terms *lesbian* and *queer* have a certain shame attached to them, causing us some hesitancy identifying with these new names. Naming is a significant part of a Black woman's identity; it provides power and autonomy, integral components to Black women's self-actualization. Not having a name for how one engages with the world causes confusion and shame. Only learning about sex and sexuality in the context of heterosexuality and inherent purity made it difficult to categorize the feeling we had toward other women. We may have assumed that these sexual urges were simply a sexual fantasy, not an actual identity marker. We could not articulate who we were outside of heterosexual and gender binaries. Without a name, there is no anchor, no power. Our queerness becomes a burden, a problem—a problem with no name.

    I knew something was different about me and that I was somehow off-kilter, but I did not have a name for what it was. I just felt different from my peers, which made me feel powerless because I could not name these differences. I did not know what it meant to be a queer lesbian. What I did know was rooted in misinformation. Growing up in the Church, I simply assumed that I had not found the "right man" who would make me feel more normal. For years I dated men, many of whom were simply good friends. I figured if I practiced heteronormativity long enough, somehow, I would catch it. Obviously, it never happened. It did not happen for many other SBQLWP either. As we realized, there was no name for how we felt internally, whether it was same-sex desire or our queerness. The only models for sex and sexuality was in the confines of heterosexuality and patriarchy. We knew we felt a stronger connection to other women, but there was no name for what this thing was. As Kea said, "I felt different, but I didn't have a name for it." Most of the time, the naming of our queer lesbian identity happened during our teenage years or while attending college, when we typically start to explore our sexualities and gender fluidity. Before that silent Black queer lesbian girl becomes a teenager or takes a gender and women's studies college course, there is this looming problem with no name.

In speaking of Church shame, many SBQLWP discussed how we felt that our feelings were a "problem" that did not have a name. This lack of naming is problematic because we no longer have an identity outside of what we have been taught. As Shay said, the Church created shame because she felt that "something was wrong with me." Kea also said, "I thought something was wrong with me," as if her identity is problematic. We can thank Betty Friedan for giving us the phrase "the problem with no name," as it applies to upper middle-class white women in post–World War II America.[26] She contends that gender constructs still position women in the confines of the domestic sphere. Friedan argued that there was a problem with how these individuals existed in certain patriarchal structures of domesticity and submission. This problem also manifests in our lives. Although I am sure Friedan would cringe knowing her words were being applied to Southern Black queer lesbians,[27] this phrasing best describes the conflict SBQLWP experience being socialized by the Church. Ultimately, it becomes a problem with no name that we carry with shame. Our very existence is perceived as a problem. The problem is the negotiation between how we were raised to understand gender, sex, and sexuality versus our real same-sex desires and queer fluidity. Who we are differs from what we were brought up to believe by the Church about female sex and sexuality. This internal conflict resonates with many of us as we recollect Church shame.

This problem with no name invokes a level of shame for being different in some way. While Friedan's women were unhappy wealthy white housewives, SBQLWP were unhappy performing in heteronormativity. The Church limits our sexual autonomy, while also shaming us to see our sexual and gender differences as a problem. When we hear the way Southern folks describe those who are not heterosexual, they are often mentioned with a level of disdain, disgust, and hatred. Unfortunately, we were hearing manifestations of homophobia. We hear names such as bulldagger, dyke, and carpet munchers—all words and names rooted in homophobic shame associated with lesbianism and queerness. As we grapple with the shame of naming, we attach our lesbian and queer identities to all things hated by Southern Black folks. To avoid being defined by these terms, we may not even call ourselves lesbian or queer but use more malleable terminologies.

SBQLWP discussed how we first identify ourselves in general (presumably safe) names before embracing the fullness of our queer lesbian identities. When we are finding a name to describe our sexual and gender fluidity, we would first identify ourselves as bisexual. This naming was partially to avoid the shame associated with lesbianism. Naming oneself as lesbian or queer was initially problematic for many. We would use phrasing such as "I dated women" or "I'm with a woman" instead of identifying ourselves as lesbian or queer. For example, Cassie came out a year before our conversation and said, "I'll be honest with you—I am struggling with calling myself a lesbian." Another interlocutor, Torrey, noted that she preferred to be labeled as *gay* over *lesbian* because, as a masculine-embodied lesbian, the term *lesbian* seemed "too feminine" for her. Cassie and Torrey both knew they were different in some way, but they were not ready to label themselves as a lesbian. Torrey joked that she thought the term *lesbian* was "a religion where you couldn't have sex." We both laughed at that comment. I responded, "Like a nun?" Torrey replied, "I figured nuns were lesbians since they couldn't have sex." We both found the idea amusing, joking about that for some time before moving on with our conversation. To Torrey, the term *lesbianism* comes with a level of shame because it is associated with asexuality. After all, based on what we learned from the Church, how can a Southern Black woman sexually express themselves without having sex with men? By existing in this patriarchal dualism, a lesbian is either considered a man-hating, hairy-legged feminist or an asexual mammy prototype.

Like Cassie and Torrey, I recalled moments where I had to come to grips with naming my sexual difference. As a Southern Black girl raised in the African Methodist Episcopal Church, I did not know how to name my queer lesbian identity. After my first crush on a woman in high school (a track athlete at another school), I assumed I was bisexual. I secretly identified as bisexual and believed that I would still eventually marry a cisgender heterosexual Southern Black man. As I was coming out, I struggled to call myself a lesbian. I would practice saying "lesbian" to remove the stigma and shame attached to the word. Admittedly, it took some time to unlearn the shame associated with *gay* or *lesbian*. When Cassie mentioned her struggle with naming herself as a lesbian, I recalled that time in my own queer lesbian actualization. Identifying ourselves as gay or lesbian solidifies our coming-out process because we are dealing with the shameful stigmas associated with lesbianism and queerness.

Why would we first identify as bisexual versus lesbian? As many SBQLWP noted, calling oneself bisexual alleviates the shame associated with lesbianism. As Brooksley Smith noted, "Bisexual is more acceptable for people looking in." Identifying oneself as bisexual gives others hope that we will somehow return to heteronormativity and align with Church teachings related to Black female sexuality. According to Cheryl Clarke, bisexuality is "a safer label than lesbian, for it posits the possibility of a relationship with a man, regardless of how infrequent or nonexistent the female bisexual's relationships with men might be."[28] In the Church, it is safer to be perceived as bisexual than a lesbian. One can benefit from that heterosexist permission, granting a person some permission to explore their sexuality as long as they return to heteronormativity. As we actualize our lesbian and queerness, we lean on bisexuality to give ourselves and others hope of heteronormativity. After all, the terms *lesbian* and *queer* appear absolute to someone who is coming to terms with who they are. Identifying as lesbian removes that hope. Like Cassie and me, SBQLWP have to come to grips with this perceived permanent position. This reality is especially prevalent for feminine-embodying lesbians, who gain some level of privilege in the South because of our cisgender presentation. Identifying as lesbian removes the privileges we may enjoy for being feminine presenting. Claiming bisexuality was a way for femme-identified SBQLWP to explore our sexualities and take advantage of heterosexist privilege. After all, many Black women had sexual relations with women and later married cisgender, heterosexual men. In this context, claiming bisexuality provided the sexual freedom to explore while also providing a sense of relief to others that this was merely a "phase" they would outgrow. Of course, this assumption about bisexuality is inaccurate and rooted in misinformation. Bisexuality remains an understudied and undervalued sexual identity in the Black queer community. SBQLWP outline how claiming bisexuality is part of the process that we encounter as we come to terms with our sexual and queer identities.

SBQLWP who identify as queer had additional layers of shame to unlearn. Maezah (they/them) discussed how, even though they were attracted to the same gender, they did not see themself as "just a lesbian." To them, the term *lesbian* attached more to sexual orientation than to gender identity. Moreover, lesbianism is perceived by some SBQLWP to exist in a sexual binary. In some cases, lesbians can adopt some level of heteronormativity in our lives and relationships. Maezah further stated, "Fluidity is the reality, but folks love boxes." In the South, we are socialized by the Church to value gender binaries. Shame is attached to anyone who challenges or embodies gender fluidity. As Maezah began to name their gender identity, they stated how there "wasn't a term for what it meant to be sexually or gender fluid." Like lesbianism, queerness became associated with social vagrancy, where one cannot be queer and fully exist in Southern society. In the South, queerness became linked to whiteness and white deviancy. *Queer* became the antithesis of all things Southern and Black. Southern Church folks understand sex and sexuality as a binary concept, the opposite of the embodiment of queerness. Because of this reality, there is typically social shame attached to being queer. We may have heard a family member or Church parishioner say that someone was "funny," but there is no positive affirmation of that person's existence. They are simply gossiped about while existing in the margins in silence and shame.

Because of the silence and shame, there are limited public representations of queerness in the South. This reality causes an obstacle to naming, where we must detach the social shame associated to queerness. Even with this reality, SBQLWP who identify as queer recognized the fluidity in their gender and sexual embodiments. When Maezah heard the term queer, they immediately identified a home for their gender and sexual fluidity. Queerness freed them and many other SBQLWP. However, they also grappled with the shame associated with naming themself as queer. This complex discussion of queerness provides an opportunity to evaluate the ways we could possibly integrate E. Patrick Johnson's quare theory as it detaches the shame and whiteness associated with queerness and integrates sexual and gender fluidity in a Black Southern landscape. Perhaps the terminology of *quare* can free us even more.

Why identify as lesbian first versus queer? Lesbianism, though still viewed as revolutionary in the South and Church, has a definitive line and embodiment of gender binaries that can show up in lesbian relationships. Queerness has many gray areas, which challenge the norms of Southern Black Church folks, who love a gender binary. In queerness, the gender binaries are insignificant in determining how one shows up in the world. Queer fluidity is a threat because it ultimately challenges the binaries honored and valued by Southern Black Church folks. Calling someone queer in the South automatically places them on the margins of society. Queerness is equated with darkness, the opposite of what Southern Black folks expect from Southern Black women. In other words, calling someone queer is a way of shaming someone for challenging the status quo and embracing gender and sexual fluidity. Lesbians coming to terms with our queer identities struggled with this shame from the term *queer*.

"She's a Friend": Shame in Our Queer Lesbian Romantic Relationships

Many SBQLWP discussed how their queer lesbian romantic relationships are usually minimized out of shame. In one conversation, Kris told me a story of the time she brought her college girlfriend to her family home in rural North Carolina. While she knew of her lesbian identity while in high school, it was not until college that she was able to openly exist as a masculine-embodied lesbian. She informed her grandmother that she was bringing a "friend" home. Obviously, her grandmother was not pleased to find out that the "friend" was a woman she was dating. Our mothers were notorious for labeling our partners as "friends" because it diminishes that person's role in our lives. It is not unusual for SBQLWP to refer to our partners or girlfriends as "our friends" to our Southern families. Regardless of one's sexual orientation, Southern Black families will label our girlfriends and boyfriends as "friends" until the promise of marriage. When we bring a significant other around our families, they will often say that is "so-and-so's li'l friend." I am not even sure they ever call the people by their names. They are just our li'l friend. While Southern Black folks like to use *friend* to minimize any relationship that is not marriage, this use is more deliberate for queer lesbian relationships. The "friend" attempts to remove the validation of our relationships. Saying someone is a "friend" becomes a coded language for us, a survival tactic to avoid Church and family shame. Because of Church shame, identifying our partners/girlfriends as friends minimizes the validity of our queer lesbian relationships. Remi mentioned how they referred to their partners as friends because "it was rooted in shame from the Black Church."

In the South, the Church validates a relationship. As we actualize our queerness, we are ashamed of our relationships because we knew the Church would not validate our relationship. We are socialized to see queer lesbian relationships as insignificant because it is not aligned with a traditional heteronormative relationship that the Church values. It takes time to see our romantic relationships as valuable. For many SBQLWP, calling our partner's "friend" delegitimizes and limits our relationships because we know we will not receive family or Church validation. Minimizing our romantic relationships as a friendship makes it insignificant and invisible to Church folks and family. As LaDawn noted, "it is a separate but equal treatment in Church," where we can exist but cannot be visible in Church. According to her, we can pay tithes and heavily participate in Church, but unlike heterosexual partitioners, we cannot rely on the Church to provide a space for us to bring our girlfriends and get married. The Church legitimizes heteronormative unions, demonizing queer or same-sex unions. Openly queer unions are not legitimized by the Church. June said that heteronormative relationships are worthy to be witnessed by the Church and notes that the Church celebrates heteronormative relationships because they are blessed directly by God. She critiqued the assumption that queer unions should not be blessed or celebrated because "there's no way God can live in our [queer lesbian] marriage." This stark value system dismisses queerness and gender fluidity in the South because it is rooted in an insidious myth taught by the Church—that lesbian and queer folk cannot have a healthy relationship or a heteronormative family. Because of these heteronormative assumptions, there is no other way the Church will validate our same-sex relationships. Same-sex relationships do not deserve to receive God's blessings, nor will they be celebrated by Church folks. While that notion of the "friend" is a running joke among us, it also invokes memories of Church shame.

The "Dark Cloud": The Looming Realities of Internal Condemnation

In our conversations about the Church, many SBQLWP brought up conversations that centered on condemnation. Once the silent Southern Black queer girl starts actualizing her queer lesbian identity, the shame she encounters from Church folks and toxic norms translates into condemnation. Pushing back against these preestablished gender and sexual norms and expectations of the Church causes an internal conflict. As we deal with shame, it manifests in an internal struggle filled with confusion, embarrassment, hurt, disappointment, guilt, and fear. What was once an external manifestation of shame becomes an internal battle where we experience self-hate. This period of condemnation becomes an isolated process and represents our moment in the mythical closet. The duality is our closeted moment. During this time, we were "existing in two worlds," living a double life. This duality leads to an internal turmoil that is often not fully discussed in our coming-out narratives. Perhaps it is too painful and too dark to discuss. The Church shame puts us in this mythical closet, and condemnation keeps us in there. We are no longer free but stuck in a purgatory of self-hatred. Kea cited this time of condemnation as a "dark cloud" looming in her life. No one around us saw this cloud, but it hovered over us daily, causing external harm and internal pain.

"I Felt Like I Was Living a Double Life": Wearing the Mask and Existing in Duality

Perhaps the most damaging manifestation of the Church shame for SBQLWP is living in a duality, a time period where we felt that we had to live a double life to avoid shame from the Church. This shame leads to condemnation, causing us to have one life that aligns with what was expected of us by Church and family and another life where we could live out our lesbian/queer lives. This duality was a way for us to protect ourselves, hiding from the scrutiny that may come from Church mothers and family. We felt the pressure to conform to traditional notions of femininity while remaining silent about our fluid sexualities and/or gender identities. Existing in this duality became a method of survival. After all, living in this duality leads to fewer questions and provides a level of acceptance from others. Even as a queer lesbian person is coming out, we know we cannot immediately or fully live our truth. As Remi put it, "You start to prepare yourself to live this double life." Remi recognized that they could not fully exist as a queer person, especially because they were still heavily involved in the Church when they came out. Because of this reality, Remi and other SBQLWP anticipated living with the mask of duality. This preparation is designing this mask, determining what it will look like, and how we plan to live in the duality. Some interlocutors did not post outings on social media. Those who attended college kept their queer lesbian life only on their respective college campuses and reverted to what was expected of them when they visited home. While many of the SBQLWP I spoke to eventually came out and reconciled with their Southern Black queer identities, some remain in this duality. As Cayce told me, "My two worlds never collided," due to the nature of her job. As an elementary school teacher, she kept her sexuality a secret to protect herself from potential rumors and judgment. At the time of our conversation, she noted that these worlds between her work and her personal life never merged. She said that the Church trauma of being disfellowshipped from the Jehovah's Witnesses has caused her to keep her two worlds separate. Regardless of whether we continue to exist in the duality, we find ways to exist by playing Black girl double Dutch in our lives.

The duality exists in this racialized sexual queer geography, where race and gender in a certain location incorporate an additional context in our coming-out narratives. Incorporating the racialized sexual queer geography, we uncover a new dimension of this infamous closet. As many SBQLWP mentioned, coming out was a gradual (sometimes slow) process that begins with existing in this duality. Due to the overarching Church norms and socialization, SBQLWP experience a unique kind of closet where we dabbled in the queer lesbian world while also participating in Southern communities. We played the role of heteronormativity while simultaneously exploring our queer lesbian identities. In this duality, we would trick others to think we were heteronormative. After all, this duality allows SBQLWP to exist in the societal DADT Southern policy. If nobody asks, then nobody needs to know. We can fly under the societal radar and continue to exist. We tricked our mothers, families, and Church community into thinking we engaged in heteronormativity and embodied traditional Southern femininity while simultaneously existing in this queer lesbian world. The duality is a new reality of the infamous closet where SBQLWP exists inside and outside our respective communities. We vacillate between the Southern Black world and our queer lesbian world to avoid Church shame and hide our queer lesbian selves. As we were coming out, we knew we had to find a way to exist in both worlds. We secretly and discreetly exist in two worlds.

This duality reminded me of Paul Laurence Dunbar's poem "We Wear the Mask." Dunbar writes, "We wear the mask that grins and lies. It hides our cheeks and shades our eyes."[29] SBQLWP wear that mask that grins and lies. The mask causes us to remain secret about our queer lesbian selves and compartmentalize our lives to avoid shame. Cassie said, "I felt like I was wearing a mask." During this time of condemnation, she talked about how she had "secret hookups" with other women. She noted how she wore this mask as a shield that protects her from the shame that comes from the Church and family. We wear the mask to hide from others and, in some cases, to hide from ourselves. The process of hiding from ourselves is a form of condemnation. The mask that grins and lies acts as a survival method against the cultural shame from mothers, family, and Church folks. The mask is intended to keep a part of us hidden from others. But it causes us to internalize Church shame, planting the seeds of condemnation. Our journey to actualization is done in silence even after we come to terms with who we are. The secrecy and wearing the mask of duality is a normal part of Black queer lesbian life in the South. We learn quickly to exist in secret and wear the mask. We are taught by the Southern cultural tradition of silence how to construct our masks and seal our lips. We are forced into a duality, the infamous closet, where we wear the mask.

Knowing that presentation and aesthetics are essential to Church life, SBQLWP are extremely careful about how we present ourselves publicly while living in this duality. We are mindful of these aesthetics when we return to our mother's homes in the South. In this homeplace, we must be aware of what we wear and how we wear it. As Star said, "When you are in your parent's house, there's no other option." We knew we had to present ourselves as straight, feminine-presenting Southern Black women. There were no other options. We understood that we had to perform and put on the mask of cisgender heteronormativity when we returned to mama's house. While we began to accept our sexual identities during our time away from home for work or college, we knew that coming home would require us to minimize our queerness. We put on the mask in this homeplace while existing in this duality. We put on the mask to pass for straight or heterosexual in our families and Churches. Sweet said how she wore the mask to "remain neutral." As we existed in this duality, we would put on a performance of femininity to pass as cisgender and heterosexual. The performance of femininity became our mask. Many gender-nonconforming and masculine-embodied queer lesbians cited the pressures to present as more feminine with family and Church while simultaneously embracing their masculinity or gender-nonconforming identities in queer lesbian spaces. As a masculine-embodied lesbian, Jae said she would hide behind feminine clothing. Leah, another masculine-embodied lesbian, noted that she kept her long hair to maintain a level of femininity. They knew to wear the blouse for Church and the button-down men's polo shirt in gay/lesbian spaces. Masculine-embodied SBQLWP were constantly mindful of their gender performance to avoid drawing attention to themselves. They wore the mask, while grinning and performing as cisgender, heteronormative Southern Black women.

Why go through all this duality? Why wear the mask? We internalize the shame of others, and we are embarrassed by our queerness. We ultimately condemn ourselves. The shame from others becomes internalized, determining how we see ourselves. The duality allows us to remain hidden from the chastisement and embarrassment from embodying queerness in the South. Existing in this duality is an example of active coping outlined by Bettina Love.[30] The mask is intended to minimize our queerness. We live in duality to cope with being queer in the South. We see our queerness as a problem we want to hide from others. We are embarrassed by this perceived problem. We hear our mothers and other maternal figures telling us to not embarrass them. Even as an adult, my mother still tells me not to embarrass her. As Cassie said, she lived the double life because "I heard the words of my mother saying, 'Don't do anything to embarrass me.'" Embarrassment starts as shame from our Black mothers, vilifying us to a point where we condemn ourselves. Embarrassment becomes an external exercise of shame that queer lesbian daughters internalize. We feel the need to wear this mask and hide from others and ourselves. Ultimately, the duality allows us to deal with our pain.

As we exist in this duality, we are not simply in the closet. Barton describes the *toxic* closet, which is based on how Southern folks should conduct themselves in the Church. As she outlines, there are three components of this toxic closet: creation of safe space, assumption of heterosexuality, and a method of censorship (what she describes as the Bible Belt panopticon). The creation of the safe space exists in the DADT societal policy, where the people around us do not know of our sexuality. This ignorance creates a safe space for us and allows us to wear our mask. Even when there is evidence that one may be queer or lesbian, there is satisfaction in not knowing. Sometimes people prefer not to know. This creates safety for SBQLWP as we continue to wear the mask. The toxic closet also provides certain assumptions about one's sexuality. As mentioned with Southern hospitality, SBQLWP can exist in the toxic closet because of the assumption of heterosexuality. Barton argues that gender-nonconforming persons (femme men or butch women) may be treated as heterosexual by others to be polite and avoid conversations about relationship status.[31] We wear the mask because, as Barton notes, we are constantly censoring ourselves to protect ourselves from societal harm and judgment. We wear the mask to maintain safety and censor ourselves while existing in this toxic closet.

Some SBQLWP uncovered an additional facet of this duality: how it differs for interlocutors with children. Cassie (mother of two) noted, "I am a mother before anything." Motherhood caused many SBQLWP to exist in this duality, which is further complicated because there are certain preconceived notions of purity of Southern Black mothers. As mentioned already, Southern Black Church women benefit from the perception of inherent purity. Motherhood is an essential component of that purity. Lesbianism and/or queerness challenge the preconceived notion of inherent purity and Southern Black motherhood. If SBQLWP had children, then their ability to mother is questioned. They are perceived as bad mothers for engaging in sexually lewd behaviors. Her queerness and/or lesbianism are tied to selfish behaviors, which is the antithesis of Southern Black motherhood. Southern Black mothers are expected to uphold purity and focus only on the desires of their children. They are not seen as autonomous women and persons. Ultimately, the duality saved them from encountering these societal expectations of Southern Black motherhood. Moreover, the queer lesbian mothers in this duality wore the mask of heteronormativity to protect their children. They internalize the embarrassment while existing in this duality, where they saw their lifestyles as a problem and wanted to protect their children from any shame they may encounter from having a queer lesbian mother. They live in a duality to save their kids. They feared others would perceive them as flawed mothers, and they sacrificed their freedom to protect their children. This duality is a mother's true sacrifice.

Under the mask and smiles, there are tears. Dunbar writes, "We smile, but, O great Christ, our cries. To thee from tortured souls arise."[32] For SBQLWP, these smiles cover tears filled with the emotional weight, guilt, and embarrassment. The weight of the guilt translates to condemnation. Cassie felt guilty that they were not living their authentic selves. This guilt becomes an internal struggle for her, and she felt the need to wear a mask of deception. Kea agrees with Cassie, discussing how this duality felt like a weight was placed on her. They both felt guilt for living double lives and not fully living out their queerness. Kea said that the double life was "slowly killing me." She describes the weight as a secret burden she carried for several years. She proclaimed, "I did everything I was supposed to do" to get rid of the internal struggle. She heavily participated in Church (she was a Jehovah's Witness), married a man, and even attended nursing school. We stew over this internal shame daily as we exist in this duality. We feel like impostors. While others celebrate Coming Out Day or participate in Pride events, those living in duality are crying under their masks of deception, our souls tortured. We lie to friends and family members as we carry this heavy emotional weight under our mask.

"I Tried to Pray the Gay Away": Condemnation Represented in Internalized Homophobia

The tears of this duality led to internal homophobia, which SBQLWP cite as "praying the gay away." The condemnation makes us question our queer lesbian existences. We attempt to bargain with God to make us "normal." We ask God whether it is possible for us to exist as cisgender, heteronormative people to avoid pain. This kind of condemnation is perhaps the most difficult to discuss. Internalized homophobia remains the most challenging to reconcile because it results from self-hatred. Audre Lorde contends that homophobia is the terror surrounding feelings of love for others of the same sex and thereby a hatred of those feelings in others.[33] During this stage of condemnation, homophobia is manifested internally, and we direct those feelings of hate toward ourselves and other queer/lesbian folks. Griffin discusses the rage that has been projected on homosexuality, where it is "an even greater sin, as a monstrosity, a part of a wicked spirit."[34] This conflict of condemnation is an internal rage where we hate all representations of queerness or lesbianism, even if it means hating ourselves. Our internalized hatred and rage become a battle of conviction. We believe that something is wrong with us, that our existence is a problem.

Growing up in the Church, we are taught that prayer changes things, and so we assume that prayer will somehow change our internal struggle. If we prayed like our grandma said, then we will be free from the "devil" of queerness and lesbianism that lurked inside us. We cry because we did everything we could to save our souls. Star cried and prayed for God to "take this thing away from me." Before it was named, her attraction to women appeared to be a demonic spirit inside her. To combat this spirit, internalized homophobia causes us to fully immerse ourselves into Church life. Bynta noted that she became a "super Christian to get closer to God." She began volunteering and participating in multiple Church activities, thinking that would erase the queer lesbian feelings. Paulette discussed a similar path, where she became heavily involved in the Church to quiet her same-sex desires: "If I am involved in the Church more, somehow, it would get rid of these feelings [I have] about women." She realizes now that this was her attempt to pray the gay away, using service to the Church as a bargaining tool for God to remove her queer lesbian feelings.

Being raised in the Church, we often hear "hate the sin, love the sinner," a phrase that triggers many of us in our queer journey. While Church folks will use "hate the sin, love the sinner" to pacify queer folks, they will say this as a way to translate their disdain for one's queerness while proclaiming Christian love for the individual. Church folks say they love the individual, because God is love, but do not agree with their queerness. SBQLWP understand that Church folks use this phrase as a sign of tolerance for gayness. Andy recognizes how the Church is mildly accepting, using this phrasing as justification. She says, "The Church is accepting but not acknowledging." The Church will accept gayness as an acknowledgment that gay folks exist, but there is no visible affirmation of our existence. Bree (they/them) noted a similar sentiment, where they acknowledged that the Church uses this phrase to be tolerant but not affirming. "Hate the sin, love the sinner" still makes homosexuality a sin and demonizes anyone who is not heterosexual or heteronormative. But pacifying the perceived sin does not make the condemnation less hurtful;

instead, it adds to it. I hated when Church folks and family would say that to me. How can you love me and hate who I am? Jae questioned, "How can this God not love me?"

The phrase "hate the sin, love the sinner," is not a biblical quote. There is no evidence of this phrase in the Christian Bible. So why is it used? Some SBQLWP would argue that it is a way of tolerating or dealing with a person's gayness. The phrase is meant to compartmentalize how Church folks deal with Southern queer folks. The phrase "hate the sin, love the sinner," is an attempt to recognize a queer person's existence as a Southern Black person but not as a Black queer person. Church folks may affirm our attendance at Church or in Southern spaces but will not acknowledge the perceived sin. Church folks and Southern Black folks are telling the Southern Black queer person that we should be ashamed of our queerness. They weaponize this phrase to tell Southern Black queer folks that our existence is problematic and that our sin is somehow worse than other sins. We internalize this, questioning whether our existence is a problem. Phrases like "hate the sin, love the sinner" amplifies our self-hatred. Griffin argues that this phrasing is illogical. For him, "hate the sin, love the sinner" is like "loving brown eyed people while hating brown eyes."[35]

Scriptures used against queer folks are rooted in biblical misinterpretation. Many preachers do not fully understand the historical context of these Scriptures and the reasons they were written. Moreover, according to Griffin, the Bible is not an adequate source for responding to issues of homosexuality as Church folks and preachers cannot address a twenty-first-century reality with the context of first-century biblical writers.[36] The New Testament is the roadmap to Christianity, but it does not always answer all the questions related to modern-day problems. In fact, there was no phrasing or wording for homosexuality or heterosexuality until 1892, when it appeared in scientific and medical literature. According to Jonathan Ned Katz, the notion of heterosexuality became a "cultural norm" between 1900 and 1930, well into the twentieth century.[37] Unfortunately, that silent Southern Black queer lesbian girl (and even the queer lesbian adult) in the congregation may not know these Scriptures are being misinterpreted or that the Bible is not an adequate source to teach about homosexuality. We do not learn in Church about certain historical realities outside of African or Black history. In many cases, our pastors or religious leaders are not Black scholars. After all, we still view the preacher as a spiritual leader, the moral and ethical authority figure who guides our spiritual path. This type of misguided preaching can lead to years of heartache and reinforce the idea that our lives are an abomination to God. We are constantly conflicted. Unfortunately, we develop internal homophobia based on a preacher's misinterpretation.

This internalized homophobia created some tumultuous times for my interlocutors, leading some to cause physical harm to themselves. Kea attempted to end her own life by carbon monoxide poisoning, leaving the car running while the garage door was closed. Her husband at the time saved her life. After that moment, she realized she could no longer live in the duality. As Kea said, "At that moment, my life was in the balance." Others shared a similar narrative of how they coped with this duality and condemnation. Some experienced depression and panic attacks and even attempted to take their own lives. Many did not go into too much detail. They mentioned it during our conversations but did not detail those experiences. I did not push for more information. It was a dark time that many of them did not want to return to. Some SBQLWP I spoke to were in the middle of their duality and did not yet fully exist as openly queer persons. I want to assure them that their existence is not a problem and that they are not alone in the internal struggles they are experiencing.

Internalized homophobia can manifest in the ways we engage in intimate relationships and how we should embody queerness and lesbianism. This homophobia can translate into the gender binary of the stud/boi and femme.[38] SBQLWP assume that studs/bois should not exist as gender-fluid persons but should exist as representations of toxic masculinity. Studs/bois can't get their nails done. They cannot have a high-pitched voice. They must only wear men's clothing and sports bras. They shouldn't speak of their menstrual cycles or wear tampons. Most importantly, they must be sexually aggressive. Internal homophobia often becomes the litmus test for how other studs/bois and femmes judge one another.

In some instances, studs/bois internalize these toxic expectations and encourage other studs to do the same. This is a way of checking one's level of masculine embodiment. Unfortunately, femmes who experience this internalized homophobia may also reinforce these as toxic binary norms. Internal homophobia may encourage the desire to assimilate into toxic cisgender heteronormativity as much as possible. It has them hating all things queer and fluid. Because they hate themselves, they must exist as close to heteronormativity as possible. Does that mean that anyone who exists in these binaries lives in this duality and experience internal homophobia? Of course not. Does this mean that studs/bois and femmes are experiencing internal homophobia? Not at all. For studs/bois, embodying masculinity can be a form of freedom to exist in authentic gender identities. But the judgment of other types of relationships outside the binary and the desire to mimic toxic cisgender heteronormativity to make sense of our queer lesbian identity are manifestations of internalized homophobia and self-hatred. These feelings manifest in how one embodies—or chooses not to embody—queerness or gender fluidity. It is a fear and hatred for anything that exists outside of this gender binary.

This Is Not the End of the Story

The Church represents the people and their ideologies as they relate to gender and sexuality. These limited understandings of gender and sexuality ultimately plant seeds of shame in our lives. In speaking about the experiences of SBQLWP, we must frame the Southern Black Church as a sociocultural institution with certain gender and sexual politics used to shame and condemn those who do not fall in line with toxic cisgender heteronormative Church norms. These Church politics create a distinct reality as we actualize our queer lesbian identities. Shame and condemnation are a pivotal chapter in our lives. Because the Church is a significant sociocultural institution for Southern Black folks, it is imperative to consider the impact of this institution in our queer lesbian journey. We attempt to navigate these Church realities, even if that means living with the manifestations of shame and condemnation. However, the realities are not the end of the trauma. We also face the realities of judgment through the lens of Southern Black heteronormativity. The Church creates and places value on this heteronormativity, giving rise to the Southern Black personality.

"The World Is Set Up for Straight Folks"

The Judgmental South and the Southern Black Personality

> It was the time to hear things and talk. These sitters had been tongueless, earless, eyeless conveniences all day long. Mules and other brutes had occupied their skins. But now, the sun and the bossman were gone, so the skins felt powerful and human. They become lords of sounds and lesser things. They passed nations through their mouths. They sat in judgement . . . they made burning statements with questions, and killing tools out of laughs. It was a mass cruelty.[1]

For SBQLWP, the South is foundational to our Blackness and Southernness. Unfortunately, while experiencing Church trauma, we encounter a darker side of the South filled with judgment and massive cruelty. This judgment is the overarching social reality we face as we encounter heterosexism, heteronormativity, and Black heteropatriarchy in the South. We hear the voices of our mothers, aunts, uncles, cousins, or family friends that judge anyone who exist outside of heteronormativity and/or challenges Black heteropatriarchy. This societal judgment acts as mass cruelty, filled with burning questions and disdainful statements. At times, the cruelty makes SBQLWP feel that our presence is a problem. This heterosexist patriarchal cruelty makes us targets of societal judgment in our homeplace. As many SBQLWP alluded to in our conversations, heterosexist judgments from Southern Black folks operate like the townsfolk in Hurston's novel, a massive cruelty from the Southern Black community. The judgment from our own suffocated us. It embodies a person, a system, and an unspoken energy that permeates the region. Based on their encounters with this heterosexist patriarchal judgment, I heard interlocutors constructing a Southern Black personality.

In the opening scene of Zora Neale Hurston's novel *Their Eyes Were Watching God*, she paints a picture of Southern townsfolk sitting on their porches, watching protagonist Janie walk back into town after her long journey. These townsfolk worked all day for the bossman only to sit at their front porches in judgment of others, which helps them feel powerful and human. They act as the bossmen of their community. Southern Black folks can be judgmental. We love nothing more than to sit on our front porch sipping sweet tea, snapping beans, and listening to the town gossip. These Southern townsfolk of Eatonville, Florida, sat in judgment of Janie as she walked back into town wearing a pair of overalls. Janie was judged because her gender performativity did not match the Southern expectation of femininity. They gossiped about her love life, her multiple husbands, why she decided to wear overalls instead of a dress, and for not having "manners enough to stop and let folks know how she been makin' out."[2] They continued talking (or as Southern folks say, "carryin' on") until her friend Pheoby chastised them: "You mean, you mad 'cause she didn't stop and tell us all her business. Y'all make me so tired. De way you talkin' you'd think de folks in dis town didn't do nothin' in de bed 'cept praise de Lawd."[3] Pheoby was the sole voice of reason against this mass cruelty. These Southern Black folks in the novel represent the practice of heterosexist and patriarchal judgment. Like Janie, SBQLWP also experience the mass cruelty of Southern Black folks through the Southern Black personality (SBP). Like the Southern and slave mentalities, the SBP acts as a person, place, thing, or idea that uses societal judgment as a way of policing the gender and sexual behaviors of Southern Black folks. The SBP uses massive cruelty as a tool to judge and suppress those who do not align with heteronormativity and Black heteropatriarchy. The SBP limits the gender and sexual embodiment of Southern Black folks. Unlike the slave mentality, driven by certain racial norms and customs of the South, the SBP is the gatekeeper of heteronormativity and Black heteropatriarchy. The SBP is the intraracial enforcer of all things Black patriarchal and heteronormative. The SBP makes queerness and any type of gayness a social stigma in the South. The SBP act as the bossman in their community, determining whether people align with Black heteronormativity and patriarchy. They cannot judge their bossman, so they use that pseudo-power to judge others to affirm their own humanity and gain societal power. Because they have limited power in the South due to historical racial oppressions, they wield power to the Southern Black community by judging and chastising others. The same folks we call our brothers and sisters weaponize heterosexism and heteropatriarchy as a tool to judge others, rendering them silent. As Bynta noted, "The world is set up for straight folks." According to her, the world (namely, the South) creates space and provisions for straight persons to thrive, opening the door for heterosexism. The Southern world is "set up" in a way that centers heterosexuality and demonizes those who resist this societal norm. In describing the SBP, SBQLWP constructed a Southern person akin to Hurston's townsfolk who sit in judgment of their own.

This SBP has a magnetic and vibrant energy—someone who exudes a sense of self-confidence and is full of Southern charm. The SBP has a steady, thick Southern drawl that pours into our ears like honey from a jar. Those with the SBP are cultured about all things Southern and Black. Similar to the Southern and slave mentalities, the SBP is not devoid of consciousness or intellectual thought. However, the SBP has a limited perspective about gender and sexuality. This personality represents the social conditioning that takes place in the South, a result of what happens when Southern folks internalize limited constructs of gender and sexuality. While the SBP is typically seen as a cisgender heterosexual male, some Southern Black women also value, honor, and respect heteronormativity and Black heteropatriarchy, using it as a litmus test for judging other Southern Black women. The SBP can show up in the ways our Southern Black mothers and maternal figures deal with our gender and sexual identities. While the SBP is Southern and Black affirming, it is not progressive with discussions of sexual and gender fluidity. The SBP perpetuates the expectation of heterosexuality and patriarchy as the norm. Southern Black women are expected to find a husband, get married, and have children—in that order. Anything outside of this expectation will cause one to be judged. Like Janie, SBQLWP walk into a sea of judgment. This personality is a person as much as an energy that permeates the Southern air, suffocating us as we actualize our identities.

"It Is a Way of Life": Heterosexism, Heteronormativity, and Black Heteropatriarchy in the SBP

Heterosexism, heteronormativity, and Black heteropatriarchy are overarching realities in the South and become tools used by the SBP to keep Southern Black folks in line with gender and sexual value systems. The questions and statements from Southern townsfolk—the mass cruelty—are filled with heterosexist and heteronormative ideologies and assumptions. The cruelty is so magnetic that even those who embody it are also victims of sexism, patriarchy, and heterosexism. However, the SBP catches Southern folks in a web of lies; we get lost in the image of the South as a heteronormative space that we must participate in. To be considered Southern, we must engage in the mass cruelty that despises all things gay and queer and embraces heteronormativity. Heterosexism and heteronormativity have a hold on Southern Black life. As Cassie noted, heterosexism is a way of life in the South.

"It Permeates Everything": Realities of Heterosexism in the SBP

Black feminist scholars define and outline the sources of heterosexism in the Black community but do not give specific ways they manifest in the South and in the SBP. While several factors show up in the South, geographic location affects the level of heterosexism that SBQLWP face. Heterosexism represents a societal hierarchy connected to the formation of a monogamous heteronormative Black family and a method of social surveillance. During my conversations with interlocutors, I asked them to define heterosexism in the South using the definition provided by Audre Lorde. I used the following quote: "Heterosexism: A belief in the inherent superiority of one form of loving over all others and thereby the right to dominance."[4] After reading the quote, I asked them how they feel this statement aligns with their experiences. Interlocutors provided several responses to Lorde's definition of heterosexism:

> Kea: "It permeates everything."
>
> Sweet: "It's been what it is in the South."
>
> Makeda: "It shows up everywhere."
>
> Janessa: "The only way of living."
>
> Marie Dylan: "Like an imprisonment."

These responses show how heterosexism is attached to one's humanity in the South, embedded in Southern life, and perpetuated by the SBP. There is no place that heterosexism does not touch in the South and acts as an overarching reality that influences how we navigate the region. Heterosexism hinders how one actualizes their gender and sexual identity in the South.

We experience heterosexism as a significant reality in our lives because of the SBP, who uses heterosexism as a tool to hinder us from reaching our full queer lesbian authenticity. We frequently encounter the massive cruelty of the SBP, where we are reminded that our sexual identities are outside the norm and not welcomed in certain spaces. If it is welcomed, we often encounter the "don't ask, don't tell" social policy—you can *be* gay but don't *talk* about it. Heterosexuality is viewed as Southern society's default sexual orientation and the glue that holds Southern Black folks together.

Heterosexism relies on the assumption of heterosexual identity. In the South, it is the assumption that Southern Black folks are inherently cisgender and heterosexual. Heterosexism makes certain presumptions about one's gender and sexual identity, sparking tension for those who are queer, lesbian, or gender-nonconforming. Onika Rose stated that there is an assumption of heterosexuality—the social presumption of straightness in the South. Some interlocutors said that Southern folks simply assume they are heterosexual, regardless of how they present themselves. This assumption of heterosexuality allows some level of safety for some of us because there are fewer questions about our gender and sexual identities, ultimately allowing us to exist in plain sight.

The SBP also uses this assumption of heterosexuality to silence queerness or lesbianism through compulsory heterosexuality. Compulsory heterosexuality relies on the combination of assumption and discrimination: an assumption of one's heterosexual identity and discriminating against anyone who does not identify as heterosexual. This heterosexist assumption weighs heavy on Southern Black women, as it assumes that all Southern Black women engage in heterosexuality and desire to be mothers. According to Suzanne Pharr, homosexuality and heterosexuality "work together to enforce compulsory heterosexuality and that bastion of patriarchal power, the nuclear family."[5] Compulsory heterosexuality also shows up in the ways Black folks have been historically marginalized. Patricia Hill Collins notes this as hyper-heterosexuality,[6] where Black folks were deemed super heterosexual, primarily engaging in heterosexuality to breed a new generation of enslaved people. This idea of Black sexuality as only heterosexual is rooted in anti-Black rhetoric that assumes that one's race is inevitably connected to some level of heterosexual promiscuity. Unfortunately, this fuels the compulsory heterosexuality in Southern Black spaces, and the SBP internalizes this anti-Black rhetoric.

Heterosexism in the South permits cisgender heterosexual Black folks to be comfortable and silence those who exist in the margins. As LaDawn said, the silencing of sexual difference forces gay and queer folks to "keep their gayness at home." A Southern Black queer person can exist in the South, but they cannot be outwardly gay in any public space because heterosexism is designed to make heterosexual persons comfortable. If queer lesbian folks are silenced by heterosexist judgment from the SBP, then heteronormative folks feel comfortable existing and taking up space in the South. The silence is intended to limit the potential of Southern Black queerness, rendering us invisible and subjected to the cruelty of judgment.

Heterosexism also acts as a gendered value system, or what Remi described as "internalized heterosexism." In the South, heterosexism is a method of socializing Southern Black folks to believe in the value of cisgender embodiment and binary sexual identities. Heterosexism socializes Southern Black folks to value a monogamous, heterosexual marriage with the nuclear family and the limited gender roles that accompany it. In turn, Southern Blacks internalize heterosexism as the only way to exist. Southern Blacks ultimately reinforce this internalized heterosexism by training future generations to desire those same goals. Regardless of sexuality and gender identity, Southern Black people are socialized to normalize these heterosexist goals. Unfortunately, SBQLWP are also indoctrinated with these heterosexist ideologies. The socialization is foundational to what we understand about gender and sexual politics in the South. Southern Blacks are taught by the SBP to value and honor these myopic notions of heterosexism and cisgender embodiment. The internalized heterosexism puts additional value on the cisgender binary, heterosexuality, and patriarchy. As a result, this internalization provides Black Southerners with a sense of humanity. Not internalizing the heterosexist value system causes Southern Blacks to encounter the mass cruelty of judgment. It is difficult for us to dispel and unlearn heterosexism. Some SBQLWP never unlearn it. Even in our queerness, heterosexism and heteronormativity can remain evident in our lives.

Several Black feminist and womanist scholars address the significant ways heterosexism affects Black queer populations. Audre Lorde explains how heterosexism and homophobia are oppressive forces that cause a divide in the Black community. According to Cathy Cohen and Tamara Jones, heterosexism works systematically to make others conform to what is deemed to be "normal" sexuality.[7] For Collins, heterosexism has underpinnings in Black patriarchy, and homosexuality is perceived to hinder Black liberation.[8] Cheryl Clark contends that heterosexism establishes the invisibility of sexually marginalized Black people. Heterosexism ultimately refers to a set of sexual and gender preferences that align with heterosexuality and rely on it as the preferred sexuality. Heterosexism and compulsory heterosexuality provide a hierarchy associated with sexuality and sexual orientation where those who adapt to certain heterosexual normative behaviors are rewarded, and those who deviate are punished.[9]

Lorde unmasks the heterosexism that exists in the Black community and how myths associated with Black lesbianism ultimately affect the full, authentic liberation of the Black community. While she makes proclamations in all her works related to dismantling the fear of difference in feminist discord, *I Am Your Sister* is one of the first works to address how Black women are not a monolithic group. Lorde emphasizes her lesbian identity in most of her works, but this becomes an intraracial discourse uncovering heterosexism in the Black community and Black heterosexual female community. She exposes several myths she has heard from Black folks when talking about Black lesbians.[10] These myths include that Black lesbians are not normal, are apolitical, and are a threat to the Black family, which will ultimately lead to the death of the race.[11] Lorde equates this ideology with racism: "when they talk about us in whispers, tried to paint us, lynch us, bleach us, ignore us, pretend we did not exist. We call that racism."[12] What makes these myths like racism? She does not say. But like racism, heterosexism is fueled by false myths around gender and sexual difference. For Black people, heterosexism becomes a way of dealing with difference in the Black community. These myths can be applied to the heterosexism in the Southern Black community, with the Church and the SBP as the enforcers.

According to Cohen and Jones, Black identity is still missing a deeper understanding of heterosexism as a system of oppression that threatens Black queer persons.[13] Their work responds to Cheryl Clarke's "Failure to Transform" essay, which uncovered the ways homophobia becomes the divisive tactic in the Black community to suppress Black queer folks.[14] In the late 1990s, Cohen and Jones found that Black queer folks were actually confronting heterosexism, not homosexuality. With heterosexism, cisgender heterosexual (cishet) Black folks align with their conservative ideologies. For Cohen and Jones, heterosexism reinforces problematic notions of Blackness as a monolithic identity. According to them, heterosexism "blatantly rejects critical aspects of Black diversity" and "presumes and legitimizes only a single set of sexual and gender relationships: the sexual union between a man and a woman, and the social relations which flow from that union."[15] They nod to the reality set out by Lorde regarding heterosexism as a systemic societal hierarchy but focus on the unions that flow from heterosexism, namely, the heteronormative Black family unit. In a heterosexist framing, the Black family is seen as the protector from all the societal evils that suppress Black folks. According to Cohen and Jones, monogamous heterosexual marital relations were the surest way to protect Black folks from AIDS/HIV and poverty. Moreover, heterosexism is a way of policing Black sexuality. It demands an environment of constant surveillance in which individual members must adhere to strict codes of conduct or risk being attacked.[16] In other words, heterosexism dictates how one should participate in sexual activities to avoid judgment. This reality makes heterosexism a systemic problem that affects anyone who is considered sexually deviant in the Black community.

Collins provides an analysis of heterosexism, making the connection between the prison industrial system and the mythical closet that Black queer persons experience. She argues that when we discuss Black sexuality, it is often in discussions of cishet Black persons and how they engage in certain heteronormative sexual behaviors. When discussing this new racism, Collins claims that Black persons need to understand the position of Black queer persons, who see racism and heterosexism as inevitably tied together. After all, Black queer folks cannot separate these systems of oppression because they overlap in their lives.[17] She claims that heterosexism and racism have several concurring characteristics. Specifically, she addresses how the mythical closet Black queer folks experience is similar to the massive incarceration of Black folks. Collins establishes four necessary components of heterosexism in the Black community: separation, social control, limited definitions, and sexual deviancy.[18] These components have racial realities associated with them, but she argues they also are manifested in the practice of heterosexism. When discussing separation, Collins contends that Black queer persons are separated from other queer communities. Social control relies on controlling how one's sexuality is performed and actualized, telling the Black queer person that they can be gay or queer but only in ways that are comfortable and acceptable to cishet persons. Limited definitions of sexuality rely on a sexual binary of gay or straight. Limiting sexuality or sexual identities controls how one's sexuality is played out in public spaces. Sexual deviancy is the way Black queer folks are viewed as sexual deviants. In my conversations with SBQLWP, they speak to all these realities as they exist in the South and the ways the SBP often uses these cruel tactics to maintain heterosexism. SBQLWP are separated from white queer and Southern Black communities. We experience social control from the SBP, who attempts to control our gender and sexual identities. The Church uses the SBP as a way to limit definitions of sexuality.

"Heterosexism Makes Certain Presumptions of Normality": Realities of Heteronormativity in the SBP

Like heterosexism, heteronormativity is an overarching reality that we experience in the South, a tool used in the massive cruelty against SBQLWP. Heteronormativity normalizes cisgender heterosexuality, deeming all other forms of sexual and gender identity deviant and abnormal. As outlined by the following quotes, my interlocutors equated heterosexism with heteronormativity:

> ANGEL: "It is the fear of homosexuality and anything outside of the norm."

> LaDAWN: "Heterosexism makes certain presumptions of normality and does not allow you to embody all of who you are in the South."

> VANESSA: "The further South, the more heteronormative it is."

According to Cathy Cohen, heteronormativity recognizes these "localized practices and those centralized institutions which legitimize and privilege heterosexuality and heterosexual relationships as fundamental and 'normal' within society."[19] Even in queer political discourse, she critiques how heteronormativity often makes heterosexuality the norm: "All heterosexuals are represented as dominant and controlling and all queers are understood as marginalized and invisible."[20] The South operates in a similar way, where heterosexuality is considered the dominant and controlling gender and sexual identity, and queer folks are deemed as abnormal. As Cassie noted, "It [heterosexism] is superior and dominant." Heteronormativity creates a binary of deviant and normal, where heterosexuality acts as the normal and superior while queerness and gayness are seen as the deviant/inferior. The South dictates heterosexuality as a fundamentally normal and legitimate form of human interaction. Queerness and any form of gayness encounter the massive cruelty because this embodiment challenges what is considered normal. SBQLWP recognize the heteronormativity in the South and had to unlearn some of the overarching realities of heteronormativity.

Southern Black folks take a big gulp of heteronormativity like it is sweet tea. Heteronormativity is alluring and sweet, served in many Southern households, and deemed a necessity in many social and economic spaces. Like sweet tea, heteronormativity is everywhere in the South—served to us at Church, reinforced on our jobs, and honored in our family homes. While heterosexism is the systemic measure of centering heterosexuality and all other institutions that derive from it, heteronormativity is the process of making heterosexuality the societal norm. Marriage and families are the institutions that perpetuate heterosexism, but heteronormativity socializes Southerners to believe that heterosexual behaviors are the only way to exist. Heterosexism is the embodiment of heterosexuality as an institution while heteronormativity dictates what is considered normal gender and sexuality. In the SBP, heteronormativity represents cultural norms one must follow to avoid judgment and cruelty. Heteronormativity represents a preferred monolithic sexual and gendered Southern identity. The SBP are the gatekeepers of societal normalcy. They determine acceptable gender performativity and sexuality in the South, judging those who do not adequately perform their assigned gender and sexuality. Sexual and gender fluidity are the antithesis of the heteronormative consciousness of the SBP. Gender and sexual fluidity are frowned on in the South, mainly because they challenge limited gender and sexual norms. Heteronormativity employed by the SBP limits the acknowledgment of Southern Black queerness.

Furthermore, the SBP uses heteronormativity to assign value to these sexual and gender norms. Heteronormativity in the South values, honors, and respects heterosexuality as the norm. Heteronormativity values folks who emulate heterosexuality and limited gender norms. If a Southern Black person falls in line or wants to uphold heteronormativity, they are valued in the South and revered by the Church community and family. As Nyx noted, existing as heteronormative equates to success in the South: "Having a family becomes a status symbol and equated to success." Existing as heteronormative Southern Blacks gives them social value, and their existence is equated with success. If a queer person exhibits some level of heteronormativity, Southern Blacks will value them and deem them successful. While they may be queer, they still legitimize the normalcy of heterosexuality. For example, queerness can have some value in the South if it mimics a monogamous relationship. A few interlocutors noted this reality. Toni mentioned how monogamous queer couples have more value in the South because "the most important thing in the South is being married, regardless of sexuality." Allison Chase discussed how she is treated with more respect when she is in a relationship: "I notice that people treat me differently when I have a consistent partner.

Having a consistent partner is important in the South if you are out." In other words, they did something right by engaging in some type of heteronormativity. The South may not want you to get married in a Church or bring your partner to Church, but Southern Blacks love a monogamous, heteronormative relationship.

Given the racialized queer sexual geography, heteronormativity is the fear of sexual and gender fluidity in the South. This fear causes tension between SBQLWP and the rest of the Black Southern community. As many SBQLWP mentioned, heteronormativity fears any sexual or gender difference, confronting it with disdain and judgment. As Tené noted, heteronormativity results from homophobia, where there is fear of anything outside the norm. Sexual fluidity and queer identities are considered problems and something to be feared in the South. SBQLWP contend that there is no room for any form of sexual fluidity because it is encountered with fear. As Leah put it, the heteronormative lens is combative to anyone who represents sexual and gender difference, implying a question to Southern queer folks: "why are you here?" This question invokes a level of fear of and disdain for queerness. Because our queer and gay identity is seen as deviant and abnormal, it is met with fear and disgust. Ultimately, the fear of queerness in the South creates the massive cruelty we experience with the SBP. This fear ultimately makes it difficult for any queer lesbian person to fully embody who we are. We fear that we will face manifestations of massive societal cruelty. Heteronormativity cause cishet folks and the SBP to fears us and we fear their judgment.

SBQLWP assimilating into society means that sometimes we must take a gulp of heteronormativity to legitimize our relationships. Some SBQLWP may conform and internalize heteronormativity in our relationships. As Maezah noted, "You tend to mimic what you know." We are raised understanding heterosexuality and its institutions as a norm, causing us to mimic these relationships and conform to what is considered "normal" Southern life. Even when deviating from the perceived norm, there may still be a desire to engage in heteronormativity for protection and safety. This heteronormativity is rooted in the fear that our queer lesbian relationships are not real; we think that even in our queer lesbian identities, we must perform as close to a heteronormativity as possible to gain a level of social acceptance. At times, we internalize the need for a strict gender binary. Heteronormativity will make a queer lesbian person believe that there must be a masculine person in the relationship to be a "real" lesbian relationship. Sunshine Honeysuckle and Bynta, a lesbian couple from the South currently living in Northern California, mentioned this problem as they encounter heteronormative consciousness from other SBQLWP. This couple is what we call a "femme on femme" relationship—both identify as feminine-embodied SBQLWP. They said that no one takes their relationship seriously in the South. Even in Black queer lesbian spaces, Southern queer folks assume they are sisters, not a couple. They mentioned that in places like Atlanta, Georgia, Black queer lesbian relationships are accepted, but only in the stud/femme binary. The stud and femme embodiments have extremely strict boundaries. Heteronormativity can exist in the SBQLWP community, where we may actualize our queerness and lesbianism in a heteronormative context.

"The Cisgender Hetero Black Man in the South Is Central": Realities of Black Patriarchy and Heteropatriarchy

Heterosexism and heteronormativity suppress Black queerness in the South, but so do Black patriarchy and heteropatriarchy. SBQLWP mentioned how heterosexism is a weapon of Black patriarchy enforced by the SBP. Heteropatriarchy in the South is connected to how close one is to the cishet Southern Black male. As Maezah said, "The cisgender hetero Black man in the South is central." Black heteropatriarchy in the South alludes to the connection to and honoring of Black patriarchy and heteronormativity. It notes how patriarchy informs our understanding of heteronormativity and heterosexism. Black heteropatriarchy connects heterosexism and heteronormativity to Southern Black patriarchy. The SBP uses this method of psychological terrorism against anyone who steps outside of patriarchy, heterosexism, and heteronormativity. Black heteropatriarchy reiterates and maintains patriarchy and heteronormativity. The SBP internalizes the Black heteropatriarchy as a normal Southern reality.

bell hooks describes patriarchy as a "political-social system that insists that males are inherently dominating, superior to everything, and everyone deemed weak, especially females, and endowed with the right to dominate and rule over the weak and maintain that dominance through various forms of psychological terrorism and violence."[21] Black heteropatriarchy centralizes the cishet Southern Black man and dismisses or demonizes anyone else. Black heteropatriarchy assumes that the cishet Black man is superior and dominant in the South and ensures that Southern Black women remain weak, indoctrinated in the psychological terrorism that places the cishet Southern Black men on a societal pedestal. He is revered in Southern Black life and honored because he is the pathway to a heteronormative family. Proximity to the cishet Southern Black man allows Southern Black women to gain some social value as a wife or mother. Without him, the creation of the heteronormative family unit would be impossible. While the woman is the vessel, he is central to the family unit. The closer a person is to Black heteropatriarchy, the more value they have in the South. This proximity upholds Black heteropatriarchy while silencing and judging anyone not close to it. Furthermore, Black heteropatriarchy focuses primarily on how one's sexuality benefits the dominant group (in this case, cishet Southern Black men). In the SBP, if one's sexuality does not benefit Black heteropatriarchy, it is considered deviant and must be controlled, suppressed, and silenced. This method of heterosexism relies on the assumption that sexuality can only exist in connection to the cishet Southern Black man. Through a Black heteropatriarchal lens, SBQLWP are viewed as societal threats because our lifestyles do not directly benefit Black heteropatriarchy. The SBP uses this lack of heteropatriarchy as a justification for judging us.

"It's All Over the Church": The Church Is Foundational in Heterosexism, Heteronormativity, and Black Heteropatriarchy

Heterosexism, heteronormativity, and Black heteropatriarchy are experienced in many social institutions in the South, but SBQLWP describe how they all have roots in the Church. The Church fuels the heterosexist consciousness of the SBP because it is the first social institution that socializes the SBP to value heterosexism, heteronormativity, and Black heteropatriarchy. According to SBQLWP, heterosexuality in the South is preferred and assumed because it aligns with misinterpreted religious doctrines. In this context, heterosexism connects Church's beliefs to societal sexual expectations. As Byanca puts it, "There is no real separation between Church and State." Other SBQLWP cite the Church as foundational in creating heterosexism in Southern Black spaces:

ANDY: "It [heterosexism] is all over the church."

LEAH: "The Church starts all of it [heterosexism]."

While the Church plants the seed of heterosexism, the Southern Black community maintains it in Southern life. As a social institution, the Church pushes certain societal gender and sexual norms under the guise of religiosity. Heterosexuality is a Church requirement, a spiritual litmus test to determine one's societal and spiritual value. The Church places significant value on heteronormativity, marriage, and family as proof of God's blessings. Ultimately, heterosexism becomes part of a spiritual hierarchy in the South, maintained by the SBP. To denounce homosexuality, the Church uses heterosexism and heteronormativity as a spiritual test where our proximity to these societal realities brings us closer to God.

The Church perpetuates heteronormativity, heterosexism, and Black heteropatriarchy by putting significant spiritual and societal value on the creation of the heteronormative, patriarchal Southern Black family. As mentioned by Pharr, the creation of a family is foundational for compulsory heterosexuality and heterosexism. Like the claims of Cohen and Jones, heterosexism attaches sex and sexuality to the creation of the nuclear, monogamous, heteronormative Black family. SBQLWP connect this reality to the Church value system. The notion that "the family is the Church and the Church is family," extends beyond the legacy of the Church in the Southern Black community to the significance the Church places on creating and maintaining the heteronormative Black family and Black heteropatriarchy. The Church pushes religious and spiritual values on sex and heterosexuality and the institutions that come from it: family and marriage.

Regardless of sexuality, Black women's sexualities are tied to creating and maintaining nuclear heteronormative Black families. For Southern Black women, the heteronormative Southern Black family reflects her societal value. If she can perpetuate heteronormativity and be close to Black heteropatriarchy, she has spiritual and social value. Cishet Southern Black men are expected to be the financial backbone and the spiritual head of the home. Yet their gender and sexual expectations are not connected to a larger community. Black women's sexuality is directly tied to establishing the Black community. Southern Black women are held more accountable for the rise and fall of the Black family and the entire race. This burden is often placed on our womb. We are physically responsible for mothering the entire Black race. This patriarchal duty puts a lot of pressure on a Southern Black woman's womb—an unreasonable expectation. Due to this pressure and burden, Southern Black women are rarely viewed as autonomous persons. We are only considered dawtas, wives, and mothers. Even in Church vernacular of "dawta" infers a paternalistic language that connects Southern Black girls (and even grown women) to a family until we are married. Dawtas have the shackles of heteronormativity, heterosexism, and Black heteropatriarchy to ensure they fulfill their duties to the Black race.

Black heteropatriarchy exercised by the Church affects SBQLWP differently than it does Southern Black gay men. As mentioned by E. Patrick Johnson, the Church acts as a nurturing space for Black gay men.[22] The nurturing is not solely based on their ability to hide in plain sight but on the ways they benefit from Church patriarchy. Regardless of sexuality, the Church celebrates cisgender Black manhood. The cisgender Southern Black man is central, privileged, valued, and considered the epitome of God in the flesh. Because of this privilege, Black queer gay men receive a more favorable status compared with SBQLWP. While they are also victims of heteronormativity and heterosexism, they have the benefits of Black heteropatriarchy. Cisgender Black gay men are automatically seen as connected to the Church in some capacity, whether in the pulpit, church leadership, or the choir. This privilege is not to say that Southern Black gay men have a better experience in the Church than SBQLWP do, but their male privilege allows them to hide from additional layers of gender discrimination. The Church honors their cisgender Black male identity, even if they identify as gay or queer. Regardless of sexuality, men in the Church benefit from Black heteropatriarchy.

While still marginalized based on preconceived traditional notions of masculinity, Black queer gay men are allowed to exist as autonomous sexual beings like their cisgender heterosexual Black brothers. Black heteropatriarchy allows for this level of sexual freedom. As discussed by Cohen and Jones, "heterosexism and patriarchy thus results in increased freedoms for black men (mitigated by race) while severely limiting the freedoms of black women."[23] The societal and spiritual value of Southern Black women, regardless of sexuality and gender embodiment, is connected to their ability to create and maintain the Black family. Because of Church patriarchy, Southern Black women are always viewed in connection to someone else, rarely as autonomous sexual individuals. In the lens of Church patriarchy, we are not independent sexual beings and have limited sexual freedoms. Black heteropatriarchy limits the sexual autonomy of Southern Black women, which ultimately translates to how we are treated.

Ultimately, the weapons of heterosexism, heteronormativity, and Black heteropatriarchy wielded by the Church limit and remove the sexual autonomy of Southern Black women. These tools restrict Southern Black women from fully actualizing their sexual identities. These variables are taught to

Southern folks by the Church and affect how Southern Black women are treated. SBQLWP are treated with massive cruelty not just because of our queerness or lesbianism; it is the audacity we have to exist as autonomous persons. We are judged by the SBP because we dare to regain our autonomy and sexuality. We have the audacity to disregard the notion that our sexuality is tied to the procreation of the next generation. Mothering the community is not connected to our wombs. We are viewed by the Church as rebels because we do not adhere to heterosexism or bow down to Black heteropatriarchy. Our decision not to fully engage in these societal norms subjects us to judgment and cruelty by the SBP.

"I See Heterosexism in the Pastor and First Lady": Pastor and First Lady as Models of Heteronormativity

SBQLWP pinpointed the relationship between pastor and first lady as the epitome of heterosexism and models of heteronormativity. Remi noted, "I see heterosexism in the pastor and first lady as the ideal relationship for others to follow." The pastor and first lady embody preferred cisgender roles and expectations. Pastor and first lady represent the relationship goals of Church folks. Southern Black folks want to emulate their relationship. Because of this, Southern Black folks idealize the pastor and first lady. Outside immediate families, the pastor and first lady introduce Southerners to the societal value of cisgender expectations and the significance of marriage and family. The pastor and first lady aesthetically complement one another in this gender binary. This imagery causes Southerners to desire and strive for heteronormativity and Black heteropatriarchy. Ultimately, they introduce us to what a heteronormative Black relationship should be, the model of Black heteronormativity. SBQLWP note that their understandings of a heteronormative relationship and gender binaries stem from witnessing the relationship between their pastor and first lady. After all, that silent Southern Black queer lesbian girl is sitting in Church watching this relationship, internalizing it as the norm. Without this model Church couple, many Southern Black folks would not know what heteronormativity looks like on a grander scale. While the pastor and first lady relationship is honored, their image of heteronormativity also limits how Southern Blacks actualize our gender and sexual identities.

The pastor has a "masculine role,"[24] an archetype of Southern cishet Black masculinity. In the Church hierarchy, the pastor is positioned second only under God. More than that, he represents the epitome of Black patriarchal masculinity. He is a leader of his Church and home. The pastor is typically a formally educated Southern gentleman who embodies certain sensibilities and charm. He is honored and respected while fighting for racial liberation and equity. He focuses on issues of social injustice and racial liberation while wearing and embodying his Sunday Best. He is typically attractive or at least nicely dressed. His racial consciousness and physical aesthetic are pleasing to the congregation. It is gratifying for Church members to see their pastor dressed well and driving a nice car.[25] The congregation insists that their pastor preaches "in style." Cishet Southern Black men want to be him, and cishet Black Southern women want to marry him. He represents the mythical norm in the Black South. The image of the Black pastor invokes a sense of accepted hegemony in the South. He is the model of Southern Black manhood, perpetuating the role that Southern Black men are supposed to play in the Black community and family. Moreover, the preacher and the pulpit are seen as the "man's space,"[26] reiterating the Black heteropatriarchal assumption that the pulpit should only be occupied by a cishet Black male. His honor and respect also results from his perceived sexuality. He is able to benefit from inherent purity and heterosexist permission. Because he is a pastor, a cishet Southern Black man second to God, he is perceived as pure while also granted sexual immunity. He may have some societal permission to be a sexually autonomous person. The pastor is situated in a privileged gender binary and sexuality in the South.

The first lady represents traditional Southern cishet Black femininity, the epitome of inherent sexual purity. While many Southern Black Church women benefit from inherent purity, the first lady is the ultimate Black female personification of it. Other Southern Black women aim for her level of purity. After all, her marriage to the pastor meant that she proved herself to be the purist woman, exuding Southern Black respectability politics at its finest. There is an assumption about her sexual identity based on her proximity to the pastor and ultimately to God. Her inherent purity makes her the leader for all Southern Black women to follow. Whether the Southern Black woman attends Church or not, they recognize that the first lady is revered. If Southern Black women follow her, they too can find a man like the pastor. She is also held in high regard in the ways she serves her Church and community. The first lady is connected to the pastor, in proximity to Southern Black patriarchal masculinity. Like the pastor, she may be formally educated and embodies Southern sensibilities and charm. She is domesticated in two spaces. While the pastor is concerned with the entire Church and focuses on issues of racial injustices and equity, she assists with the youth and children. She is also responsible for molding the next generation of Southern Black women. She is responsible for her own home as well, ensuring that her house is a safe, peaceful place for pastor after he works hard for the Church. Perhaps the most important role she has is to complement the pastor, matching his style and values, what Church folks refer to as being "equally yoked." Together, they epitomize the goal of heteronormativity for Southern Black folks. Whether or not Southern Black folks attend Church, they see the pastor and first lady as models of heteronormativity.

These Church hierarchies represent one's responsibility to the Church, whether in the functioning of the larger institution or in a particular ministry. Everyone who enters the Church has a position in this hierarchy that is both practical and spiritual. The hierarchy determines who has value in the Church. Even in the harsh harbors and invisible churches during enslavement, individuals had certain roles during service. According to Janet Cornelius, everyone in worship had a purpose, from the elder who sang the hymn to the preacher who conducted the sermon.[27] Above all, Church folks perceive that this hierarchy is ordained by God. God is the spiritual head of the church, and the pastor is second only under God. This hierarchy assumes that only a cishet male can have a spiritual connection to God, the epitome of what is considered holy and sacred. The pastor is supported by a series of Church leaders, such as associate and assistant pastors, deacons, and/or trustees. As Jacqueline Grant discusses, the women's place is often in the pew,[28] acting as supportive members of the Church but rarely viewed as leaders. In this case, Southern Black Church women influence the Church by acting as the moral compass or prayer warriors but do not hold much authority. The pew exists as a marginalized, gendered place in the Church. While sitting in the pew, Southern Church women looked upon the pastor, first lady, and Church leaders for spiritual guidance. Sitting in the pew also situates them in a marginalized space.

The pew position represents where Southern Black women exist in the heteronormative hierarchy as well. The pew is a patriarchal position that relegates Southern Black Church women into certain subservient positions of support. While they often make up the largest population in the Church, they exist at the pew. Black women are considered the backbone of the Church, which Grant argues is the background of the church, where they are support workers who must stay in their place.[29] The Church pew is both a physical location and a hierarchal position that places Black women, regardless of sexuality, in the background. If cishet Southern Black women operate at the Church pew, then SBQLWP exist in the last pew, representing the bottom of the Church hierarchy. As Horace Griffin mentioned, they are possibly disregarded as Church partitioners and do not exist in the Church hierarchy.

The position in the last pew solidifies our position as the outsider within and extends to our worldview. Collins's outsider within theory is often cited based on positionality, but she contends that this position becomes foundational in establishing one's worldview. The position of outsider within informs one's way of knowing and learning, establishing a standpoint and epistemology. Moreover, this position "fosters new angles of vision on oppression."[30] Our positionality in the last pew highlights new angles about heterosexism, heteronormativity, and Black heteropatriarchy. SBQLWP recognize how this positionality allows us to question and challenge the gender and sexual hierarchies of the Church. While we are in the back, we can see the whole Church. From our position, we get a full picture of the Church. SBQLWP question the heteronormative nature of the Church and its influence on Southern life. We are more likely to discuss the hypocrisy within the Church and have a deeper understanding of how the Church creates and maintains heteronormativity. Many SBQLWP were critical of how heteronormativity and heterosexism from the Church create hypocrisy and inconsistencies, specifically as it relates to the dynamics of sin. As Kris noted in our conversation, "So lesbianism is a sin, but you are living in sin, too."

While Church folks judge others regarding sinful behavior, SBQLWP recognize the ways the hypocrisy from the Church perpetuates heterosexist ideologies. The pastor and Church leaders see the front of the church, looking out into the congregation, seeing a person's front, the representative of what they want pastor and 'em to see. SBQLWP sitting in the back pew witness all the ugliness that Church folks want to hide. We know the Church's flaws. We know some secrets that the deacons hold. We are aware of the Church trauma and hurt experienced by others. Our position allows for us to identify this Church hierarchy and informs our views on heterosexism, heteronormativity, and Black heteropatriarchy. Our outsider within position helps us understand the realities of Southern Black Church life, filled with hypocrisy and heteronormativity. We also recognize the lengths folks will take to maintain heteronormativity. From our standpoint in the last pew, we see the Church for what it really is: a flawed institution.

"Unspoken Rules of What Is Acceptable": Heterosexism and Heteronormativity Reiterates Unspoken Cisgender Roles and Expectations

Heterosexism and heteronormativity in the South dictate what is considered normal in terms of gender roles and expectations related to Southern manhood and womanhood. Heterosexism and heteronormativity also dictate that gender expression can only exist in a binary. Many SBQLWP cited how these limited gender roles and expectations are foundational to heterosexism and heteronormativity in the South. Both ultimately limiting gender fluidity. SBQLWP are taught that certain gender roles and expectations are socially acceptable in the South and are socialized to accept these roles and expectations of normality. As Sweet said, heterosexism and heteronormativity in the South are rooted in certain "unspoken rules of what is acceptable." She notes that these "unspoken rules" are the binary gender norms and expectations that Southern Black folks are expected to follow. As Marie Dylan detailed, heterosexism has three significant components: gendered roles, cisgender identity, and monogamy. She argues that these components make Black Southerners feel a sense of belonging, connection, and membership in mainstream Southern life. In this context, SBQLWP note that heterosexism and heteronormativity are attached to an embodiment of a cisgender binary identity. These rules are not written down on a memo anywhere for Southern Black folks to read and follow but are passed down from generation to generation like a family heirloom. We may have learned these unspoken rules while snapping beans with our grandmothers.

"It Was Shoved Down Our Throats and Became the Guiding Norm": Socialization of Binary Cisgender Embodiment

SBQLWP note that heterosexism and heteronormativity socialize Southern Black women to exude Southern femininity, with that model as the guiding norm. These cisgender normalcies are rooted in cishet behaviors and practices. Like the cult of domesticity and politics of respectability, the cisgender feminine embodiment provides Southern Black women a sense of societal status and humanity. SBQLWP recognize the value of the cisgender embodiment of femininity as an expectation in our lives. As Remi noted, we are socialized to normalize and value these feminine gender roles from a young age: "These roles happen to us." According to Kea, the socialization of gender normalcy was "shoved down our throats and became the guiding norm." Kea contends that this expectation was forced on Southern Black folks. Heterosexism and heteronormativity represent the processes of accepting these limited embodiments of femininity and masculinity as normal and any deviations as a problem. But what are these cisgender binary gender embodiments that have been shoved down our throats? What guiding norms have we been taught to assimilate to?

Cisgender binary embodiment grows out of the Southern tropes such as the Southern gentleman, the good ol' boy, and the Southern belle, as outlined by James T. Sears. Sears highlights that these gender tropes—directly tied to the antebellum South and the legacy of enslavement—ultimately create contemporary gender and sexual distinctions. These Southern tropes such as Scarlett O'Hara and Bubba are the guiding norm and are caricatures that Southerners often attempt to embody. These tropes are shoved down our throats from the moment we are born, the models of Southern humanity and the epitome of cisgender binary embodiment in the Southern landscape. While these tropes extend to all Southerners regardless of race, Southern Black folks are indoctrinated to believe that embodying them will provide a sense of racial equity and freedom. Southern Black folks believe these roles provide an opportunity to reclaim their humanity and regain respect in a racially contentious space. Regardless of race, Southern men want to be the Southern gentleman and a good ol' boy, and Southern women want to marry them. Southern women, regardless of race, believe that embodying the Southern belle trope will provide societal access to marry the Southern gentleman or the good ol' boy. These tropes influence the SBP as well. Cishet Southern Black men and the SBP understand masculinity only in the context of these hegemonic tropes. The SBP believes that cishet Southern Black women must embody the Southern belle trope because it places men in the center, ultimately validating the SBP. These tropes distinguish what is considered an acceptable embodiment of cisgender Southern femininity and masculinity. The Southern gentleman, good ol' boy, and the Southern belle are all models of Southern hegemonic masculinity and femininity. Embodying these tropes gives Southerners a more favorable societal status, where they become cisgender models of heteronormativity. The SBP uses these tropes as a measurement of heteronormativity.

In the context of traditional Southern masculinity, money and labor are attached to class and power. The Southern gentleman is the epitome of aristocratic lineage with inherited generational wealth. Sears defines the background of the Southern gentleman: "Aristocratic lineage (sometimes the product of too frequent intermarriages between first cousins) and the beneficiary of a Southern liberal education, he enjoys the prestige of his position without the accompanying power. This self-assured gentleman with natural dignity of manner is often trotted out for *Southern Living* photos and honored at annual historic events. His affable and understanding demeanor disappears only when an outsider attempts to destroy established customs or seeks membership in his social circle."[31] The Southern gentleman is the epitome of hegemonic manhood in the South. He is an educated, cishet white male who has the benefit of family heritage. He does not have to work hard for his money but only needs to maintain the inheritance (typically from generations of enslaved labor). His labor is mental instead of physical. Everyone knows his family; his last name has power and status. He may be a member of prestigious clubs. He is the Southern aristocrat, at the top of the social, economic, and political hierarchy. He represents the genteel patriarch, someone whose manhood is attached to land ownership. He is "refined, elegant, and given to casual sensuousness."[32] Southern men of all races hope to emulate him.

On the other hand, the good ol' boy represents the man who works to reach social mobility. He typically has the name "Bubba," a name designated to the family patriarch. My father is the Bubba of our family because he is the only son from my paternal grandma. Sears defines the good ol' boy trope as: "un-lettered working-class Southerner with child-like simplicity and ox-like determination. He has more erections than problems, and his colorful stories outnumber the keys hanging from his 40-inch belt. Good natured, unpretentious, and reliable, he respects the law, pays taxes, and attends Sunday church. Most often found at fishing holes, hunting grounds, and stock car tracks, the Good Ol' Boy is likeable, 100 percent American."[33] He is a cishet white man with a huge sexual appetite, but he is not of Southern noble blood. His educational attainment or military service gained him social mobility. His last name may not carry much weight in the community. If he is part of a club, it is because he gained access from his hard-earned money. He is similar to Michael Kimmel's "heroic artisan," a man who takes pride in his hard work. His manhood is attached to physical strength, economic autonomy, and participating in the democratic process.[34] Southern folks admire him for his ability to engage in the economic and political sphere as a hard worker, not an inheritor. Southern folks love a hard-working man.

According to Sears, the Southern belle is a social metaphor—an unmarried, white upper-middle-class woman who has limited education confined to the Bible, history, and well-chosen literature.[35] Joan Morgan defines the Southern belle as someone considered too virtuous and pure to be sullied with anything as nasty as independent sexual desire.[36] This cisgender femininity embodies Southern sensibilities and refinement. The belle is Southernness at its best, a model for all cishet Southern women. From a young age, the Southern belle represents a hegemonic Southern femininity that all women are expected to embody. For young Southern women, this embodiment is the only way to exude Southern femininity. The more Southern Black women fall in line with this rigid embodiment and heteropatriarchy, the more social protection they receive.

These tropes are directly tied to the value system of heteronormativity in the South and Black heteropatriarchy in the Black South. The Southern gentleman and good ol' boy not only represent hegemonic masculinity, they also contribute to the manifestation of Southern patriarchy. Besides the pastor, cishet Black men embody these archetypes of masculinity to perpetuate and maintain Black heteropatriarchy. The Southern belle is the womb of Southern heteronormativity. Sears describes the Southern belle as unmarried, but she is socialized to be a suitable wife to the Southern gentleman and the good ol' boy, providing them with a heteronormative family. This Southern feminine cisgender embodiment connects Southern folks to the imagery of a heteronormative, monogamous marriage and a nuclear family unit. Without the Southern belle, creating and sustaining heteronormative families would not be possible. SBQLWP discussed how the Southern belle (and by proxy the Southern wife) acts as a social, economic, and even political position in the South. Socially, she receives respect and value. Economically, the trope represents financial security. Through marriage, she is well taken care of. The Southern gentleman and the good ol' boy provide financial security for the family. Politically, the Southern belle assists with the political imagery of heteronormativity. Southern folks love their political leaders to have a heteronormative family, the Southern belle and wife are essential to that image. Even in our queerness/lesbianism, SBQLWP still discuss how this trope informs our Southernness.

While the Southern belle is typically considered to be a conservative white woman, Southern Black women are encouraged to adopt this archetype as well. Southerners address her as "ma'am," a sign of respect and admiration. Even while being marginalized by race and gender, Southern Black women use this trope to gain the societal benefits of heterosexism. Like Black men who use the Southern gentleman or good ol' boy types to gain power, Southern Black women use the Southern belle trope to gain societal respect. For Black women, who have historically been referred to as subhuman and sexually lewd, the cisgender feminine embodiment is an opportunity for her to regain her humanity. In aligning with definitions from Sears and Morgan, embodying the Southern belle means that the Southern Black woman is a cisgender woman in a certain socioeconomic class and has a level of formal education: an upper-middle-class Southern Black women with at least a bachelor's degree. She is a Christian woman, possibly raised in the Church, heavily believes in Church doctrines, and embodies evangelical faith. She believes that family and marriage are attached to her role and expectations as a woman. She dismisses any kind of sexual and gender fluidity, only seeing gender as blue and pink. She is extremely hospitable and does not speak loudly among cishet Black men (as Southerners say, "in mixed company"). She benefits from inherent purity, not openly speaking of anything related to sex or sexuality outside of procreating. The SBP wants to marry her or emulate her, by perception or reality. She represents heteronormativity at its best, the "good woman."

Robin Boylorn's description of the Southern rural town of Sweetwater sheds light on the ways these limited gender roles exist in Southern Black spaces. Boylorn describes these feminine categories as the good woman, the bad woman, and the in-between woman:

> Good women are churched, or too simple or ugly to be impressive. Good women stay home, except for church services, school, and missionary work. The bad ones, or the ones still young enough to be cute and still naïve enough to think they can convince a man to stay off good looks and good lovin', spending their nights out. The in-between women take turns staying home and going out, depending on the night of the week . . . good women are good cooks, modest lovers, and humble.[37]

This description represents the way the SBP perceives as socially acceptable Southern Black cisgender embodiment.

Sexuality is the significant delineation between the good woman and the bad woman, where the proximity to sexual purity is the deciding factor in cisgender Southern Black femininity. The good woman is a modest lover, while the bad woman is perceived as an experienced lover, a sexuality they use to their advantage (read: gold digger). The bad woman challenges traditional discussions related to sexual purity but still engages in heteronormative sexual behavior. These archetypes of Southern Black womanhood suggest that sexual and gender fluidity is a "stage" that Southern Black women experience, where they are the bad woman who becomes the in-between woman and then, saved by marriage, the good woman. The bad woman is what older Southern Black women could call "worldly women" or "women of the streets," where the "streets" represents a level of sexual and gender fluidity. As Shay noted, queer lesbians are considered "street people," with limited morals and success. As Higginbotham states, the street is "a metaphor for all that was unwholesome and dangerous."[38] Anything connected to the street is considered dangerous. Sexual independence and gender fluidity equate to a societal danger. The good woman becomes the standard for the Southern Black female community, the ideal hegemonic Southern Black femininity like the Southern belle or first lady. She may not be attractive, but she has social value because she is the Southern Black version of the Southern belle. The dichotomy between the good and bad woman represents a Southern Black social hierarchy rooted in a sexual value system. The good woman is the Southern belle, while the bad woman (or street people) are social vagrants and undesirables. Due to gender and sexual fluidity, SBQLWP are the antithesis to the good woman archetype in the South, only perceived as the bad or in-between women. Even if the SBQLWP embody Southern cisgender femininity, they are not automatically equated with the good women. A Southern Black woman's proximity to heteronormativity and heterosexuality is the deciding factor to determine where she fits in this good/bad woman dichotomy. This eliminates SBQLWP ability to be considered good women. Southerners who embody gender and sexual fluidity are deemed to be the bad woman.

SBQLWP equate heterosexism and heteronormativity to the embodiment of these gender binaries because these tropes affect how we are judged in the South. It is rooted in these unspoken rules related to gender roles and expectations outlined by Sears's and Boylorn's archetypes, which limit how we can actualize our queer lesbian identities. As we come to terms with our gender and sexual identities, we are still met with these binary gender expectations. For the SBP, the lesbian represents the bad or in-between woman. Because of our queer lesbianism, we are perceived to be promiscuous and engage in the unholy sexual behaviors of the bad woman. Somehow our lesbianism prevents us from being a good woman because Southerners assume that we do not (or choose not to) embody traditional femininity and respectability. We are perceived as those in-between women, who are perceived as merely going through a phase until we find God and align ourselves with sexual purity. After all, who would want to be a bad woman for a lifetime? The SBP reiterates heteronormativity by making lesbianism a phase. When coming out, many SBQLWP are met with the assumption that our lifestyles are merely a phase that would eventually end. It provides the SBP comfort that somehow, we will return to heterosexuality and engage in heteronormativity. This ideology makes Black queer lesbianism dirty and impure because it does not fit within the hegemonic Southern Black femininity. Queer lesbianism becomes equated with sexual impropriety. Because we are considered a bad or in-between woman, we are judged and encounter a massive cruelty, justified by others because we choose to blur the binary lines and challenge the embodiment of these tropes. SBQLWP who embody gender fluidity equates to a level of immorality. Our queerness and lesbianism remove us from benefitting from inherent purity. Purity becomes equated with how a woman embodies traditional Southern cisgender femininity. Without this, we are considered societal vagrants. We are double stigmatized for being not sexually pure and for not having sexual relations with men. These gender limitations are the manifestations of Southern heteronormativity, perpetuated by the SBP.

The SBP use these tropes to police Southern Black female sexuality and to limit the potential of what Southern Black femininity can be. The SBP use these binary gender norms to dictate how Southern Black women should engage in sexual and gender politics. If a Southern Black woman does not align with these roles, her sexual identity is judged. Anyone who does not embody or desire to participate in this hegemonic Southern Black cisgender femininity is relegated to the margins and silenced by the SBP. The SBP emerges as the enforcer of these rules of gender and sexual assimilation. As Maezah discusses, gender fluidity causes a level of confrontation in the South. Like Barton's discussion of the Bible Belt panopticon, the SBP use these tropes as a litmus test to police the gender and sexual behaviors of Southern folks. Southern Black women who do not fully embody and honor one or more of these cisgender tropes of purity and heterosexuality encounter a massive cruelty from the SBP.

Collins discusses how heterosexism manifests in the Black community in these limited gender definitions. She uncovers how heterosexism relies on a sexual binary and values normalizing a limited gender binary. She mentions that sexuality (like racism and sexism) relies on the binary of normal/deviant. The "normal" race is white, and the "normal" gender is male. Heterosexuality is perceived as the norm, while interaction outside of that is considered deviant. In this context, sexuality is part of this mythical norm that produces hegemonic ideologies that are often taken for granted.[39] The Southern feminine tropes represent a hegemonic ideology and hierarchy that Southern Black folks frequently take for granted and fuel the SBP. Further, they represent a mythical norm in the South, where cishet Black folks are normal and Black queer folks are considered deviant. Southern Blacks are socialized to accept and normalize this binary. Collins asserts that this sexual deviancy demonizes white homosexuality, but heterosexism in the SBP views any Southern Black woman who steps outside of these limited gender roles and expectations as a sexual deviant. While these limited gender roles and hegemonic hierarchies were established to combat racism, this same hierarchy determines who is sexually deviant in the Southern Black community. As a result, these deviants encounter massive societal cruelty.

"Go Outside Those Lines, and That's a White Person's Thang": The Whitening of Homosexuality and Queerness

The SBP maintains heterosexism through an unspoken rule that somehow heterosexuality and cisgender identity are connected to one's racial identity. SBQLWP discussed how heterosexism makes gender and sexual fluidity a "white person's thang." Yes, "thang," spoken in true Southern Black vernacular. As Maezah said, "We [Southern Blacks] stay in the lines; go outside those lines, and that's a white person's thang. Fluidity is a 'white thang.'" This ideology equates racial identity to cisgender, heterosexual identity. Whitening homosexuality and queerness limits Black sexual, freedom, exploration, and autonomy. We learn that there is no room for fluidity or sexual difference in Southern Black spaces. For Southern Black folks, gayness and queerness represent a proximity to whiteness. According to Collins, homosexuality causes queer folks to be perceived as less authentically Black, as if Blackness somehow is attached to heterosexuality.[40] As Collins outlines, by making queerness and homosexuality a "white thing," heterosexism creates intraracial separation and tension where the SBP can dismiss the experiences of SBQLWP because our problems are perceived as an adoption of whiteness. We encounter this massive cruelty because our sexualities and queerness are considered a "white person thang," outside the norm of what is considered Southern and Black. The idea of gayness and queerness as a connection to whiteness is a foundational element of heterosexism in the Southern Black community.

This perspective is linked to weak assumptions about racial liberation and empowerment. Heterosexuality in the Southern Black community is a litmus test for one's Blackness and a badge of honor for those who uphold heterosexist norms. The whitening of queerness and homosexuality becomes a method of making Black sexuality monolithic. Anyone who steps out of Black heterosexuality is perceived as a racial traitor and would encounter judgment and cruelty. Heterosexism and heteronormativity cause a Southern Black queer person to be viewed as somehow disconnected from their authentic Blackness. The whitening of queerness and homosexuality is not new to Black studies and Black queer studies. Many Black nationalist ideologies focused on adopting a pan-African perspective, focusing on racial liberation while reiterating the whitening of homosexuality and queerness. For example, Molefi Asante discusses Afrocentricity and claims that homosexuality is considered a deviation from Afrocentric thought because it is inferred that the queer person focuses more on personal needs over those of national consciousness.[41] Since the European/Western ideology focuses on personal needs, it is assumed that homosexuality is rooted in the European ideology of individualism over the African consciousness of community. This ideology inspired a virulent racial ideology that assumed that Black queer persons adopted this individual worldview, where they think of themselves above the Black and African diasporic community. This perspective whitens homosexuality and is seen as counterproductive to Black liberation. Black queer folks purportedly hinder Black liberation and align themselves with whiteness. This inference of white allegiance is faulty, as I found that many SBQLWP are racially conscious people. Many interlocutors internalized an African-centered consciousness and cosmology. The Afrocentric theory attempts to reinforce heteronormativity; however, it is not a reflection of the consciousness of SBQLWP.

Southern Black folks also assume that queer lesbianism is attached to the white female experience. The assumption of whiteness in queer lesbianism attempts to stir tension in the Black female community, separating lesbians from their cishet sisters. Lorde contends that Black folks consider lesbianism a "white woman's" problem.[42] This unspoken ideology explains why Black lesbians are ignored, silenced, or discounted as contributors to Black culture, history, and life.[43] As many SBQLWP are connected to our Blackness, we are also connected to our feminist and womanist consciousness as a significant part of our identities. We often exist at the intersections of several Black feminist discourses, integrating a radical Black feminist political framework while advocating for a womanist theology. We have a sprinkle of hip-hop feminism, with a drop of Africana womanism in recognizing the significance of family and community. However, it is assumed that we exist solely in a white feminist framework. The idea that our lesbianism is somehow a white woman's thing places us as outsiders within the Black female community.

The idea of lesbianism and queerness as somehow connected to white womanhood uncovers the heteropatriarchy in the Black community. This contention assumes that a Black woman's sexuality and identity must be attached to cishet men. This myth uncovers how the SBP attempts to police Southern Black women's sexuality. The SBP uses lesbian baiting to separate SBQLWP from our cishet sisters, who fear being labeled lesbians (or in Southern life, the street women). As Lorde argues, Black women's sexuality is often stifled out of fear of being accused a lesbian.[44] Pharr defines lesbian baiting as the ways homophobia affects sexism and how women are treated in a patriarchal society. Lesbian baiting has little to do with acknowledging someone's sexuality and more about pointing out the fact that a woman is out of her place.

Regardless of sexuality, all women are threatened to be called a lesbian if they are claiming some autonomy or control:

> Lesbian baiting is an attempt to control women by labeling us [women in general] as lesbians because our behavior is not acceptable, that is, when we are being independent, going our own way, living our own lives, fighting for our rights, demanding equal pay, saying no to violence, being assertive, bonding with and loving the company of women, assuming the right to our bodies, insisting upon our own authority, making changes that include us in society's decision-making; lesbian baiting occurs when women are called lesbians because we resist male dominance and control. And it has little or nothing to do with one's sexual identity.[45]

No woman wants to be labeled as a lesbian, especially a cishet Black woman. This baiting has as much to do with patriarchal validation as it does with privilege and power. Regardless of their sexuality, this baiting removes the desire for sexual autonomy. Lesbian baiting is a method of patriarchal control over women. Consequently, this baiting and fear planted the seeds for Southern Black heteropatriarchy to thrive. The SBP plants the seeds by using lesbian baiting as a tactic to whiten queer lesbianism, invoke fear, police Black female sexuality, and silence us.

A combination of this baiting and fear attempts to make SBQLWP feel less authentically Black or connected to the Black female community.

We are perceived as outsiders. Whitening queer lesbianism places a level of racial shame on SBQLWP. This racial litmus test makes us feel the need to prove our Blackness in some way, causing intraracial tensions when coming out. Even though many SBQLWP are racially conscious persons, we are being separated from our Blackness and Southernness. Fear disconnects us from those foundational institutions that inform who we are as Southern Black persons. Many SBQLWP disconnect from Southern Black spaces because we actually thought we were adopting some level of whiteness. We were coming to terms with the possibility of separating from one or all institutions because we felt we had this "white disease." We may conceal this part of ourselves from the SBP out of fear of being connected to whiteness and ultimately dismissed from the Southern Black community.

"Black Lesbianism Is a Threat to the Heterosexual Black Male": Black Queer Lesbianism a Societal Threat to SBP

Southern Black queer lesbianism is a direct social threat to the heteropatriarchy of the SBP. Black lesbianism is perceived as the antithesis to the heterosexual, cisgender Black man. Because we are a threat to Southern Black heteropatriarchy and heteronormativity, we encounter mass cruelty. As Maezah put it, "Black lesbianism is a threat to the heterosexual Black male, and it is not okay to threaten the Black man." Our queer lesbian presence challenges the hold that Black heteropatriarchy has in the South. SBQLWP are silenced and suppressed because we threaten the normalcy of Black heteropatriarchy, which is not acceptable for the SBP. Because we are not sexually attached to the cishet Black man, we cannot be controlled by his patriarchy. Queer lesbian identity allows a woman or individual to be a sexually autonomous being, a direct threat to patriarchal manhood. We choose to define ourselves for ourselves. The presence of SBQLWP is a direct contradiction to heteronormativity, patriarchy, and the taken-for-granted gender and sexual hegemony because our existence does not serve heteropatriarchy in any way. We not only challenge heteropatriarchy, we challenge traditional Southern feminine and masculine cisgender binaries, both of which are critical to Southern Black living.

Black queer lesbians are a threat because we do not uphold the strict Southern heteronormative value system that centralizes the Black heteropatriarchy. SBQLWP threatens the Southern Black heteronormative family rooted in heteropatriarchy. For us, marriage, family, and monogamy are considered options, not a requirement, in our gender and sexual identities. SBQLWP threaten Black heteropatriarchy because we decide how we want to engage with these social institutions of marriage and family. If we choose to engage in some level of heteronormativity, it is not out of fear of the Southern Black heteropatriarchy. Of course, many of us decide to get married or have children, but it is not to serve the Black heteropatriarchy. In fact, we participate in these institutions as a form of resistance against the Black heteropatriarchy. We engage in these social institutions to remind the SBP that his presence is not required for us to become wives or mothers.

Despite popular belief, the Southern Black cishet man is not a factor in our decision to be lesbian or queer or whether to engage in some level of heteronormativity. The myth that we somehow become queer or lesbian because of some trauma from the cishet Black male is an idea fueled by the SBP to make the man relevant in our queer lesbian identities. This notion reiterates Black heteropatriarchy. Also, the idea that somehow the removal of a Black cishet male figure will feminize Black youth is merely a perpetuation of the Black heteropatriarchal consciousness. The lesbian threat challenges this toxic consciousness. Kelly Douglas addresses this lesbian threat: "lesbians are often thought of as a betrayal of manhood by simple virtue of who they are. Malicious references to 'dykes' and 'bulldaggers' insinuate that they are some deviant form of a wanna-be man. In actuality, there is perhaps no individual perceived more challenging to male prerogatives than a lesbian."[46] The lesbian threat stresses the belief that lesbianism is a threat to Black manhood. The naming of lesbians as man-hating dykes and bulldaggers only reiterate that threat. We are a threat because we challenge the embodiment of Southern Black womanhood and manhood. SBQLWP become the enemy of the SBP because we do not center Black masculinity and manhood. Our presence makes the Southern Black cishet man expendable in Southern Black life. While we do value the Black family and community, we do not need to center Black heteropatriarchy to prove it. Ultimately SBQLWP are a threat because we shed light on the toxic traits of Black heteropatriarchy.

The presence of gender-nonconforming SBQLWP and studs/bois are a larger threat to Southern masculinity and the SBP. Masculine-embodied lesbians and gender-nonconforming persons directly challenge toxic masculinity. The Southern masculine hegemony is clouded by patriarchal notions related to limited gender identity, performance, and roles. Jae, a masculine-embodied SBQLWP, noted during our discussion how she is often "sized up" by Southern Black cishet men. According to Jae, her masculine embodiment is perceived as a threat, causing them to challenge her embodiment of masculinity. Sizing up is a method of toxic masculinity and Black heteropatriarchy used by the SBP to keep masculine-embodied and gender-nonconforming lesbians in a position of marginalization. Because the SBP is threatened, the embodiment of masculinity by studs/bois or gender nonconforming persons are deemed as superficial by the SBP and minimized by the myth that they want to be men. To lower their societal threat, the masculinity of studs/bois are not taken seriously. Southern Black cishet men are threatened by the ways studs/bois and gender-nonconforming SBQLWP embody masculinity as their authentic selves. Studs/bois are given derogatory names and treated negatively because it is assumed that they want to benefit from Southern Black heteropatriarchy. However, the Southern Black cishet man is not so much threatened by the embodiment of masculinity as by the ways this embodiment challenges their own preconceived notions of Southern Black masculinity.

The Southern Black cishet man's quest for manhood is based on the white patriarchal notion of manhood,[47] which relies on economic class, dominance, power, and control. Hegemonic Southern manhood is rooted in the tropes of the Southern gentleman and the good ol' boy, representing a masculine binary tied to control, power, and dominance. The lesbian threat stems from the idea that only Southern Black cishet men can embody this Southern white patriarchal notion of manhood. Gender-nonconforming persons and studs/bois threaten the Southern Black men's ability to uphold and gain proximity to Southern white patriarchal manhood. They appear to disrupt the Southern masculine hegemony. Moreover, when SBQLWP embody masculinity, Southern Black cishet men begin to question their own preconceived notions of Southern hegemonic masculinity. The Southern Black cishet man and the SBP question how studs/bois and gender-nonconforming folks can embody masculinity and perpetuate gender norms and expectations related to manhood without actually identifying as male. SBQLWP embodying masculinity forces the Southern Black cishet man to question the gender realities they were raised to understand. They may ask themselves, consciously or subconsciously, how these studs/bois can embody masculinity without actually being a cishet man.

Furthermore, the presence of studs/bois and gender-nonconforming SBQLWP have Southern Black cishet men questioning what they have been socialized to understand about sex and gender. Young cishet Black men are taught that because they were born biologically male, they have societal power, control, and domination over women and girls. More important, they understand that patriarchy works to their advantage. The presence of studs/bois or gender-nonconforming SBQLWP threatens the perceived control, power, and dominance of the Southern Black cishet man. Someone who is not a cishet male embodies that power. The person they thought they could dominate and control is now perceived to have proximity to that patriarchal power. The Southern Black cishet man can no longer dominate by wielding heteropatriarchy or using their penis as a method of control. As Clarke mentions, the Black lesbian is "not interested in his penis, she undermines the black man's only source of power over her, viz., his heterosexuality."[48] Without his heteropatriarchy or his penis, the Southern Black cishet man does not have control, power, or dominance over Southern Black women, making us a threat. The Southern Black cishet man may ask how we can embody masculinity without a penis. These questions and concerns are only brought to consciousness in the presence of the stud and gender-nonconforming SBQLWP.

Clarke and hooks tie the Southern Black cishet man's need for power and control to some historical realities, particularly relating to his lack of proximity to benefit from traditional patriarchy. As bell hooks contends, Black men were not emasculated by white imperialist institutions such as slavery, they just did not benefit from patriarchy the same way their white male counterparts did.[49] His only ownership over persons is over Black women through the use of his penis and heteropatriarchy. Southern Black cishet men use heteropatriarchy as a way to reclaim their societal power and control in the South. This threat is further exaggerated because the cishet Black man's penis is perceived to be the only gateway to the heteronormative family and marriage, a significant pathway for Southern Black women to obtain societal value and status. Making a heteronormative family and marriage a choice dismantles the Southern value system. SBQLWP are the wrenches in this heterosexist value system and a threat to this societal control. Once Black heteropatriarchy is challenged, Black cishet male power is ultimately dismantled. Clarke infers that this places the Black lesbian in a threatening position. This threat causes the SBP to weaponize Black heteropatriarchy to make others view queer lesbians as a patriarchal threat, a force of evil. Clarke contends, "For a long time, the lesbian has been a personification of evil."[50] We are evil to the SBP for our audacity to dismantle heteronormativity and heteropatriarchy. The SBP thus found a way to demonize SBQLWP to the rest of the Southern Black community, justifying the massive cruelty we encounter. Because we threaten the societal positioning of the Southern Black cishet men, the SBP sees us as evil and convinces others that our presence is problematic.

Ultimately, our presence challenges the use of Black heteropatriarchy and heteronormativity to control cishet Southern Black women. According to Cohen and Jones, the idea of the traditional nuclear family attacks single heterosexual Black women and demonizes lesbians and gays.[51] Moreover, Clarke contends that Black lesbians "threaten Black man's predatory control of Black women."[52] She further asserts that Black lesbians remove control from Black heterosexual men. SBQLWP threaten patriarchal societal gender relations in the South. SBQLWP having freedom from the Black heteropatriarchy and heteronormativity ultimately opens up the possibility that all Southern Black women can claim some level of sexual and gender autonomy. SBQLWP challenge the manifestations of Black heteropatriarchy that have controlled Southern Black women for generations. Our presence gives Southern Black women options in actualizing their gender and sexual identities. Our visibility makes heteronormativity and heterosexuality an option, not a requirement. This possibility loosens the control of the SBP and Southern Black heteropatriarchy. This possibility ultimately makes the Southern Black cishet male socially expendable, unable to use heteropatriarchy as a method of societal control. SBQLWP ultimately threaten the societal hold the SBP has on Southern Black cishet women.

"You Are Never Enough": Heterosexism, Heteronormativity, and Black Heteropatriarchy as Massive Cruelty in the SBP

No matter what SBQLWP do, our existence is a threat to heterosexism, heteronormativity, and heteropatriarchy in the South, solidifying our marginalized societal status. As Star noted, "You are never enough" in the South. We are never perceived as the good woman, the Southern belle, or the first lady. Even if we exist in these archetypes, we are still considered a threat. No matter what we do, we will encounter massive cruelty. Our existence will be met with cruelty, being perceived as part of some societal and racial problem. We encounter this cruelty because our authentic selves are not valued. The SBP discredits our existence because we choose to live freely. We are never enough because we challenge all things the SBP values. We are not enough because we engage in a level of autonomy against heterosexism, heteronormativity, and Black heteropatriarchy. The SBP is an energy that perpetuates heterosexism and heteropatriarchy through judgment and suppression. Like the townsfolk in Hurston's piece, the SBP sits in town gossiping and judging those on the margins of society. We experience this judgment as we walk through our Southern towns because we do not fully immerse ourselves in heteronormativity and heteropatriarchy. We do not usually fall into the trap that heterosexuality is the only way to exist in the South. But we also know that we will encounter cruelty for not fully engaging in heteronormativity and heteropatriarchy.

The SBP personifies the social judgment we encounter in the South. Like Hurston's townsfolk, the massive cruelty wielded by the SBP dehumanizes the SBQLWP. This SBP uses judgment as a method of exuding power and maintaining all things patriarchal and heteronormative. The SBP recognizes the Southern Black community as their kingdom where they can reign supreme. Unfortunately, they use their power of influence to marginalize those who do not fit properly in this Southern kingdom. SBQLWP are a direct threat to their reign. Even speaking with these interlocutors, I realize that the SBP continues to have a tight hold on the Southern Black community. The SBP is a part of a Southern backdrop where we learn that our existence is never enough, ultimately silencing us. The manifestations of societal judgment based on heterosexism, heteronormativity, and Black heteropatriarchy create pain and trauma for SBQLWP.

As they say in the Church, after the storm, joy comes in the morning. Another great thing about the storm is that it is temporary, a season. As we snap beans, we discuss the Church trauma and the massive cruelty of the SBP. We recognize that this is only part of our story. These experiences become the catalyst that leads us to our freedom. We are no longer silenced, bounded by shame, condemnation, or judgment. Our shackles loosen as we reach freedom and reconciliation. A traumatic storm becomes the entryway for coming out and reaching reconciliation. When studying Southern Black queerness, there is a desire to stop our work with the storm. But trauma does not encompass the entire story of what it means to be a Black queer lesbian in the South. The trauma is not the end of the story but a part of this narrative. As we continue to snap beans, we uncover our journey to self-love, authenticity, and reconciliation. As we actualize our queer and lesbian selves, our story becomes brighter.

"I Am Standing in My Truth"
The Authentic and Reconciled South

> Freedom is acquired by conquest, not by gift. It must be pursued constantly and responsibly. Freedom is not an ideal located outside of man; nor is it an idea which becomes myth. It is rather the indispensable condition for the quest for human completion.[1]

> Lesbianism is a recognition, an awakening, a reawakening of our passion for each (woman) other (woman) and for same (woman).[2]

According to Paulo Freire, liberation is the process of reconnecting an individual to a sense of humanity to achieve freedom.[3] He contends that freedom is a condition for human completion. In our journey to queer lesbian actualization, we desire that same level of freedom to reaffirm our humanity. The Southern oppressions of silence, shame, condemnation, and judgment try to remove our humanity. Regardless of these oppressions that attempt to hinder our humanity, we continue to strive for liberation and freedom. When coming out, we recognize the oppressive nature of these realities and begin doing the spiritual and intellectual work to unlearn the societal harm we encountered. We aim to live freely as Southern Black queer lesbians. But what does freedom and liberation look like for us? While our narratives on Southern Black queerness are filled with pain, there is an additional story of freedom and liberation. We often speak of Black queer experiences in a deficit, but we rarely discuss how Black queer folks reclaim our freedom and humanity. We rarely speak of Black queer love and joy or the ways Black queer folks find to thrive. With all the problems that

SBQLWP experience, why do we stay in the South? Why identify as Southern when Southernness is connected to so much trauma? The discussions of coming out and reconciliation in this collective narrative help us to address these questions. Our stories of authenticity, coming out, and reconciliation represent a renewed sense of wholeness and freedom for us.

In my conversations with SBQLWP, we discussed ways we reached personal and communal healing and wholeness through love. As we reach liberation, we find love. We find the beauty in our authentic selves, recognizing that we are fearfully, wonderfully, and uniquely made. We no longer see our existence as a problem. We begin to love our authentic selves. Even with the trauma we experienced, our journey of self-love allowed us to find new ways to fully live our queer lesbian lives. Part of this journey means reconciling with the beauty of our Southernness, recognizing that our Southernness reflects both Southern pain and healing. We uncover a love for all things Southern, Black, and queer lesbian. In coming out and reconciliation, many of us found a new love for ourselves and all the communities we represent. We are dedicated to living for us, on terms that work best for us. As Tisha profoundly said: "I've always lived for others, now I am living for me." This is a proclamation of resistance and self-love. Other SBQLWP expressed similar sentiments:

> STAR: "I love me, nobody can shape me. I no longer downplay my sexuality."
>
> SUNSHINE HONEYSUCKLE: "I was consumed with being a perfect Christian. I learned how resilient I was."
>
> KRIS: "Nobody can live your life but you."
>
> TONI: "I continue to be who I am."
>
> LEILA: "If it makes you happy, do what you want to do."
>
> CASSIE: "I only live for me."
>
> BREE: "I am not going to beat myself up for being who I am."

Living for others meant that Tisha and other SBQLWP existed in silence, experienced shame and condemnation, and feared judgment from the

Southern Black personality (SBP). In some cases, living for others means existing in heteronormativity: marrying a man, having children, and putting family ahead of one's own desires. As Southern Black women, our existence is limited to the expectation of being a suitable wife and mother. In coming out and reaching reconciliation, we begin to leave that behind and decide to exist as our authentic selves and engage in self-love. We are free from the heteronormative expectations of Southern Black womanhood. We understood that before our liberation, we were Southern Black women living for others, and our existence was for the benefit of others. As we become liberated, we begin to live for ourselves. We start to pour into ourselves and find wholeness. We begin to discover love for self.

In our journey to wholeness, we pursue freedom that is not some ideal myth located outside of ourselves. Instead, our freedom comes from reconnecting to our humanity. Coming out and existing as a queer lesbian is a form of resistance, an act of liberation. This self-love is a practice of autonomy. We decide how we want to exist in the South as our authentic selves. We internalize this autonomy, making it part of our process of reconciliation. We resist the heteronormativity, patriarchy, and heteropatriarchy that have shackled us. As we come out, we renegotiate with who we are and how we want to exist in the world. We uncover what it means to be a Black queer lesbian who embraces our Southernness without shame. For us, coming out and reconciliation integrate our queerness and Southernness as complementary elements, integral to our narrative. This journey to freedom is very real for us, not some myth or idea that seems unattainable. This freedom from silence, shame, condemnation, and judgment. It is a reality in our narratives, reaffirms our humanity. We reclaim our joy.

"That's When My Liberation Started": Manifestations of Coming Out

As a result of the damage established by the toxic traits of the SBP and the Southern Christian Black Church, many SBQLWP felt compelled to exist in a duality as we negotiate our sexual and gender identities. The duality is a metaphorical weight hindering us from fully existing as our authentic selves. For SBQLWP, coming out lifts the weight of existing in that duality. Coming out is often referred to as the way LGBTQIA+ persons publicly present our authentic sexual and/or queer identities in public spaces. In our narratives, coming out does not represent a door toward freedom but lifting the baggage of oppression. It's the difference between metaphorically walking through a door and removing an imaginary weight from our shoulders. Removing this weight is not easy, but it lifts the trauma and leads to liberation. As Byanca said, "As painful as it was [coming out], that's when my true liberation started." For her, coming out occurred when she stopped existing in this duality, a painful process with a beautiful result: an imagined freedom that becomes a reality. Liberation and freedom are not easy, but without them, we cannot exist authentically. Freire describes liberation as a painful birth,[4] a distressful experience that creates a new life. For SBQLWP, this painful birth allows us to live a new authentic life. Unfortunately, our new authentic existence came with some obstacles. This process could mean that some family members no longer want to associate with us. Childhood friends refuse to speak to us. We encounter conflict and challenging discourse with our Southern cishet family. The pain of liberation may mean that we stop attending certain social institutions, such as Church and family functions. We may move away from our homeplace. Holidays are no longer spent with biological family members. While we may have snapped beans with grandma and 'em while we existed in the duality, we may no longer do so. There may be moments of isolation as we go inward, finding inner validation and peace. After that pain, there is freedom and liberation. To reach true freedom and authenticity, we must remove the shackles placed on us by the SBP and the Church. In our freedom, we reach pure authenticity.

Coming out has internal and external realities, essential to our self-actualization. The internal affirmation of our lesbianism or queerness is manifested externally. Coming out is reconciling with the internal homophobia experienced during condemnation. Existing in the duality is strictly an internal struggle, rooted in internalized homophobia. Coming out is an internal battle, a moment (or series of moments) where we had to tune out the world that shamed and condemned us. Internally, we are making sense of our lesbianism and queerness. Externally, we are publicly showing up as our authentic selves and making the intentional effort to be visible and take up space in the South. Coming out is a journey to actualization that manifests externally, versus the duality, which often happens internally. First, we articulate how shame and condemnation affected our consciousness and manifested in our lives. After we recognize these effects, we intentionally embody our queer lesbian selves without shame. We take pride in fully existing as our queer lesbian selves. Previously, we existed in silence as we encountered shame, condemnation, and judgment. Coming out combats this trauma, allowing us to find a place and space for us to fully live our queer lesbian selves. Before we can make a public display of our sexual and queer identities, we must have an internal shift in consciousness that occurs away from the watchful eyes of others. Coming out is a period of self-reflection that very few people know about. We go inward to find our truth.

"It Was a Weight Lifted Off Me": Coming Out of the Duality

Coming out removes the shackles and the negative self-perception we experienced during our duality. It is the conscious effort to remove the weight of societal oppressions that hindered our humanity. Reign discussed how she made a conscious choice to come out of the duality. She notes, "Living in two worlds was stressful, coming out was a weight lifted off of me." Sunshine Honeysuckle agreed with this discussion, saying how "coming out meant I do not have to live two lives." SBQLWP described this internal condemnation as a weight, with emotional, spiritual, and physical implications. For us, coming out is not the moment of recognizing or identifying as queer or lesbian, but the moment we get out of the duality of condemnation. Coming out is the moment the weight of duality is lifted, and we metaphorically remove the shackles of silence, judgment, and shame attached to our fluid sexual and gender identities. We are no longer silent about our gender and sexual identity, no longer weighed down with the burden of judgment and shame.

Coming out includes intentionality, deciding how we want live out our queer/lesbian selves. We are intentional about combatting the culture of silence that permeates the South, choosing to exist out loud, and unapologetically embodying our lesbianism or queerness. Coming out gives us the necessary armor to combat the judgmental nature, heterosexism, heteronormativity, and Black heteropatriarchy of the SBP. We finally remove the shackles of homophobia and heterosexism from our lives so we can exist authentically. Coming out means minimizing the massive cruelty in the South. We decide to live our lives for us, even if that means that we must emotionally or physically separate ourselves from those oppressions and oppressors. Coming out also means establishing boundaries with those who choose not to acknowledge our queer lesbianism. As we come out, we desire that liberation, regardless of what others think.

Coming out varies among SBQLWP. The process is not a monolithic set of experiences; it is manifested in different ways. For some of us, it was making the conscious decision to wear masculine clothing in public spaces.

For others, it is identifying as queer. For some, it is openly dating and/or marrying a woman. For others, it is posting about their significant other on social media without feelings of embarrassment. For Torrey, coming out came in the form of a rainbow tattoo. Leah decided to cut her long hair. Sometimes it is an internal revelation, as Andy stated—she started to "see a change" within herself and started to live more authentically. Regardless of how the painful birth manifests, coming out is a constant negotiation with the world around us. We remove those elements that hindered us from fully existing in our authentic selves. Whatever the physical or internal manifestation, coming out is challenging what we have been socialized to accept in terms of sexuality and gender in the South so that we can fully embody our queer lesbian selves.

"I Have Been Coming Out My Entire Gay Life!": Coming Out as a Continuous Process

Coming out is a continuous, complicated process in the South as we combat the landscape of silence, shame, and judgment. Any journey to actualization is not a linear process. Coming out is not one isolated event, but a series of events where we unpack the complex layers of our multifaceted identities. It is the process of peeling back layers to find out who we are. Not one SBQLWP spoke of having a single epiphany but revealed a culmination of experiences that led to their coming out. Many SBQLWP described how the process took some time. Coming out is a set of experiences, a progression to get us to the point of coming to terms with the fullness of who we are. Sunshine Honeysuckle noted: "You [a SBQLWP] are always coming out." Leah mentions a similar sentiment: "You are a lifelong grower and changer. It [coming out] is an ongoing process." In my conversation with Maezah, they said, "I have been coming out my entire gay life!"

When it comes to our actualizations, there are certain life changes (such as getting married or having children) that brings our lesbianism and queerness back to the center of conversation. In some cases, SBQLWP may return to heteronormativity or the duality that provides us with a sense of safety. June mentioned her years of what she calls "misplaced energy," a time in her queer lesbian actualization where she began dating cishet men. While she identified herself as a queer lesbian at the age of sixteen, in her early twenties she began dating cishet men. As a Southern Black woman, she said it was easy to be with men. She noted that this was her first experience with heterosexual privilege. However, June recognized she had to "silence so much of myself to be with men." That silence of heterosexism, heteronormativity, and Black heteropatriarchy led her to reconnect to her queer lesbian identity.

My own coming out came in a multitude of experiences. I remembered how I felt when my cousin called me one evening, asking me if I was a lesbian. I whispered: "Yes, I am with a woman," as if saying I was a lesbian too loud would somehow make it real. I recall telling my father late one evening while my mom was sleep. I asked him, "Would you still love me if I never married a man?" As I waited for his response, my heart was beating so hard I could hear it ringing in my ears. The ringing calmed down when he said, "My love for you is not limited to who you are with." But the pivotal moment was telling my mother, who was not thrilled hearing her daughter was a lesbian, but asked me a few months later whether my girlfriend and I were going to Black Pride in Atlanta. But my coming out did not end there; it was identifying myself as a lesbian out loud in public spaces, recognizing my queerness while embracing my feminine embodiment, acknowledging my partner in public spaces, marrying a woman, and even writing this book. While I considered myself an openly queer lesbian woman, when I informed my family of my engagement, it was like coming out again. While it is already difficult to come out as a queer lesbian person, it is even more challenging to make a lifelong public commitment to another woman. As Maezah said, I have been coming out my whole life.

Coming out involves reconciling with one's fluid or fixed gender identity, embracing and redefining the gender binary we have been socialized to accept. In some instances, the coming-out process includes embracing our queer, gender-nonconforming, or gender-fluid identities. Coming out is the process of actualizing how we want to embody our gender fluidity and how our gender embodiment forces us to constantly come out. When Maezah mentioned that they were coming out their entire life, they included the process related to their gender fluidity. Their coming out process included coming to terms with their queer identity. They felt that the terms "lesbian" or "stud" did not fully address how they existed and navigated in the world. They participated in a queer practice, uncovering and embracing fluidity. They said that once they heard "queer," they automatically attached themselves to that identity. The connection to their queerness was part of their coming-out narrative.

Allison Chase's cisgender feminine embodiment provided some protection from the shame and judgment in the South, but it also means that she is constantly coming out. She said: "I am always coming out. It got to the point where I just don't talk about it so I don't always have to explain myself or answer questions all the time." June discusses how, as a feminine-embodied SBQLWP, "I gotta let you know I was gay." Because femmes are perceived as being heterosexual and/or heteronormative by Southerners, we are constantly coming out about our sexualities and/or queer identities. Existing as a cisgender person causes our queer lesbian identity to be questioned, and we are constantly coming out to those who think we are queer or lesbian. This oversight makes certain assumptions about cisgender embodiment. Cisgender embodiment is perceived to have ties to heterosexuality and heteronormativity, making it difficult for cishet folks to recognize that lesbians can be cisgender women. The cisgender embodiment assumes one's sexual identity is attached to their gender presentation and that an individual cannot possibly exist as a cisgender lesbian. This embodiment challenges the traditional imagery of lesbians as only masculine-embodied individuals. This myth causes additional hurdles for femmes. The stereotypical image of a queer lesbian is the caricature of the hairy, leather boot–wearing, short-haired woman in oversized men's clothing. The imagery invokes the idea that a lesbian is simply a woman posing as a man. The cisgender lesbian is the antithesis of this caricature. Because of this heterosexist assumption, femme SBQLWP are always coming out and reminding others of our queer lesbian identities.

Coming out is a consistent process that seldom ends. For the gender-nonconforming or masculine-embodied interlocutors, coming out as a queer lesbian was one step toward actualizing their gender fluidities. Identifying themselves as queer, gender-nonconforming, or a variation of stud is a part of coming out. On the other hand, some SBQLWP found ways to adopt and embrace these gender binaries. Whether embracing or redefining the gender binary, coming out incorporates coming to terms with how we want to live out our queer lesbian lives and express it in public spaces. This process includes finding ways to publicly embrace our fixed gender identity, gender fluidity, and/or masculine embodiment in an uncompromising, unapologetic way. Whether going to a family event, going to work, or attending a social event in the South, we show up as our full selves. Coming out means that we no longer exist as silent Southern Black queer lesbian girls snapping beans in grandma's kitchen. Instead, we snap beans in the fullness of who we are.

"Standing in My Truth": Coming Out as Lessons of Authenticity and Self-Love

As a result of coming out internally and externally, we ultimately "find our truth" or "stand in our truth." There is a vernacular of truth-telling associated with coming out. While SBQLWP speak about coming out, the word choice is rooted in myriad responses that align with the process of truth-telling or lessons of authenticity that infers a level of self-love. As we challenge realities of silence, shame, condemnation, and judgment, we find our truth and reach internal validation. We may use the terminology of "coming out" for others (namely, cishet folks) to help them understand that we identify as queer and/or lesbian. But when speaking with one another, SBQLWP refer to coming out as a journey of authenticity, truth-telling, and uncovering who we are. SBQLWP had various responses for what they define as "finding my truth":

FATIMA: "Standing in my truth."

NEILE: "Just being who I am and existing."

ANGEL: "Continue to live in your truth."

MAKEDA: "I just showed up and I am who I am. I just show up as my whole self."

CASSIE: "I found my voice."

MAEZAH: "I am true to who I am."

The practice of standing in one's truth is a level of self-affirmation as one is coming out of the self-hatred and duality of condemnation. The truth of who we are liberates us from the lies we told ourselves while experiencing internalized homophobia. Star realized she could "no longer live a lie." The freedom and liberation in truth-telling help us develop a sense of self-love. Finding our truth allows us to gain a sense of wholeness.

Finding our truth is not for pomp and circumstance—it is an external proclamation of self-love, truth, and authenticity. Truth-telling is the internal validation and actualization, a proclamation of self-love. Jae directly discussed self-love: "Self-love is intricate, grounded in who we are."

Star mentioned this self-love when she recognized her internal strength: "I am much bolder than I thought." She discussed how timid she was during her marriage to a cishet Black man. Finding her truth allowed her to exist boldly and love herself. Her boldness came from existing in her truth and coming out as a lesbian woman. Sometimes we marry or date cishet men out of societal expectations to engage in heteronormativity. As Tisha noted, we often live and exist for others and not ourselves. The idea of truth-telling is the process of removing the mask we created in our duality moments. We decide to no longer live up to the heteronormative expectations of others. Star's comment suggests that our internal strength is not fully recognized (by ourselves or others) until we make the conscious decision to exist on our own terms. We choose to love ourselves first. The desire for freedom is bold and often scary. But as we reach liberation, we find our truth, reclaim a love for ourselves, and cling on to it. Self-love is the direct antithesis of the shame and condemnation. While living in the duality, we hate ourselves and all we represent. Truth-telling is the difficult journey to exist authentically. We tell ourselves our truth so we may tell others. Grandma and 'em may not affirm our queerness, but we learn to affirm ourselves. We learn to pour into ourselves. The process of truth telling is different from simply coming out: our coming out is for others, while truth-telling is for ourselves. We come out to others, and we tell ourselves who we truly are. Simply put, coming out is an external practice, while truth-telling is a consciousness-raising journey. Truth-telling is the shift in acknowledging and naming our queer lesbian identity. We are less concerned about what others think of us. Instead, truth-telling is for internal validation. Coming out is more of a courtesy for others, not strictly necessary in queer lesbian actualization. Truth-telling is the epitome of loving all of who we are.

    Reign personified the internal validation that occurs during the truth-telling process she described: "I no longer wanted to deprive her." The "her" is her authentic self and desire to live a life outside of the oppressive Southern gaze. She wanted to start living a life that she felt was truly authentic to who she was. She even gendered that inner self as "her." She did not want her inner self, her inner woman, to feel that she had to hide any more or live up to the expectations of others. The inner girl was deprived of love (for self and community), truth, joy, liberation, and freedom. Truth-telling freed that inner woman. For many of us, truth-telling stopped us from being that silent Black queer girl in our grandma's kitchen. Now we are providing that younger self a voice and an opportunity to experience liberation and freedom. My queer lesbian actualization gave me a chance to connect with my childhood self, reassuring her that the journey of liberation will be painful but fruitful. That inner girl is fed and no longer suffering. Like Reign, I stopped depriving her.

The recognition of our truth is the first step for SBQLWP to reach wholeness. Does this mean that we wave Pride flags the moment we decide to live outside of this duality? Of course not. It simply means that we recognized we had been living our lives for others and how we wanted to live authentically. Staying in the duality provided safety in the South, but it also was a life lived for others (namely, our mothers and family). Truth-telling meant making a conscious effort to live our lives for ourselves. While existing in our truth, we want to establish a level of autonomy. As Star bluntly put it: "I love my life, so why should I give a damn what others think of me?" We stop caring what the SBP thinks and what our grandma and 'em say about us as they snap beans. This truth-telling not only informs others of our queer lesbian identities but is also a reawakening of ourselves—a step toward autonomy.

Our queer lesbian actualization becomes a method of loving all of who we are. Truth-telling became an entryway for us to explore all of our other identities. It allowed us to recognize how our sexual orientation leads to more critical discussions of our multifaceted identities and allows us to uncover other ways of being. Truth-telling peels back additional layers of self-discovery. Janessa noted that identifying as a queer lesbian meant embracing herself as a Southern Black, femme, fat-affirming person. Her queerness became the pathway to discover other identity markers. While she noted that she had tried to shy away from identifying as fat, Black, and queer, exploring her queerness allowed her to find wholeness with these additional identity markers. As Janessa said, "It's something I don't have the privilege of not saying. They [other persons] see I am fat, and Black first." Further, many SBQLWP noted that truth-telling and adopting a queer consciousness challenges traditional structures of Southern life. Marie Dylan noted an additional layer of coming out as polyamorous in the South, which challenges the traditional institution of monogamy.

These examples prove that truth-telling represents a consciousness-raising activity, not simply a manifestation of one's sexual orientation. Truth-telling is a radical Black feminist discourse that results from life sharing. Once the truth of who we are is expressed, it raises our awareness about other realities in our lives. We use our queerness as a chance to uncover nuances of various identities and lifestyles. Engaging in truth-telling allows us to become more conscious, discovering new ways to exist in the world. This helps us discover new possibilities, providing an opportunity to see and explore new ways of being. Truth-telling becomes foundational in discovering and appreciating the additional layers to our identity. As we come out, we learn to love all parts of ourselves, even our Southern Black selves.

The truth-telling vernacular not only describes an internal actualization, it also provides evidence of how we adopt our Southernness to our queer lesbian actualization. The terminology of truth-telling is rooted in our Southernness, where one phrase has multiple meanings. In the South, we live in euphemisms, whether it is "carryin' on,"[5] "bless your heart," "fixing to do/finna do," "Lord willing and the creek don't rise," "over yonder," "hilla beans," "reckon," "making groceries," "telling stories," "the devil is beating his wife," and countless others. It makes sense that SBQLWP adopt a multifaceted Southern phrasing to discuss our queer lesbian selves. The statement "finding my truth" or "living in my truth" are Southern-coded phrases. If we speak to another Southern Black queer person, this terminology needs no additional explanation. We engage in a practice, rooted in our Southernness, as a way of exposing our queer lesbian selves to others. The language of "coming out" reinforces how queerness and lesbianism can be viewed in proximity to whiteness. Using the phrase "finding my truth" connects to our Southern Black identity, where we affirm and reclaim our Southern Blackness and queerness. Compared to the language of coming out, the phrase "finding my truth" has a stronger practical and vernacular meaning as it fully describes our journey to wholeness and reiterates our Southernness.

"It Is a Means of Reclaiming That Which Is Mine": Journey toward Reconciliation

In truth-telling, we reconcile with our preconceived notions about Southern Black queerness and Southern Black womanhood. For SBQLWP, reconciliation means to reclaim that which was almost lost in the silence, judgment, shame, and condemnation. Cheryl Clarke provides context for how we reach reconciliation. Clarke says, "Lesbianism is a recognition, an awakening, a reawakening of our passion for each (woman) other (woman) and for same (woman)."[6] Our lesbianism has always existed within us, waiting to be recognized and awakened from its slumber. It was that inner voice we dismissed because we were ashamed of her and we feared that we would be judged by the SBP. This inner woman did not have a name. But identifying as a queer lesbian and finding our truth allows us to recognize and hear the power of her voice. Reconciliation is the process of tuning into that inner voice, letting her guide us to wholeness. Although this quote does not directly address the South, Clark addresses the ways truth-telling helps us to reconcile with our individual queer lesbian identities, our communities, and the South. Lesbianism and queerness are not simply about being in a same-sex romantic relationship or embracing queer fluidity but about an awakening passion for ourselves and all the communities we represent: Southern Black, Southern Black queer, and Southern Black women. Truth-telling awakens and reaffirms all those identity markers. In this sense, reconciliation becomes a journey of love, one that is often overlooked in our narratives. The liberation that comes from truth-telling ultimately leads to our reconciliation.

But what does it mean for a SBQLWP to reconcile with the South? We are healing from the trauma manifested from the Southern tradition of silence, Church shame, and the SBP. But the traumas that cause pain are not the end of our narratives. The reconciliation and subsequent healing help us reach wholeness that allows us to thrive in this region. Reconciliation addresses why we decided to stay in the South and refer to ourselves as Southern. Even amid the tumultuous cultural landscape of the South, reconciliation allows us an opportunity to recognize how we can embrace both our Southernness and queerness. We stay in the South and/or remain connected to our Southernness because we love our Southern selves and communities. Reconciliation allows us to exist in the intersection of our Black, queer, lesbian, female, gender fluid, and Southern selves. Reaching reconciliation is also an act of resistance, as it allows us to contest dominant values and norms in the South that hinder how we actualize our queer lesbian selves. In this consciousness-raising queer exercise, we reconcile with these Southern traumas, adequately naming them and their roles in our queer actualization. We challenge the monolithic heteronormative Southern narrative, expanding the cultural landscape of the South.

In our reconciliation, we are awakening the identity that has been silenced in the South, reestablishing love for ourselves, even in our lesbianism and/or queerness. Like truth-telling, reconciliation is a practice of self-love. Truth-telling and reconciliation lead us to loving our queer lesbian identity. Reconciliation means dismissing the heteropatriarchy and heteronormativity associated with Southern Black womanhood by challenging the inherent purity, heterosexist permission and the limited embodiments of Southern cisgender femininity. Reconciliation through self-love is the process of finding internal validation because we know that we may not find external validation from the SBP. We reclaim a love for ourselves despite how we have been socialized to see ourselves. In reconciliation, we dispel the myths associated with Black lesbianism and queerness in the South. Reconciliation with self means that we dismiss societal suppressions and oppressions that hinder us from making the intentional effort to engage in self-love. We can find reconciliation with who we are, not what others expect us to be. Reconciliation is the direct pathway to reach wholeness.

Reconciliation is also a womanist practice—we are reawakening a passion for Southern Black female culture. Alice Walker makes this notation in her definition of womanism: "A woman who loves other women, sexually and/or nonsexually. Appreciates and prefers women's culture, women's emotional flexibility (values tears as natural counterbalance of laughter) and women's strength."[7] In reconciliation, we find a new love and appreciation for Southern Black female culture, both sexually and nonsexually. The womanist practice is the catalyst for exploring communal love with other Southern Black women and the desire to reconnect to Southern Black female communities. Even as we think back on the memories of snapping beans with our female elders, the passion to explore and reconnect to the Southern Black female community is awakened. In reconciliation, we reaffirm our love for our Southern Black female elders and the lessons of Southern Black womanhood. We can see that some of the lessons from grandma and 'em are rooted in patriarchy and heteronormativity and understand the hold these societal structures had on our Southern Black female elders.

In this reconciliation, we uncover the value and beauty from those communal experiences with grandma and 'em, where we gain lessons of authenticity and resistance. We are able to apply these lessons to our experiences as Southern Black queer persons. We recognize the significance of these communal spaces as we establish community with other SBQLWP. With that in mind, reconciliation solidifies our love for other SBQLWP and the significance of establishing community with one another. In some cases, the stage when SBQLWP developed an intimate relationship with other women marks the catalyst for coming out and reconciliation. Once we have a sustaining intimate relationship with another woman—romantic or platonic—then we find our awakening with another woman. When I am among other SBQLWP, it is a safe space to receive the external validation we rarely get from cishet communities. Reconciliation establishes this safe space. In this community, our humanity is restored.

Reconciliation is the act of addressing how we reconnect to our Southern Blackness. As Shay alludes to, reconciliation allows us to take ownership of the South and our Southernness. While the traumas attempt to place a wedge between us and our Southern Blackness, reconciliation reconnects us to our Southern Blackness with our queer lesbian identity. All the overarching cultural experiences attempt to separate us from our Southernness. Reconciliation is the understanding that one's Southernness is inevitably connected to our Black queerness. Shay reflected, "It is a means of reclaiming that which is mine." She elaborated, "It is a part of it that is mine." The "it" refers to her connection to the South: the culture, history, ideology, cosmology, and even how the South is an African diasporic space. Reclaiming that which is hers is reimagining a future of what it now means to be a Southern Black queer person, reconnected to one's racial and locational identity.

Often the concept of the New South is connected to Southern industrialization and modernization, describing how the South economically thrived after the antebellum period. The New South is rooted in a capitalist framing, proving that the South can economically participate in a global market. In these discussions of reconciliation, we are imagining the New South in a humanistic context that includes Southern Black queerness in this Southern cultural landscape. In the New South, we are reconciling with other possible ways to exist in the South outside of the traumas of silence, shame, and judgment. The New South means establishing a South that is inclusive of all. Reconciling with the South means establishing a new Southern narrative from the vantage point of those marginalized by race, gender, and sexuality. Uncovering the New South as an intersectional place and space makes the South inclusive of all Southerners, not just cishet Church going Southerners. We can reconcile with who we are as Southern persons in this New South. This New South provides a level of freedom and autonomy for those who traditionally exist in the margins of the South. SBQLWP (and all Southern queer folks, for that matter) find themselves to be fixtures in the South instead of victims of Black heteropatriarchy, heteronormativity, silence, and shame. The New South provides options for how we choose to exist as Southern Black persons. Reconciliation establishes the New South, where one has the freedom of choice to thrive and exist out loud. We reclaim our Southernness without diminishing our queer lesbianism. Reconciliation allows for the expansiveness of what it means to be Southern.

"These Southern Belles Like Women, Too": Reckoning with Cisgender Binary Labels

Reconciliation helps SBQLWP redefine the ways they embody and resist the Southern masculine and feminine heteronormative binaries. As we negotiate with our Southern queer lesbian identities, we can reconcile with how these cisgender binaries can be oppressive and liberating. We resist and adopt these Southern cisgender binaries while also contesting the heteronormative roots of these binaries. Because we have been socialized to understand gender in the context of these cisgender binaries, we may incorporate them into our queer lesbian lives. We are not assimilating, but rather embodying new dimensions of femininity and masculinity within the South. This negotiation opens the door for us to reconcile with the South and our Southernness. The way we play with these cisgender binaries allows us to connect our Southernness, Blackness, and queerness. But what labels are we embracing and contesting? What about these cisgender binaries are we resisting? How are we challenging these traditional cisgender embodiments of masculinity and femininity?

Conversations about traditional cisgender embodiments led to some fascinating discussions. Allison Chase proclaimed: "Southern belles like women, too!" I initially laughed with her. Then I realized that she was taking pride in identifying herself as a Southern belle. While this role is within this cisgender binary, there are new elements that challenge heteronormativity. She proudly identified herself as a lesbian *and* a Southern belle. She claimed how she enjoyed "feeling like a lady," discussing at length how there are "lesbians who happen to be girly." There is a pride in being able to move between the cisgender feminine embodiment of Southern Black femininity and lesbianism. Her comment challenged the myth that lesbianism is only recognized in the embodiment of masculinity. Her statement also incorporates the way femmes proudly embrace their cisgender femininity. During this phase of reconciliation, we are recognizing and embracing the aesthetic and spiritual power of the feminine. Audre Lorde's erotic as power[8] framework also infers that the embodiment of femininity has certain spiritual powers that inform how we live our lives. In queer scholarship, there is an assumption that cisgender embodiment is oppressive and limiting. While there may be certain oppressive elements to cisgender embodiment, it does not mean it cannot be liberating for queer persons. Cisgender embodiment of a queer lesbian or gay person does not make them any less queer, gay, or lesbian than our gender-nonconforming counterparts. Instead, we remove the heterosexist notion that cisgender embodiment is linked to heterosexuality. The feminine embodiment reconnects us to that spiritual power of the erotic. Our presence proves that cisgender feminine embodiment does not belong to heteronormativity. More important, femmes remind us of the aesthetic beauty and spiritual power that can exist in the feminine.

In a few conversations with femmes, they embrace and challenge the traditional ideals associated with Southern Black femininity. According to Kaila Story, femme acts as a gender expression that comes from a queer space and community,[9] embodying the power of the feminine in queer spaces. Femme challenges heteronormativity and cisgender privilege, where lesbianism and queerness do not automatically equate to a masculine-embodied lesbian or gender-nonconforming folks. Femme SBQLWP adopt Southern femininity as a form of resistance against Black heteropatriarchy and heteronormativity. Simply put, this feminine embodiment means that femininity is not the sole property of Black heteropatriarchy. While we may embody some traditional performances of Southern Black femininity, we use these sensibilities to engage in the queer lesbian world. In some ways, we use traditional Southern feminine sensibilities to attract a gender-nonconforming person or stud. In other ways, we embody femininity to incorporate our queerness with our understanding of Southern Black womanhood. Femme SBQLWP remove the Southern belle trope from the realms of heteronormativity and applies it to our queer lesbian lives.

The Southern belle is an honored Southern trope, connected to status and privilege. For femme SBQLWP, embodying the Southern belle directly challenges traditional imagery of Southern femininity. First, Southern belle embodiment is no longer tied to a heteronormative marriage to a cishet man. This establishes that lesbianism no longer equates them as Boylorn's "bad," wayward, or "street" Southern Black women. In our adaptation of the Southern belle, we are reclaiming our worth and value as Southern Black women. Black femmes adopting the Southern belle also challenges the idea that only those of a certain race or class status can embody femininity. This reclamation removes the racialized heteronormative ownership of the Southern archetype, where the Southern belle is no longer the domain of elite Southern white womanhood. Cisgender feminine embodiment removes the hegemony of Southern womanhood for Southern Black women and SBQLWP, reclaiming a sense of humanity. Embodying this trope is an act of resistance for us and provides a new narrative of Southern cisgender feminine identity. This is how femme SBQLWP reclaim our Southernness.

On the other hand, studs/bois discussed how they adopt some elements of the Southern gentleman trope. Their Southernness and masculine embodiment influence how they enter public spaces and how they court or date femmes. Makeda, a masculine-embodied SBQLWP, noted how she "shows up in the world as my whole self." Her whole self includes her Southern Black identity and her masculine embodiment. She further stated that she would often "take the lead" in courting a woman. Like the traditional notions of Southern masculinity, studs/bois can take a more assertive role in same-sex relationships. Some take pride in the work they do to financially provide for their partners. Studs/bois can challenge traditional notions of toxic Southern masculinity and the Black heteropatriarchy and help Southern Blacks redefine what masculinity can entail without the toxic elements. While some studs/bois do embody toxic masculine characteristics, the interlocutors in this work embody masculinity as a means of expressing their authentic selves. Unlike the Southern gentleman or the good ol' boy, whose masculinity is rooted in capitalist assumptions related to manhood, masculine-embodied SBQLWP adopt an embodiment of power that is not oppressive. Their notion of masculinity is a means of protecting femme SBQLWP and presents a complex physical aesthetic that integrates both feminine and masculine spiritual elements.

Studs/bois do not necessarily adopt the normalcies of the infamous butch, but instead integrate certain elements of cishet Black manhood. They adopt Southern Black cishet male gender roles, expectations, and attributes. While they may take certain traits from the SBP, they remove the oppressive elements. The sexual behaviors and the embodiment of Southern Black female masculinity closely reflect that of Southern Black male culture. After all, the embodiment of masculine-embodied SBQLWP is based on how they are socialized to understand Southern Black masculinity. Like Moraga, who was socialized to view masculinity in the context of Chicano/Mexican culture, studs and bois are socialized to adopt a type of racialized masculinity that closely matches their Southern Black identities. For some masculine-embodied SBQLWP, this may include the adaptation and resistance to certain heteronormative elements of Black masculinity. This racially situated masculine queer embodiment challenges the notion that queer or sexual identities are attached to whiteness. Like femmes taking on the Southern belle trope, masculine-embodied SBQLWP resist traditional notions of Black masculinity. This negotiation is how studs/bois reclaim their Southern Black selves.

Embodying and resisting these cisgender binaries in racialized queerness is a revolutionary act. For SBQLWP, these binaries act as a pathway to reconciliation and liberation. Our queerness and lesbianism do not automatically separate us from adopting and embodying cisgender binaries and redefining them in the context of the Southern Black queer lesbian experience. Contrary to popular belief of the SBP, identifying as queer lesbians does not mean that we are not embodying whiteness. While the gender binaries appear to limit our gender fluidity, they provide an opportunity to redefine how we embody masculinity and femininity. It also provides a new Southern narrative, where adopting these gender binaries does not necessarily equate to heteronormativity. We can reconcile with cisgender binaries by having the audacity to find ways to incorporate our Southernness and Blackness with our queer lesbian selves. This redefining and embodying represent a method of reconciling with what it means for us to fully exist as our queer lesbian selves. Adopting some elements of the cisgender binary while resisting its oppressive nature allows us to reconcile with our Southern Black identity.

"God Loves Me, Regardless": Reconciling with the Church

To be free, we must reconcile with the Church. Directly or indirectly, the Church permeates all things in the South. Reconciliation with the Church is essential, as this is the first institution where we first actualize our queer lesbian identities. Because of the Church, we are introduced to the trauma of being a queer lesbian and our outsider-within placement. Reconciling with the Church is tied to reconciling with grandma and 'em, who once chastised and shamed us. To find reconciliation with the South, we must determine what the Church means for us. We gain spiritual validation and reconnect to our spiritual selves without taking on the traumas from the Church. We discovered several methods to reconnect to the Church and redefine what spirituality means for us in our lives. Many SBQLWP find this spiritual journey essential in reclaiming our Southern Black selves.

While the Church established shame and condemnation for SBQLWP, the institution also gave us spiritual grounding. We still want the spiritual connection the Church provided for us without the societal trauma. In the process of reconciling with the Church and all other remnants of this institution, we would experience at least one of the following: separation from the Church and religious practices altogether, reconnecting to a queer-affirming Church space, or redefining what spirituality means for us outside of the Church. These methods provide spiritual validation outside of the Church shame. As Bynta noted, "God loves me, regardless." She further said, "Once I knew God loved me, I was good." Bynta, a former

Church of God in Christ and Missionary Baptist Church congregant who believed God was some "big guy in the sky," she realized that "God can love me in the full expansion of me." She further stated: "I was born a masterpiece." Leah noted, "I believe now that I am created in God's image. I don't condemn myself." These spiritual validations occurred as a means of reconciling with the Church and reconnecting to a new level of spirituality. We counteract the condemnation of internalized homophobia. We find that spiritual validation can only occur through expanding our understanding of God and evangelical Christianity. We start to see God as love. Because God is love, God loves us regardless of our queer lesbian selves. We heard these spiritual lessons of love while growing up sitting in Bible studies, sermons, and Sunday School. We hear that God is love within the gospel lyrics we grew up listening to and contemporary praise and worship songs. We simply applied this lesson to our queer lesbian actualization. Similar to what E. Patrick Johnson notes, SBQLWP will find ways to seek spiritual grounding: "These women sought out forms of worship that were more woman centered or turned inward to a self-discovery of a communion with a higher power."[10] Even as we reconcile with our queerness and/or lesbianism, we seek to remain connected to a spiritual entity in multiple ways.

In the process of reconciling with the Church, SBQLWP are the epitome of what the Church folks say about religion and spirituality being an individual journey. Pastors often speak of having a personal relationship with God and that we cannot "ride on the coattails" of our mothers and grandmothers. This individual spiritual journey is necessary for our reconciliation. As Reign said, in reconnecting to her faith and spirituality, she can no longer "ride the coattails of mom." Our mothers and grandmothers provided us with the spiritual foundations of evangelical Christianity. Whether directly or indirectly, grandma and 'em taught us the significance of incorporating and maintaining some level of spirituality in our daily lives. These spiritual foundations also connects us to our Southern Black selves and our roots as Southern Black women. Even in our queerness and/or lesbianism, we desire that spiritual connection. As we reconcile with our lesbian/queer identities, our spiritualities are still a significant component in our lives. For some SBQLWP, queerness helped us build a stronger spiritual foundation. The journey to reconciliation leads us to reconnect to that spiritual source and our Southern Black selves.

The need for spiritual connection dispels the notion that queer folks are devoid of spirituality or do not have a desire to maintain a spiritual anchoring. Because lesbianism and queerness are often seen as the antithesis of anything holy and sanctified, Southern Black folks assume SBQLWP are disconnected from a spiritual or religious grounding. Our queerness does not make us nonspiritual beings. We still want the spiritual anchoring introduced to us by the Church. We still want a spiritual practice. Our lives are filled with the stressors and emotional burdens that cause us to seek some form of spiritual refuge. In many ways, we still need lessons of faith to maintain our sanity and peace. The desire for spiritual peace does not go away as we actualize our queer lesbian selves. We find ourselves needing a faith practice more as we come out of the duality and internalized homophobia. We need the faith lessons of peace to heal us from the Church trauma and our mothers' dismissal. A spiritual connection fills our voids and heals our wounds. As ironic as it sounds, the spiritual grounding we gained from grandma and 'em heals us from the Church trauma. We want to continue that spiritual tradition of our maternal figures without the culture of shame. Finding our truth and reaching reconciliation with the Church is essential to finding our peace and joy.

Even in my newfound queer identity, I yearned for that sense of spirituality and faith practice my paternal grandma gave me. I wanted the spiritual aspect without the dogmatic religious undertones. I wanted the praise and worship without suppression and oppression. I yearned for Church fellowship without encountering the SBP. After all, the Church reminds us of our Southernness and Southern Blackness. As we reconnect to that faith practice of Southern Black evangelical Christianity, there are certain elements of the Church and family we want to maintain. We love the music, praise and worship, fellowship, moments of reflection, and words of inspiration. Endesha noted that the Church laid the foundation for the spiritual work she later did as a pastor and spiritual leader. She witnessed women's roles, recognizing how they often functioned as the backbone of the Church. Endesha reconciled with the Church by recognizing how it was foundational for Southern Black culture, provided a space where we engaged in public speaking (from Christmas plays to Easter speeches), and established the connection to our community. Reconciling with the Church means we desire a spiritual practice and anchoring that connects us to our Southernness and provides us healing, albeit in different ways.

Some SBQLWP reconcile with the Church by completely separating from the institution altogether. When first discovering our truth, our first instinct is to separate from the Church altogether. While living in duality, I went to Church every Sunday without fail. There were not many Sundays Church folks did not see me in Church. But as I was uncovering my truth,

I stopped attending services because I did not know what spirituality meant for me in my queerness. Reconciliation meant separating from what I was familiar with. The same thing happened with other SBQLWP, where they decided to leave the Church and the South altogether to reach some sense of reconciliation. For those SBQLWP who grew up in the Jehovah's Witness faith, the separation was not by choice. Once their queerness or lesbianism was known, they would be forced to disfellowship from their Kingdom Hall. For other SBQLWP, the separation meant leaving the South. The time away was a separation from the Church, family, mothers, grandma and 'em, and the SBP that caused emotional and spiritual harm. It is easier for some to reconcile when they are not living in the place that caused the trauma. For example, Makeda, originally from Atlanta, Georgia, recounted moving to Portland, Oregon for a job, which gave her a chance to reconcile with her lesbianism. While she eventually returned to Atlanta, her separation from the South helped her heal from the trauma experienced by Church and family. In some cases, this separation occurred simply by moving to a more progressive Southern city. For example, Brooksley Smith noted that moving from Chattanooga, Tennessee, to Atlanta allowed her to embrace her lesbianism: "I got to be my own person in Atlanta." In Chattanooga, she said, "I was just this Black girl," where her identity was connected to her family. She felt that she was the token Black girl. Moving to Atlanta allowed her to authentically explore her lesbian identity. June agreed with this assessment, proclaiming that "Atlanta is the first place where I felt safe." Atlanta is a unique Southern location, where one's Southerness, Blackness and queerness can be affirmed. The traumas while existing in the duality can become too burdensome, causing us to separate from these institutions, by choice or force, to find peace. Sometimes we simply remove ourselves from the space and place that caused trauma. Even though we are separating from the South, Church, family, mothers, and the SBP, the separation is an opportunity for us to reconcile with the shame and judgment and provides a space to reestablish our faith. Some SBQLWP who separated from the Church never return to a traditional Christian Church. Instead, they found other forms of spiritual reconciliation. As Star reminded me, "The Church is in you." This statement reveals an internal spiritual validation while separated from the institution itself. We lean on our spiritual grounding from the Church without entering the Church itself. For these SBQLWP, the separation became the solution to reach reconciliation.

Separating from the institution was not the end goal for other SBQLWP. In our reconciliation, many of us attempt to find a queer-affirming spiritual place and space where we do not have to hide our queerness. Many SBQLWP need to connect to a Church institution in some capacity, for it represents part of a larger spiritual process of reconciliation. While the Church often is a space of trauma for us, there are progressive subsets of certain religions that are more LGBTQIA+-affirming. These churches may be in urban Southern spaces such as Richmond or Atlanta. Reign discussed the Progressive Pentecostal/Holiness religious subset that is queer affirming while also having tenets of Pentecostal religion. In Atlanta, a few Methodist and Baptist churches are progressive and queer-affirming with queer or LGBTQIA+ pastors. While reconciling with the Church, I attended these churches in hopes of finding my home. I found a queer-affirming church in the area that allowed me to worship and connect to what I grew up with. On the other hand, some SBQLWP continue to attend traditional Churches knowing they will not be affirmed. As Andy noted, "I do not expect the Church to acknowledge it." While attending Church—and even working as a media operator there—she accepted that the Church would not be a queer-affirming space for her. Essentially, she sees the Church and family as "it is meant to be," and does not try to change the institution. Andy conceded that "everyone is not going to accept me." These realizations act as a form of reconciliation, the recognition that we may never receive queer affirmation by the Church or family.

Another form of spiritual reconciliation occurs through reconnecting to another spiritual or faith practice. Southern Black folks often conflate religion with spirituality or faith. Reconciliation connects spirituality and faith over the traditional Christian religion. We recognize the difference between faith and religion. As Bree noted, their journey to reconciliation meant removing faith from the sole domain of conservative, heterosexual folks. Bree did not have "a crisis of faith." For them, spiritual reconciliation meant they could practice faith or spirituality without automatically connecting it to a religious institution. The internal homophobia we experience was a manifestation of flawed religious institutions that adopted hierarchies of oppression and discrimination, not faith. But in reconciliation, we recognize that spirituality, faith, and the Church are not synonymous.

In our reconciliation, we are reconnecting to our faith. Growing up in the Church, we received lessons of faith, understanding that faith is the substance of things hoped for, evidence of things not seen. This language stems from the New Testament, Hebrews 11:1: "Now faith is the substance of things hoped for, the evidence of things not seen." This belief has roots in evangelical Christianity, and many of us continue that tradition as we reconcile with our spirituality, where the Church is merely where one celebrates their faith. In moments of condemnation, where our faith was questioned, we remember the lessons of faith as we reconnect to our spirituality. We realize that it is not the Church building or the people we want to reconnect to, but the faith that sustains us and reaffirms us. We reconnect to a faith system and spirituality as it removes the cloud of self-hatred. E. Patrick Johnson recognizes this dichotomy: "I found that the church and spirituality play out a very different role in the lives of black queer southern women."[11] We understand how faith is a daily spiritual practice that does not require a building. I am now able to enter churches with a level of freedom, knowing that my faith and spirituality are not tied to an institution. As Reign assessed, reconciliation means that we "get to know God for ourselves." In other words, our connection to faith and spirituality is no longer connected to the hurtful messages from grandma and 'em. Reign realized, like I did, that we had to find the God within us to affirm our faith, spirituality, and queerness. Reconciliation is the epitome of the faith practice we learned in Sunday school. Through this reconciliation, we find other ways to reconnect to our faith without experiencing the conviction related to internalized homophobia. Reconnecting to our faith and spirituality allows us to enter spaces that were once designed to silence, shame, and judge us with a newfound understanding and appreciation for what this institution can do, but also acknowledging what it does not do for our healing.

We can see this practice of faith manifesting in other spiritual practices. Many SBQLWP found other ways to gain spiritual fulfillment outside of evangelical Christianity by practicing traditional African-centered spiritualities that are queer-affirming such as Ifa, a Yoruba monotheistic religious practice. Ifa's focus on going inward to find spiritual validation through prayer and meditation is an important part of combatting the internalized homophobia we experienced. Toni addresses how Ifa is a more queer-affirming spiritual practice because it allowed for gender fluidity: "Ifa is more queer in practice, it affirmed who I was and the fluidity of spirit and gender." African-centered spiritual systems align with what many of us grew up with in the Southern Black Church. African spiritual systems have prayer and meditation, a spiritual leader/counselor, and a connection to elders and ancestors. Even though Southern Black folks adopted Christianity as their spiritual anchor, the religion still had elements of traditional African spirituality. It is not far-fetched for us to adopt an African spiritual path as we actualize our queerness. Not only is it a part of our Southern Black identities, it is also a queering practice of finding new, innovative ways to engage with our spiritual selves outside the confines of the traditional Church.

In 1976, playwright Ntozake Shange premiered her work *For Colored Girls Who Considered Suicide/When the Rainbow Is Enuf*. This work represents an array of Black women's experiences with pain, joy, and reconciliation. Filled with Black women in various colors and stories, the performance contains narratives of death, betrayal, and oppression. There are moments of laughter and tears from each character. In the end, they came together for the piece titled "a laying of hands." In it, they spoke of the laying of hands that provided wholeness and peace from one another and within themselves. This piece is an intentional affirmation of self and communal love. The Lady in Red states, "i found God in myself and i loved her / i loved her fiercely."[12] I vividly remember being frozen with tears when I first heard that line at a local theater in Atlanta. As I reached reconciliation with the Church, those words continued to resonate with me. First, this statement was an affirmation of self-love, affirming the love for all the communities we represent. Second, this notion of God challenges what we traditionally view as divine. We are raised in the Church to refer to God as "Him." Making God "her" challenges preconceived notions of what God can be. God can be me, in the female form. Third, this notion of God living within us, as Black women, changes our spiritual lens. No longer do we feel the need to reach out to an institution to find spiritual fulfillment; we can find that within ourselves. God is not an external being in the universe somewhere but is living and breathing within us. The principle of having an internal God is also integral to Ifa spiritual practice and internal validation.

Toni discussed this internal validation, saying that we must stop looking externally to find spiritual validation. She said that she "stopped letting these spaces try and affirm me." Internal validation is a laying of hands and finding God within us. She recognized that the struggles that SBQLWP have is attempting to find external validation over finding internal peace. Reconciliation comes with the understanding that these institutions may not validate our existence. Finding God within ourselves destroys the internalized self-hatred, helping us reach new levels of spiritual enlightenment. We find the God within us, and we love her fiercely. While other SBQLWP discussed what that meant for us, Janessa offered an example of what this means in her daily life. She detailed her Sundays, which she still spends as a day of spiritual reconnection, even if not inside a physical Church. She described her ritual faith practice of listening to gospel music in the park.

She would turn off her phone and pray or meditate. She found God in herself, taking some spiritual practices learned from her Church upbringing to her queer-affirming life. This practice provides spiritual affirmation. We find ways to reconnect to the God within us, finding wholeness and spiritual reconciliation to maintain that spiritual anchoring.

"The South Is a Reclamation": Reclaiming the South and Southern Identity

Even with all the pain and trauma experienced in the South, the majority of SBQLWP still identify themselves as Southern. Doing so is a method of reconciliation. Taking ownership of the South is not merely stating where one is born and raised; we recognize what the South provided in actualizing our Black, gender, and queer identities. In my conversation with Shay, she said that "the South itself is reclamation." She is reclaiming ownership of the South: "it is a part of it [the South] that is mine." Reconnecting to Black and African diasporic history is rooted in the South and our Southern Black female identity. Even though we identify as queer and/or lesbian, we still recognize our Southern lineage. Our families, history, culture, and spirituality are anchored in this region. Our queerness becomes the pathway to reconciling with those elements that affirm our Southernness.

In my conversations with SBQLWP, I recognized how they saw the South as an anchor. Our relationship with the South is complex, as it causes pain and trauma, it also connects us to our ontological selves and reminds us of our homeplace. The South is a significant part of our roots, even if we leave. Our roots in the South are strong and fertile. We can clearly define the South as our homeplace, a connection to our ancestral roots. Even for those not born and raised in the South, placing their feet on Southern ground helps them get a spiritual connection to the South and the way it can still operate as a homeplace. As Toni mentioned, the South is her spiritual home. While she is a native of Ohio, she found her ancestral roots and a spiritual anchoring in the South. In reclaiming what is ours, we recognize how the South acts as a spiritual anchor. As a few SBQLWP mentioned, the South contains the footprint of our African ancestry. They claim that the energy of the South is spiritually African. Toni confided that she moved to the South to connect to that African energy. She said the "South gave me the most spiritual transformation." We find ways to reconnect to our spiritual selves by connecting to the South as a spiritual space.

Our queerness informs our Southernness. As we connect to our queer lesbian identity, we reconcile with our Southern selves as well. We take some ownership of the South and see ourselves in the Southern cultural landscape. Our connection to the South helped us grow stronger in our Blackness and queerness as the Southern cultural landscape has racialized, sexual, and queer elements. The South is not in conflict with our racialized sexual queer identities but is complementary to them. The landscape raises our consciousness about our interlocking identities and the role the South plays in overlapping realities. I knew what the South meant to me, but it was through conversations with other SBQLWP that I understood it as a multifaceted space foundational in how we view our queer lesbian selves. On Southern fertile ground, we reclaim what always belonged to us: our Southernness. Reconciliation is the process of naming and reclaiming our Southernness. As Endesha noted, reclamation is "coming home to myself." The "home" representing the South and "myself" recognizes the totality of who we are: our history, family, culture, and spirituality. Through reconciliation SBQLWP found healing from the trauma of the South. Endesha described how her queer lesbian actualization led to her healing with the South. Reconciling with the South is reclaiming that which was lost in our trauma. We are no longer held down by the weight of pain and oppression—we are reclaiming what is ours.

Moreover, we connect to the South through our family ancestry. In this sense, reconciliation is a reconnection to our Southern Black families. While the family became a site of trauma for SBQLWP, they can also be sites for us to reconnect to our Southern Black identity. Those who separate from the Church recognize the historical and cultural significance of the Church in their families and its impact on their spiritual journeys. When Shay mentioned reclaiming that which was hers, she was referring to her attempt to reconnect to her estranged Southern Black family. She is reclaiming her position and space in that family, taking ownership of the family name and legacy. This reclamation means that we are no longer outcasts but are integral parts of the family history and legacy. It also means that we are intentional about being visible in our families, no longer silenced, shamed, or judged. We may not be fully accepted by all family members because of the lurking SBP. But reconciliation with family is not for acceptance or affirmation but to make ourselves unapologetically visible, positioning ourselves as part of the Southern family legacy.

"My Queerness Became Secondary": Reconnecting with Southern Black Womanhood

In some cases, reconciliation occurs by making queerness secondary in reconnecting to our understanding of Southern Black womanhood. Onika Rose said, "my queerness became secondary," to her identity as a Southern Black woman. She further said: "The one [identity] I cherish the most is being a Black woman." Her queerness does not make her any less of a Southern Black woman, and her queerness is not central to her identity. As we come out and find reconciliation, our queer lesbian identities become a component of our intersectional identities. Our queerness helps us reconnect to other facets of our lives. While our queerness informs and influences how we see the world, it does not consume us to the point where we cannot exist in other ways of being. Our queerness becomes a pathway to evaluate our additional identities. We find ways to incorporate our queerness into those identities. Many SBQLWP connect their queer lesbian identity into other ways of being. We are not only queer lesbians but also mothers, educators, entrepreneurs, and activists. In those varying ways of being, we can reconcile with the fullness of who we are. Reconciliation means that our queer lesbian identities are parts of our lived experiences that inform additional identities and ways of being. We decentralize our sexual and gender identities, integrating them as part of our lives. In reconciliation, our queerness is part of being a Black person and/or a Southern Black woman. It is an opportunity to reconnect with our notions of Southern Black womanhood and/or our Southern Black selves.

"It's Not Where You Live, But How You Live"
The South as a Place and Space for Liberation, Authenticity, and Reconciliation

The South became less a space of hindrance and more a space to reach liberation, authenticity, and reconciliation. We reconcile with the South and find ways to authentically live out our lives. Truth-telling and reconciliation are relevant lessons of authenticity in our Southern queer lesbian actualization. As Cassie noted, "It's not where you live, but how you live." The South is often viewed as a contentious space, but it can also be a space for helping one reach freedom, liberation, autonomy, and authenticity. As Cassie puts it, where we live is not as significant as how we live in that place. We live by reaching a space where we can reconcile with our love for self, community, and the South. Truth-telling, authenticity, and reconciliation represent the love of our queer lesbian identities, our Southern Black and Black female communities and families, and the South. Even if we don't live in the South, we find liberation, authenticity, and reconciliation. We fall back in love with our Southernness.

In the healing comes an affirmation of our Southernness. I learned more about my identity as a Southern woman once I reconciled with my queer lesbian identity. Like Endesha discussed, I found my queerness through my healing. I was able to come home to myself, to her, the South. I was more invested in my Southern family lineage. Even in my queerness, I reconnected with my Southern Black female ancestral roots. This reconnection was the beginning of my reconciliation with the South. Coming out is often described as the process of sharing one's sexual identity with family and friends. In this collective narrative, coming out was the realization of what it meant to be queer lesbian in or from the South. This processes of coming out and finding our truths brought us closer to our racial and locational identities. Our queerness becomes the vantage point to evaluate all the ways the South exists in our lives. Reconnection leads to healing. We reach autonomy, freedom, joy, and peace. Even if we are not fully whole, we are in the process of healing. We return to the South, where we reach reconciliation and liberation. Once we return home (metaphorically or physically), we carve a unique space for us to not only exist but thrive and find wholeness in the Black queer lesbian South.

The Black Queer Lesbian South

Driving through the South at the beginning of spring, a Southerner may notice lavender-colored jacaranda trees growing, with a sweet, honeyed smell from the blooms. In this season of renewal, one may recognize these trees either standing alone or as accented leaves popping out among the greenery of other trees. The jacaranda colors stand out among the earth tones of browns and greens. The trees almost look displaced, like a toddler adding color to a green and brown canvas. These trees remind us of the beauty that blooms during the season of renewal. Your eyes may gaze over them as you are driving, but once you start paying attention to the jacaranda trees, you cannot miss them. SBQLWP are like those trees—fixtures of the South that seem displaced but bring brightness, beauties hidden in plain sight among the cultural landscape. Like the jacaranda trees, SBQLWP bloom after the harsh winters of pain, sprouting a sense of renewal. After experiencing the darkness of silence, shame, condemnation, and judgment, SBQLWP find ways to express our truth. Like the jacaranda trees, the Black queer lesbian South is a fixture of the South, often ignored but bringing additional aesthetic beauty to the region. As we uncover these narratives, we find a new colorful tree in the Southern landscape. Similar to the jacaranda tree, we provide a pop of color in the Southern landscape. It is also interesting that these jacaranda trees bloom in light purple, a color that often aligns with queer or LGBTQIA+ identities. When I see these trees, I think of our Southern queer ancestors who painted the landscape purple to remind us that they were here. These lavender trees remind us to reclaim and take up place and space in the South. But like the jacaranda trees, Southerners disregard SBQLWP, minimizing our beauty and our role in the Southern landscape. The Black queer lesbian South reminds us to stop and listen to these queer lesbian narratives, amplifying our voices so we may add new colors to the Southern landscape.

The Black queer lesbian South does the following: (1) uncovers the existence and contributions of SBQLWP to Southern life; (2) represents a homeplace within a homeplace, a racialized sexual queer lesbian home established in the South; and (3) operates as a place and space of resistance against Southern silence, oppressive manifestations of the Church, and the Southern Black personality. The Black queer lesbian South helps other Southerners understand how the South is a racial, sexual, gendered, and queer place and space. The Black queer lesbian South represents what happens when SBQLWP find our truth and reach a level of reconciliation with the South. We may not automatically leave the South once we find our truth. Instead, we find ways to exist and thrive in the South and/or come to terms with the manifestations of our Southernness. This place and space explains how we can identify as Southern and authentically exist here. In the Black queer lesbian South, we authentically decide to unapologetically exist out loud in the South, celebrate our Southern Black queerness, and find ways to thrive. We can see ourselves as fixtures in the South, no longer in the margins of society. The South has a place and space for us to exist and thrive in Southern life. The experiences of SBQLWP are uncovered and celebrated. We are affirmed in this space, even if we just affirm one another. This South also provides a pathway to authenticity and freedom as Southern people. SBQLWP carve a space for us in the South so we can fully exist in the Southern landscape and reconnect to our Southernness.

The Black Queer Lesbian South as a Place and Space

The Black queer lesbian South represents the ways that place and space are not automatically synonymous entities. Place reiterates traditional notions of geography, the geographic boundaries that define the South and exposes certain cultural elements of the South. SBQLWP desire to carve a physical place for ourselves, to be in community with other SBQLWP. Space is a metaphorical connection, a location not dictated by geographic boundaries. Discussions of our Southernness remind us of this notion of space, where one's Southern identity is not limited by whether one presently lives or grew up in the South but is based on the cultural connection to what the South means for the individual. It is not limited by place but represents the way the South manifests externally. When speaking of a Black queer lesbian South, I speak of a place and space where we can exist and thrive inside the closet, fully existing out loud, or somewhere in between. In the journey to reach wholeness, we decide to create a space for ourselves. Finding this space is not an option—as we must find places and spaces to exist and thrive or we may be devoured by the trauma of the South. The Black queer lesbian South becomes an essential place and space to finding wholeness and healing.

The Black queer lesbian South provides evidence of a racially gender-based sexualized queer geography positioned like the jacaranda tree—where our presence uncovers intersectional elements of the Southern landscape. The Black queer lesbian South operates as an intersectional place and space that informs our interlocking identity markers. The Black queer lesbian South as a racialized sexual queer place and space helps Southerners understand how our interlocking identities can be actualized by a specific location. The Black queer lesbian South allows Southerners to uncover how race, gender, and sexual identity formations can be determined by geography. My conversations with SBQLWP showed how the South informs and molds our queer, sexual, and gender identities. While it is birthed within certain geographic boundaries, the racialized sexual queer location is not restricted by those boundaries. SBQLWP who live outside of the South or those from other areas outside the South can also exist in the Black queer lesbian South because their interlocking identities were further actualized by their Southern experiences. These realities create new possibilities for the South. With that in mind, I contend that the Black queer lesbian South is situated as a space that dictates our Southernness. Because of it, we do not need to physically live in the South to embody Southernness because we understand that the South is part of our ontological selves and informs our sociocultural viewpoint. Whether or not we currently live in the South, the Black queer lesbian South as a place and space affects how we actualize our queer lesbian selves.

The Black queer lesbian South is also a method of gaining citizenship and (re)claiming a geographic place and space. It challenges the assumption that our queerness somehow removes our Southern citizenship. Citizenship typically has political implications related to one's relationship with a particular state or governing body. While this definition remains relevant to Southern citizenship, it also infers a level of belonging to a certain place and space. Citizenship is a way of staking a claim to a place and having a sense of ownership, nationalism, and allegiance to a specific place. Citizenship also includes receiving certain benefits from the state or political entity. In the United States, this could look like freedom of expression, the right to vote, the right to privacy, and so on. The fight for citizenship is a battle that Southern Black folks have experienced for generations. Historically, one's race and/or ties to slavery challenged one's state and federal citizenship status. Southern Black folks always understood that citizenship to a particular state provided them a sense of protection and belonging to a particular location. For Southern Black folks, this determination is attached to our desire to gain a sense of nationalism. We may not be able to pinpoint where we come from in the African diaspora, but we know what Southern state our ancestors lived in. Southern Black folks have attempted to claim a state to gain a sense of belonging and citizenship. With that in mind, the establishment of the Black queer lesbian South as a physical space is the opportunity for SBQLWP to claim physical territory, maintain ties to the state (the South), and establish a sense of Southern citizenship and identity. SBQLWP carry on this tradition of citizenship, attempting to reclaim our Southern citizenship and to gain a sense of physical autonomy. Even with all the present political realities in the South that target LGBTQIA+ folks, Southern Black and Southern Black queer folks still stake claim to their Southern citizenship. We are reclaiming what is rightfully ours, staking ownership of the Southern place. Reclaiming a physical territory establishes our citizenship to our Southern state.

The history of Southern citizenship is rooted in the use of and access to physical space. According to W. Fitzhugh Brundage, this represents "social permission," detailing one's societal permission to physically occupy and exist in certain public spaces.[1] This access to physical spaces is central to Southern historical memory and identity. In our Southern memory, this social permission was (and sometimes still is) based on racial identity. Brundage claims that the struggle over social control over one's physical place informed both white and Black Southern culture.[2] The social permission relies on the assumption that certain persons are "worthy of access to public life," while others are deemed unworthy to exist in Southern public spaces.[3] In other words, our access to social spaces relies on whether we are socially valued. Being marginalized in the South means that one cannot exist publicly and is thus relegated to the dark corners of the South, invisible in public spaces. These dark corners are filled with those who do not fit in the heteronormative white supremacist model of the South. Social permission assumes that these marginalized populations are not worthy of being visible or gaining access to public spaces. For Southern Blacks, fighting for physical space is the ability to fully live their lives without the fear of racial tension. Southern queer folks attempt to carve out a space to congregate with one another without the harsh backlash from overzealous fundamentalist Christians. Southern

Black queer folks want to occupy spaces where our racial and sexual queer identities are affirmed. This perception does not mean marginalized Southern queer folks did not publicly exist in Southern places, but we would often minimize ourselves to make others comfortable. Since social permission in the South relegates us to the margins, SBQLWP use the Black queer lesbian South to create a physical place and metaphorical space in the South, where we can feel safe, build community, and thrive. SBQLWP construct visible places for us to commune with one another and further actualize our Southern queer lesbian identities. Even without social permission, we desire to fully exist and live in the South.

The Black queer lesbian South is a method of resistance, taking physical space without social permission. The Black queer lesbian South represents the audacity for us to find spaces and places that do not require social permission or validation from the Southern Black personality, family, and Church norms. Because of that, the Black queer lesbian South acts as a place and space of resistance. The Black queer lesbian South is an attempt for us to navigate and resist this social permission, determining how and where we decide to safely take up physical space in the South on our own terms. Research shows other ways Southern Black queer folks resist this social permission and take up physical space. For example, Craig Washington cites that Black gay men in Atlanta establish place to exist in dance clubs.[4] He looks at how the club acts as a space of vision, resilience, and improvisation among Southern Black gay men. As an extension of that, since the 1990s, we have celebrations like Black Pride in Atlanta and Richmond to take up space in urban Southern areas. These celebrations were documented in *Venus* magazine,[5] a Southern Black lesbian-owned magazine that distributed information imperative to Southern Black queer life. This locally based magazine provided visibility and representation of Black LGBTQIA+ communities in American South. In addition, SBQLWP in urban Southern spaces find social gatherings such as clubs and lounges as places to congregate. In many cases, party promoters in urban Southern places would rent spaces for queer lesbians to hold events. SBQLWP entrepreneurs establish businesses for Southern Black queer folks to congregate, such as coffee shops. SBQLWP would even congregate at the few lesbian bars that are open to all Southern queer folks regardless of race. These businesses are open to the public but provide a safe space for SBQLWP. These businesses may include dance clubs or bookstores, LGBTQIA+ support groups, comedy shows, and drag shows. SBQLWP even take up physical space in the Church, where we serve as Church leaders, volunteers, and congregants. Some SBQLWP take up physical place and spiritual space as pastors and priests. For example, Endesha is both a spiritual leader in both a nondenominational Christian Church and an African spiritual priestess. Some SBQLWP would create independent social gathering spaces specifically for us to gather together. Makeda hosts a monthly book club for SBQLWP in Atlanta. She mentions how she uses this platform to provide visibility for SBQLWP and a safe space for us to gather. We can thrive in the South when we can find, establish, and maintain physical space. The decision to create and establish safe spaces is an act of resistance against the Southern societal permission.

The Black queer lesbian South operates as a space that connects SBQLWP to each other. This community space transcends physical boundaries. Speaking to SBQLWP for this book revealed how the Black queer lesbian South acts as a space. While I was speaking to people who were connected to a physical Southern place, we are ultimately connected by our Southernness. Those living in the South wanted to connect to a community with other SBQLWP. Those not living in the South at the time of our conversation connected through this metaphorical space of the Black queer lesbian South. We are connected to the physical and cultural South, establishing a network with other SBQLWP that transcends physical location. Finding and establishing that space allows us to create a sense of community. The desire to return to the South was not just a physical return to the geographic location but a wish to connect with other SBQLWP. This community space allows for us to thrive.

As a space, the Black queer lesbian South represents love for other SBQLWP by creating and maintaining fictitious, nonbiological families. In the South, we simply call it "fam" to represent our connection to the SBQLWP community and a safe spaces for us to actualize our identities. Regardless of sexuality, Southern Black women are socialized to understand the significance of creating and maintaining community among other Black women. Although we consider homeplace to be a physical location, the notion of a homeplace also includes a community space. For SBQLWP, the fam is this homeplace, an intimate space that allows us to connect to our Southern Black queer female communities. SBQLWP often connect to this nonbiological family as we exist in duality. The fam will not urge us to come out, but it will provide a safety net when we finally decide to fully live our truth and reach reconciliation. Through the connection with the fam, we can reimagine what our homeplace can look like. Bernadette Barton discusses a similar phenomenon where she reveals how Bible Belt gays find ways to navigate their sexualities by developing communities with other gay/lesbian folks. The participants in her work felt like they were part of an exclusive club.[6] Instead of feeling like outsiders within the South, we are members of an exclusive community where our Southern Black queerness is affirmed and validated. We are drawn together by our shared experiences with the South. Ultimately, the fam provides a sense of belonging we may not always receive from other Southern Black folks. By creating and maintaining the fam, the Black queer lesbian South establishes a homeplace within a homeplace. The Southern culture of silence, judgment, and shame attempts to limit our potential, but we ultimately create a new homeplace in the Black queer lesbian South through the fam.

The Black queer lesbian South allows us to unapologetically exist, resisting silence, judgment, and shame. This space and place allows us to combat the silence of the South, challenge the validity of the Southern Black personality, and uncover the implications of shame and condemnation in our lives. The Black queer lesbian South provides an opportunity for us to uncover a South that is inclusive of our sexual and gender identities. Many marginalized population finds ways to resist oppression. According to bell hooks, a Black woman's homeplace is a site of resistance. Black women use the homeplace as a mechanism to combat oppression, establishing a core of resistance. The Black queer lesbian South is no exception to this reality. We carry on the tradition of homeplace, finding ways to resist the oppressive realities of the South. For hooks, resistance comes in the form of affirmation and self-love: "Working to create a homeplace that affirmed our beings, our blackness, our love for one another was necessary resistance."[7] The Black queer lesbian South exists in that same form of resistance, where our Southern Blackness, Southernness, queer lesbianism, and humanity are affirmed. Here we continue our process of reconciliation, where we love our Southern Black queer lesbian selves. But in the Black queer lesbian South, we want other SBQLWP to reach self-love as well. The Black queer lesbian South signifies an external act of resistance for SBQLWP by sharing and receiving communal affirmation. The intentional decision to affirm one's existence is a form of resistance.

The Black queer lesbian Southern space also offers an opportunity for future generations of SBQLWP to find safety. Once we create communities for ourselves to actualize our identities, we want the same for the next generations. Vanessa said she felt "indebted to make sure I tell the next generation" to exist and thrive as a Black queer lesbian in the South. Toni remains visible to help with the "queer babies." She said, "I will continue to be who I am in hopes that a queer baby sees me." She wanted to be a representative for Black LGBTQIA+ youth, a role model for "queer babies" in their queer lesbian journeys. While we may find wholeness and reconciliation, the oppressive realities of the South still exist. The closet is always there. Even as one person comes out, others remain closeted and endure duality. The culture of silence, Southern Black personality, shame, and condemnation still permeate the region. These oppressive realities can devour Southern Black queer lesbian youth who do not have safe spaces to take refuge. Existing in our truth and reconciling with the South is not just for us but for the queer generation coming after us. Being visible in the South and taking up physical space creates opportunities for Black queer lesbian youth to find safe communities. Even as I teach undergraduate courses, I find myself becoming more visible for my Black queer lesbian students because I, too, recognize the significance of representation. Being an openly Black queer lesbian while embracing my Southernness allows my students to see that they can exist in the fullness of all their identities. Our representation of the Black queer lesbian South creates new possibilities for future generations to thrive. The Black queer lesbian South acknowledges that representation and visibility are essential components of our resistance.

As a historically marginalized person, taking physical place and finding space in the South is a method of resisting the cultural Conservative landscape of the South. Taking up physical place and finding space means more than merely living passively; it is the intentional act of existing out loud and unapologetically against the cultural norms established by the Church and the Southern Black personality. As John Howard noted, it is unusual to see "Southern" and "LGBTQIA+" used in the same sentence, as if the South is only a heteronormative space. According to Howard, Southern queer folks do not seem to fit in the narrative of American lesbian and gay history or in Southern history.[8] When SBQLWP find spaces of their own, they challenge the notion that the South belongs only to cishet Southern Black folks. SBQLWP taking up space in this Southern setting—even amid these heteronormative assumptions—serves as a method of resistance. The Black queer lesbian South signifies a possibility for those marginalized in the South to establish our right to exist in the South.

Furthermore, the Black queer lesbian South resists by refusing to be a product of oppressive components of the South, namely, the culture of silence, the manifestations of shameful Church realities, and the Southern Black personality. SBQLWP can exist as a Southern person and embody Southernness without conceding to toxic cisgender identities or heteronormativity. Part of this refusal to belong signifies a sense of deviancy that exists in the Black queer lesbian South. SBQLWP are deviants to the traditional Southern cishet white heteropatriarchal narrative and geography. This also explains why we are considered societal threats in the South. SBQLWP use deviancy as a method of resistance in this Black queer lesbian South in order for SQLWP to gain agency in the South. In this context, being deviant to the heterosexist South is an act of establishing autonomy in the Black queer lesbian South, which ultimately resists heteronormativity and Black heteropatriarchy and restructures a new Southern reality. Cathy Cohen refers to this practice as the politics of deviancy, where decisions or acts of "deviants" result from attempting to "create autonomous spaces absent the continuous streams of power from outside authorities or normative structures."[9] The way SBQLWP live out our lives, whether in the South or outside of it, we intentionally make decisions and actions that challenge or shed light on patriarchy and heteronormativity in the South. Once we find our truth, we may appear deviant to maintain that truth and establish a sense of autonomy and agency. The Black queer lesbian South uses the politics of deviancy to maintain a newfound freedom. The deviancy in the Black queer lesbian South is not just a personal process, but an opportunity for any Southern queer person to reclaim place and space.

Snapping Beans Reiterates the Black Queer Lesbian South

By snapping beans, literally or metaphorically, we can create and sustain the Black queer lesbian South. Grandma and 'em gave us the blueprint to establish the Black queer lesbian South as a safe place and space. Snapping beans with them provided the tools to carve out place and space for ourselves, foundational in how SBQLWP establish the Black queer lesbian South. The sound of the green bean snapping reminds us of our connection to our Southern Black female community and our desire to maintain that connection with other SBQLWP. The Southern practice of snapping beans reminds us of the need to create community with other women and recognize the significance of creating communal spaces that can help us affirm one another. While our foremothers could not tell us how to be a queer lesbian person in the South, they gave us a space to speak about it, through the connection to the Southern kitchen and snapping beans. While snapping beans, we learn from an early age the significance of and need for community. We are socialized to recognize that without community, snapping beans would not happen. Although we may not physically snap beans, we continue the tradition of finding ways to connect to our Black queer community in the Black queer lesbian South.

Snapping beans represents a Southern Black female practice of freedom and authenticity, integral in establishing a Black queer lesbian South. We can exist as our authentic selves in the company of other SBQLWP. Queerness represents a level of authenticity and freedom to simply be. Snapping beans creates this space for Southern Black women. SBQLWP recalled snapping beans as an intimate, vulnerable space of freedom. Of course, as the silent Black queer lesbian girl comes out and fully embraces her queer lesbianism, she would want to return to that space of authenticity and freedom. In the Black queer lesbian South, we re-create a space of vulnerability, authenticity, and freedom among other SBQLWP. Like the memories of snapping beans, the Black queer lesbian South provides an opportunity for SBQLWP to authentically engage with one another in an intimate practice with other SBQLWP outside the watchful eyes of others. We do not have to worry about being silent, judged, or shamed by others. We are free.

The Black queer lesbian South is essential in finding our truth and reaching reconciliation by reconnecting us to our Southernness and healing from our traumas. In many cases, SBQLWP leaned on the Black queer lesbian South to gain the affirmation needed to live our lives authentically. While reaching my own truth and reconciliation, connecting to a Black queer lesbian South was pivotal. Connecting to the Southern Black queer female community provided me a safe space to fully actualize my queer lesbian identity in a Southern landscape. It reminded me of the safety I had while in the kitchen with grandma and 'em. While we were often silent about our queerness with grandma, she gave us the desire to establish and maintain community while snapping beans. Now the silent Black queer lesbian girl can exist out loud. The Black queer lesbian South sees her, all of her. And like grandma and 'em, embraces her with open arms. She returns home to a place where she belongs. Moreover, snapping beans in the Black queer lesbian South becomes the opportunity for SBQLWP to reconnect to our Southernness. We are given a chance to reconnect to our Southern Black female selves. We snap beans to remind us of our Southern Black and female identities. Now when we think of snapping beans, it is no longer in the oppressive context of our girlhood but in a space to recognize what it means to be Southern. With each snap, there is knowledge of what the South does provide for us in our queer lesbian journey. Each snap is an affirmation of our Southernness and that we belong in the Southern landscape.

Like snapping beans, the Black queer lesbian South creates a pathway for SBQLWP to find wholeness and healing. This homeplace within a homeplace gives us space we speak our truths, both the trauma and the joy. We can metaphorically engage in a Southern practice that allows us to fully speak our truths. Coming out and living in our truth is one thing; being able to articulate our truth to others is a practice that leads to healing. These conversations are essential in establishing the Black queer lesbian South. We recognize how we have been silenced, shamed, and judged. What is happening in our brain will now be spoken. Our experiences will breathe life into our existence. Those hot, dry Southern streets that used to silence, shame, and judge us become a place where we can find freedom in the Black queer lesbian South. By snapping beans in the Black queer lesbian South, the South is transformed to a potential landscape of freedom.

Types and Tropes of the Black Queer Lesbian South

Regardless of racial, gender, or sexual differences, the South births several personalities that are simultaneously oppressive and liberating. As discussed in previous chapters, James T. Sears established some tropes of the South that represent oppressive racial and socioeconomic realities, such as the Southern belle, the Southern gentleman, and the good ol' boy. This work included additional Southern Black tropes to expose heteronormativity: pastor, first lady, good woman, bad woman, and the in-between woman. In the Black queer lesbian South, similar archetypes and members exist, acting as extensions to these Southern personalities. The tropes of the Black queer lesbian South are liberatory acts of redefining oneself in the Southern landscape. These character types represent autonomy and authenticity for SBQLWP. They also allow us to embody our Southernness and queerness. This argument does not suggest that there are no oppressive personalities here. Heteronormative SBQLWP adopt patriarchy and misogyny. Some SBQLWP adopt the heteropatriarchal and heteronormative tropes of the South because there is a presumed power associated with them. Once we attempt to establish and maintain this Black queer lesbian South, there is an opportunity for us to redefine and embody new Southern archetypes. Finding our truth and finding reconciliation in the Black queer lesbian South allows for us to embody new forms of being that are not in opposition to their Southernness but complement it.

The tropes that exist within the Black queer lesbian South are Southern Black femme, Southern Black gentlelady, Southern stud, Southern good ol' boi, and Southern Black nonbinary person. This is not an exclusive list, but these tropes are integrated into the Black queer lesbian South. The more we uncover additional ways we bend gender norms, I am sure additional tropes and archetypes will emerge. These identities are rooted in certain character types that exist in the South but have been redefined based on their role in the Black queer lesbian South. These metaphors exist in a racialized sexual queer geography, positioned in the intersection of race, gender, and sexuality in the South. Similar to Sears's tropes, these also expose some relevant class elements. Even in our Southern Black queerness, we still find ways to emulate these class dynamics, specifically as they relate to educational attainment and employment. Moreover, these tropes represent a spectrum of how SBQLWP adopt certain traditional Southern tropes in the Black queer lesbian South.

The Southern Black Femme

The Southern Black femme problematizes and embraces traditional cishet Southern femininity. The Black queer lesbian South dispels the myth that one's feminine identity is ultimately connected to a monogamous, heteronormative marriage. As explored earlier, the South imbues value on those who uphold femininity in the traditional sense, specifically as it relates to heteronormative institutions such as family and the Church. Southern Black women are socialized to consider femininity only in these strict terms to gain societal privilege and value. If the embodiment of femininity is not related to purity, submissiveness, domesticity, and the creation of family, then it challenges what is considered feminine in the South. Southern Black women strive for femininity to gain a sense of humanity. If one's presentation or embodiment does not align with the Southern belle, first lady, or the good woman, then they are considered wayward, worldly, bad women, not worthy of honor and respect. The Black queer lesbian South allows us to reconcile what it means to be a feminine-presenting person without adopting the traditional societal patriarchy that accompanies it. Problematizing the Southern belle in this way allows SBQLWP to adopt the Southern feminine value system without the accompanying oppressions. This new value system pushes back against the Southern Black heteronormativity and heteropatriarchy in the Southern

Black personality. The Southern Black femme identity allows SBQLWP (and even heteronormative Southerners) to see variations of femininity that are not limited to the Southern belle, first lady, or a good woman. Finding our truth and identifying as a Southern Black femme person means embracing our Southern femininity in a Southern Black queer place while dispelling traditional assumptions of femininity in Southern heteronormative spaces.

The embodiment of the Southern femme is not a contemporary phenomenon. There are some historical examples of this Southern femme. Jazz and blues artists such as Ma Rainey and Bessie Smith (both Southern Black women) embodied the Southern femme by challenging traditional assumptions of Southern Black cisgender femininity. According to Angela Y. Davis, "the female portraits created by the early blues women served as reminders of African-American women's tradition of womanhood, a tradition that directly challenged prevailing notions of femininity."[10] Jazz and blues allowed these pioneers to express their fluid sexualities while protesting the traditional Southern notions of cisgender femininity. Their performances incorporated some level of Southernness, and their embodiment of femininity was not limited to heteronormativity. SBQLWP in this book continued this tradition that problematizes the Southern belle and first lady while also embracing some elements of Southernness that these tropes present.

The Southern Black femme is an extension of our Southernness. This embodiment aligns with what we consider feminine and femme in the Southern Black queer community. In the Black queer lesbian South, the Southern Black femme embraces the feminine gender expression, recognizing the ancestral power of Southern Black womanhood. The Southern femme recognizes the power of the feminine in the South and adopts this identity in the Southern Black queer community. The Black queer lesbian South allows SBQLWP to actualize what femininity can look like in a Southern queer space. We often consider femme in the context of queer studies as anyone who embodies femininity. Yet when incorporating a racialized queer sexualized geography, the Southern Black femme embodiment adds a layer to this notion of femme that embraces elements of the South. The Black queer lesbian South highlights the ways femme embodiment can have some Southern elements as well.

Like the Southern belle and the first lady, the Southern Black femme may be formally educated, middle to upper-class, and a model for femininity in the Southern Black queer community. She presents herself as the feminine embodiment of Southernness. Femmes may enjoy engaging in Southern hospitality, volunteering in a local Church, cooking for their families, and taking care of elderly families. The Southern femme may engage in the traditional aesthetics of feminine beauty in public spaces. When a Southerner sees them, they may not automatically recognize them as queer and/or lesbian. She can hide in plain sight, contributing to the Southern Black community as a cisgender femme. She could pass for heterosexual in the South and may benefit from heteronormativity and heteropatriarchy. Because she can hide in plain sight, she receives some level of protection and respect from both the Black heterosexual community and the Black queer lesbian community. She proves her femininity through the lack of manual labor, adopting traditional cisgender femininity as a means of gaining social status. The Southern Black femme identity reconnects to that Southern feminine identity Southern women were socialized with, where we adopt some characteristics of the Southern belle and first lady, but knowing we can redefine what those can mean in a Southern Black queer lesbian space and place. While the Southern Black femme can adopt some elements of the Southern belle and the first lady, that is neither constrained nor limited by those elements. In redefining Southern Black femininity, we also embody some elements of what is traditionally viewed as feminine and femme.

As I was finding my truth, reconciling, and finding space for myself in the South, I often dealt with an internal struggle of what it meant to identify as femme in a Southern queer space. Once we identify as lesbian or queer, it is assumed that we dismiss all notions of cisgender femininity as oppressive or binary. I realized that this dismissal is a manifestation of internalized heterosexism, where Southern femininity can only manifest in one way. I did not see myself in what I traditionally understood as feminine in the South. I have never been a "girly girl," nor did I grow up viewing heteronormative marriage or family as the only way to exist in the world. I am certainly not the Southern belle or the first lady. But in finding my truth in the South, I reconciled with a Southern femme identity that allows me to embrace the power of the feminine and how it manifests in my Southernness. Furthermore, this femme identity provided a space for me to express my femininity in a queer context, helping me delineate how the femme embodiment can be liberating even in my Southernness. This reality allowed me to recognize even the ways I do not have to be a "girly girl" to be considered femme because femininity has a spectrum that is inclusive of stems and aggressive femmes in the Southern Black queer lesbian community.[11] Connecting to my Southernness allowed me to see the expansion of what Southern Black femininity can encompass.

This Southern Black femme places value on her femininity, connecting it to the Southern femininity gained from the maternal figures before her. This identity connects us to what our foremothers taught us about what it means to be a feminine-identified individual in the South and how our femininity can be honored outside the confines of oppressive gender norms. While Southern Black maternal figures may be an oppressive element in the collective narrative, they show their queer lesbian daughters the power of Southern feminine energy. While they were cishet Southern Black women who benefited (and were oppressed by) the societal value system related to femininity in the South, they provided the framework for what Southern femininity can look like. SBQLWP embodying a femme identity in the South is a form of resistance against preconceived notions related to queerness and lesbianism. This lesson was provided by our foremothers and indoctrinated in the Black queer lesbian South in the form of the Southern Black femme.

The Southern Black femme represents a homeplace in the Black queer lesbian South. The Southern Black femme yields the possibility that Southern femininity represents a reclamation of power and agency. The Southern Black femme is a part of how femme-embodied SBQLWP reclaim the South. It is a life force, especially Southern Black queer folks, to reconnect to our Southernness. The Southern Black femme archetype represents a person and energy that reminds SBQLWP that we are home, like getting a hug and a kiss from an auntie. Like bell hooks's notion of homeplace, this same energy and life force is what SBQWLP attempt to re-create through the femme, where other SBQLWP can feel comfort, safety, and peace. The Southern Black femme identity provides comfort, safety, and peace for the Southern Black queer community. Similar to other Southern Black women, the femme maintains and sustains the Black queer lesbian South, providing a homeplace in a contentious place and space.

Southern Queer Masculine Embodiment: The Southern Gentlelady, the Southern Stud, and the Southern Good Ol' Boi

According to Michael Kimmel, masculinity is historical and socially constructed.[12] Our understanding of what masculinity looks like in the Black queer lesbian South is dictated by certain racial and cultural realities. There are certainly SBQLWP who understand masculinity in the context of the Southern Black personality, one that is heteropatriarchal, toxic, and oppressive. After all, the Southern Black personality establishes a hegemonic model of masculinity for others to follow. The question becomes how masculine-embodied SBQLWP align with and challenge this hegemonic masculinity. Southern culture attaches masculinity to social status, namely, property and power. However, given the historical realities of the South, many of the people who benefited from traditional notions of masculinity were upper-class white men with generational wealth. They represent the hegemonic masculinity that all Southern men attempt to emulate, including Black cishet men.

Masculine-embodied SBQLWP adopt and problematize this traditional embodiment of masculinity. Their masculine embodiment challenges what we traditionally associate with masculinity in the South. Like Sears's Southern gentleman and good ol' boy tropes, the Black queer lesbian South has similar masculine-embodied personalities. Masculine-embodied SBQLWP are considered either studs or bois. Differences among these are debatable. Some masculine-identified SBQLWP pointed to a generational difference in the terminology, where bois are young and immature while studs are older and mature. Some discuss individual preferences, depending on how that masculine-identified SBQLWP choose to define themselves. They provide a context for how Southern masculine queer identity manifests in the Black queer lesbian South. There appears to be a spectrum of Southern Black queer lesbian masculinity that include Southern gentleladies, Southern studs, and Southern good ol' bois.

Some masculine-embodied SBQLWP I interviewed referred to themselves as "gentleladies," who embody the characteristics of the traditional Southern gentleman and aristocrat without the oppressive patriarchy associated with it. Southern gentleladies seem to garner more respect in the Black queer lesbian community because they embody what we traditionally see as masculine in the South, rooted in power and protection. In the South, regardless of where masculinity is embodied, it is respected. Although it may be rooted in some patriarchal notions, Southern Black folks love to see Southern masculinity at its best. SBQLWP are no exception to this. Masculine-embodied SBQLWP garner a level of respect in the Black queer lesbian South that is inherited. Southern gentleladies will even perform and embody the same characteristics as the Southern gentleman: refined, genteel, and aesthetically pleasing. This embodiment transfers to how they engage with Southern femme persons. Similar to the Southern gentleman, the Southern gentlelady may have more education and higher-paying jobs. This is how they prove their masculinity. They prove their masculinity through their ability to engage in mental work. Southern gentleladies can vacillate between their femininity and masculinity based on necessity and preference. Gentleladies may outwardly perform a level of femininity if their work environments necessitate it, especially if they work in the South. The outward performance of femininity is often for the benefit of others, making the other person comfortable in their presence. Like Kimmel's historic construct of manhood, the gentlelady appears to have some feminine characteristics of the genteel patriarch, who is considered "an anachronistic feminized dandy—sweet but ineffective and outmoded."[13] The gentlelady is what the genteel patriarch and Southern gentleman appear to be—feminine and masculine wrapped up into one body.

On the other hand, the Southern studs and good ol' bois traditionally use their hands to prove their masculinity. Like Sears's good ol' boy and Kimmel's heroic artisan, the Southern studs and good ol' bois believe in social mobility through manual labor. They value physical strength and using their hands to build their lives. Like the heroic artisan, they take pride in their work.[14] They are more likely to engage in a craft of sorts and less likely to sit at a desk job. They may have a limited formal education, but their masculinity is connected to their ability and desire to work to attract the Southern Black femme counterpart. The necessity of working and using their hands is essential to maintaining and embodying their masculinity. They are respected because they use their hands to gain social mobility and status in the South. Regardless of race or gender, Southern folks love to see a hard worker. The Black queer lesbian South is no exception. Moreover, unlike the Southern gentlelady who vacillates between femininity and masculinity, studs and good ol' bois hold on to their masculinity to maintain a sense of power in the Black queer lesbian South. Based on what they do for a living, they rarely operate outside of their masculinity. They consistently show up as their masculine selves in all spaces.

These Southern masculine queer identities challenge and adopt traditional and hegemonic masculinity and the Southern Black personality. These masculine embodiments remove the "he" pronoun associated with masculinity, challenging the idea that cisgender men are the only ones who can embody masculinity. Southern masculine embodiment removes masculinity from the attachment to the hegemonic, white supremacist model. Simply put, this challenges the idea that cisgender Southern men are the sole owners of Southern masculinity. Their embodiment of masculinity has little to do with land, property, and power. These archetypes in the Black queer lesbian South have some overlapping characteristics related to class status and social mobility even though they are not manifested in the same way. After all, as Black people in the South, they do not automatically benefit from power associated with land ownership or generational wealth. Their embodiment of masculinity is connected more to educational attainment and employment, both of which seem to focus more on protection and perceived social status than on generational wealth.

These Southern masculine queer identities also use masculinity as a method of protection. They are the ones who stand in the gap between the Southern Black personality and the Southern Black femme. They are automatically a threat to the Southern Black personality and heteropatriarchy. The spectrum of Southern female masculinity offers the possibility that masculinity is not automatically toxic. SBQLWP typically do not use their masculinity as a patriarchal tool to oppress femmes or other women. They represent traditional Southern masculinity related to strength and protection that includes their Southern Blackness and queer lesbian identity. While traditional hegemonic cisgender masculinity is the antithesis of anything feminine, SBQLWP embodying masculinity is the opposite of that, showing how masculine and feminine can exist in one person.

The Embodiment of Southern Queer Fluidity

Even though the Black queer lesbian South challenges certain cisgender realities, it can adopt some of its binary elements. The visibility of gender-nonconforming queer persons in the Black queer lesbian South provides a new narrative that challenges all cisgender embodiment. Southern queer fluidity allows some flexibility as it relates to the masculine/feminine cisgender binary, especially for those Southern Black queer lesbian persons who do not fit neatly in the Southern Black femme or queer masculine spectrums. These people may exist in the Southern queer femme and masculine tropes, but their identities are not fixed in it. Because they embody a queer fluidity, they do not have a specific trope name. Instead, they are a representation of what queer identity looks like in a Southern landscape. The Southern queer embodiment exists outside of binary tropes.

In finding our truth, we are expected to exist within these cisgender binary tropes. Instead, we find ways to vacillate between the masculine/feminine binary tropes or create a new space to embrace our Southernness outside of the confines of any trope. A gender-fluid person in the Black queer lesbian South do not need to exist in the binary that plagues the region. Southern folks may look at these individuals as "funny" or "off" because they cannot be placed as either a stud/boi or femme lesbian. Like the Southern gentlelady, this queerness recognizes a twoness (or threeness or fourness) in one Southern body. The Southern queer-fluid person establishes a new South that normalizes the embodiment of multifaceted and multidimensional identities. They embrace the normalcy of gender bending and fluidity in the South. This fluidity allows Southerners and those in the Black queer lesbian South to understand how to embody Southernness without automatically attaching it to certain binaries. These individuals provide a blueprint for how one can integrate Southernness and queerness without Southern binaries. Southern Black queer fluidity combats the urge to fit into a cisgender binary, showing the Black queer lesbian South (and the South in general) the myriad possibilities of what it means to be queer and Southern with pride and dignity.

SBQLWP who embody Southern nonbinary queerness challenge cisgender heteronormativity. Their existence allows Southern folks to challenge heteronormativity in all social areas, especially in the Church and family. Queer embodiment provides the possibility of seeing humanity, gender, and sexuality outside the confines of cisgender heteropatriarchy and heteronormativity. In challenging heteronormativity, Southern Black queerness directly threatens the shame, silence, judgment, and condemnation that permeates the South. Southern queerness challenges myriad traditional norms in the South and removes the value system associated with Southern heteronormativity. Southern fluidity is a representation of the reconciliation that a queer person can have with their queer and Southern selves, where they do not have to be separate entities but are complementary to one another.

The Black Queer Lesbian South: Place and Space for Southern Black Queer Joy

The Black queer lesbian South is a place and space for SBQLWP to find Southern Black queer joy. All those with multiple marginalized identities can find peace and wholeness because we can integrate our Southernness with our queerness. That integration is the starting point to reach wholeness and healing. The Black queer lesbian South creates space and place for this integration, with less emphasis on nostalgia and more focus on claiming ownership. Reclamation is the pathway to gaining wholeness and healing that does not require external validation from other Southern people. The Black queer lesbian South provides us with that human and Southern affirmation.

The Black queer lesbian South is an awakening that Black queer joy and love can exist in the South. Our joy can be actualized as we reach wholeness. We can laugh, cry, and carry on as Southerners. We celebrate ourselves and who we have become as a result of our experiences in the South. While trauma attempted to keep us in a place of marginalized silence, we decided to carve out a space for ourselves in our homeplace. Our joy is resistance to the trauma that we experienced. In this joy, we find ways to thrive by building community. This joy represents the fullness of what it means to be Black and queer from the South. With the audacity to love ourselves and all the communities we represent, we do not have to exist in silence. Even if we do not physically live in the South, we can still carry the South with us without shame or embarrassment. Our roots are strong, fertile, and grounded. We plant our feet on the Southern dirt, take a breath of the humid air, and feel reassured that we are home, where we belong. The smell of the Southern dirt will no longer remind us only of the trauma but also the joys of being from the South and embodying our Southernness. It is the place and space where we can sit on our porches and snap beans in peace and joy, knowing that we are at home.

Epilogue

We Continue to Carry On

I want to thank the readers for taking this journey with me, with all the twists and turns that come with any captivating narrative. To my Southern Black cishet folks, I hope this provided you with some insight into what many people in your life may have or are currently experiencing. Send those people love and affirmation, not daggers of judgment and tolerance. For my Southern Black queer folks, I hope it freed you and perhaps helped you in your healing and reconciliation. That's all I want for you: to live a life that is authentic for you, whatever that may look like. I want to apologize if there were moments you had to relive pain or trauma as you think of your journey to queer actualization. For those Southern Black queer folks who remain silent, I hope this book provides you a voice, even if it's shaky.

I have to be honest, I was reluctant to write about something that means so much me personally and professionally. Through this writing process, I grappled with being bold enough to share my story alongside these interlocutors. But I realized that excluding myself from this collective narrative would be a disservice to the readers. Although this work certainly contains scholarly elements that attracts academics, it also had to be authentic for me. If my phenomenal and insightful interlocutors could be bold enough to share their stories with me, knowing I was writing a book about them, the least I could do was stand with them and say, "Me too, sis." I also dealt with the silence, shame, condemnation, and reconciliation. I also encountered the Southern Black personality in my family and the community. I too experienced the ways my mother played the role of the Church. I became intentional in saying "we" and "our" in this story because it is our story. Do not let this bold action of telling our stories fall into the abyss or be archived somewhere. Do not let our voices be silenced. Do not let our bold actions of storytelling be a waste of our time. Let our voices be a call to action for that next scholar, activist, or practitioner.

Snapping Beans is not the first text about Black queer lesbians, and it won't be the last. This work is merely a launching pad of what will come. This is the beginning, not the end of sharing our stories. We are not done with snapping beans. Now it is time to preserve the green beans, canning them for future use. While this book may be criticized for being too "woke" or part of a "leftist agenda," no one cannot ban the internet. They cannot void and silence our experiences. Folks cannot stop us from sharing our stories, nor can they stop us from establishing safe spaces for us to exist and thrive. Our Southern Black queer ancestors did so; certainly we can create ways to virtually snap beans, making the medium accessible for everyone. We will create a virtual front porch, where we snap beans and share our stories, laugh with each other, share love and affirmation with one another, and be in community. As we move on to the next phase of establishing the visibility of the Black queer lesbian South, we must remember to pay homage to the past while recognizing that this work has a sustaining, viable future. Our stories will not be silenced and erased; they will continue to be shared, loudly and proudly. We will continue to be bold enough to carry on.

Notes

Preface

1. In this context, I refer to the interlocutors of this work and myself as queer lesbians, as many interlocutors identified themselves as both lesbian and queer. However, as this book will outline, one's experience with sexuality does not automatically equate to a queer fluidity and queerness.

2. E. Patrick Johnson, *Sweet Tea: Black Gay Men of the South: An Oral History* (Chapel Hill: University of North Carolina Press, 2008), 2.

3. SBQLWP describes a whole population, whom I grammatically refer to as a plural noun. Because of this, there will be cases where it appears grammatically incorrect, but it is the correct subject-verb agreement because I am referring to a group of individuals.

4. Anna J. Cooper, *A Voice from the South* (Xenia, OH: Aldine, 1892).

5. E. Patrick Johnson, *Black. Queer. Southern. Women: An Oral History* (Chapel Hill: University of North Carolina Press, 2018), 10–11.

6. Johnson, *Black. Queer. Southern. Women*, 15.

7. Qiana Cutts, "My Labels Are [Not] Too Many," in *Queer South Rising: Voices of a Contested Places*, edited by Reta Ugena Whitlock (Charlotte, NC: Information Age, 2013), 298.

8. *Dawta* is the Southern African American vernacular referring to young Black women in the Southern Black community. This term is a universal name Southern Black elders use to address younger generations of Southern Black women. We refer to one another using family terminologies to represent racial unity.

Introduction

1. Johnson, *Sweet Tea*, 1.

2. See Old Farmer's Almanac, "Green Beans," https://www.almanac.com/plant/beans/.

3. Old Farmer's Almanac, "Green Beans."

4. Streak o' lean is a hardened bacon with salt, similar to fatback, that when added to water softens up so you do not have to use ham hock. Tangentially, some individuals mentioned adding potatoes, whereas others said that potatoes actually take away from the green bean flavor.

5. Christopher Stapel, "Dismantling Metrocentric and Metronormative Curricula: Toward a Critical Queer Pedagogy of Southern Rural Space and Place," in *Queer South Rising: Voices of a Contested Place*, edited by Reta Ugena Whitlock (Charlotte, NC: Information Age, 2013), 61.

6. Combahee River Collective, "A Black Feminist Statement," in *Words of Fire: An Anthology of African American Feminist Thought*, edited by Beverly Guy-Sheftall (New York: New Press, 1995), 233.

7. Layli Phillips, "Introduction—Womanism On Its Own," in *The Womanist Reader*, edited by Layli Phillips (New York: Routledge, 2006), xxiv.

8. Combahee River Collective, "A Black Feminist Statement," 233.

9. Combahee River Collective, "A Black Feminist Statement," 233.

10. Phillips, "Introduction," xxiv.

11. Phillips, "Introduction," xxiv.

12. Patricia Hill Collins, *Black Feminist Thought: Knowledge, Consciousness, and the Politics of Empowerment* (New York: Routledge, 2000), 266.

13. Collins, *Black Feminist Thought*, 271.

14. The American South is a region in the United States that consists of people who live below the state of Pennsylvania, also known as the Mason-Dixon Line. In this context, the region includes the states in the Southeast corner of the United States. Sixteen states are included in this region, which the US Census Bureau divided into three smaller groups: South Atlantic states, East South Central states, and West South Central states. The South Atlantic states are Delaware, Florida, Georgia, Maryland, North Carolina, South Carolina, Virginia, and West Virginia. East South Central states consist of Alabama, Kentucky, Mississippi, and Tennessee. The West South Central states are Arkansas, Louisiana, Oklahoma, and Texas. Participants for this research were derived from the broad geographic location of the American South.

15. Reta Ugena Whitlock, "Introduction: Loving, Telling, and Reconstructing the South," in *Queer South Rising: Voices of a Contested Place*, edited by Reta Ugena Whitlock (Charlotte, NC: Information Age, 2013), xxvii.

16. James T. Sears, *Growing Up Gay in the South: Race, Gender, and Journeys of the Spirit* (New York: Harrington Park Press, 1991), 9.

17. W. Fitzhugh Brundage, *The Southern Past: A Clash of Race and Memory* (Cambridge, MA: Belknap Press of Harvard University, 2005), 3.

18. Brundage, *The Southern Past*, 11.

19. Katherine McKittrick, *Demonic Grounds: Black Women and The Cartographies of Struggle* (Minneapolis: University of Minnesota Press, 2006), xiv.

20. McKittrick, *Demonic Grounds*, xiii.
21. McKittrick, *Demonic Grounds*, xiv.
22. McKittrick, *Demonic Grounds*, xiv.
23. These predominantly white towns and cities in the American South would terrorize Black persons who stayed there after sunset as a way to enforce racial segregation and oppression. If a Black person stayed after sunset, they might have encountered racial violence in the forms of lynching. This type of racial violence hindered Blacks from owning property or housing in these towns and cities.
24. Tera W. Hunter, *To 'Joy My Freedom: Southern Black Women's Lives and Labors after the Civil War* (Cambridge, MA: Harvard University Press, 1997), 20.
25. LaToya E. Eaves, "Outside Forces: Black Southern Sexuality," in *Queering the Countryside: New Frontiers in Rural Queer Studies*, edited by Mary L. Gray, Colin R. Johnson, and Brian J. Gilley (New York: New York University Press, 2016), 155.
26. Eaves, "Outside Forces," 155.
27. bell hooks, *Yearning: Race, Gender, and Cultural Politics* (Boston: South End Press, 1990), 43.
28. hooks, *Yearning*, 48.
29. Collins, *Black Feminist Thought*, 114.
30. Collins, *Black Feminist Thought*, 99.
31. Collins, *Black Feminist Thought*, 114.
32. Clenora Hudson-Weems, *Africana Womanism: Reclaiming Ourselves* (Lambertville, MI: Bedford, 2004), 58.
33. Janheinz Jahn, *Muntu: African Culture and the Western World* (New York: Grove Press, 1990), 124.
34. Jahn, *Muntu*, 124.
35. Cherríe L. Moraga, *Loving in the War Years* (Cambridge, MA: South End Press, 1983), 109.
36. Cheryl Clarke, "Lesbianism: An Act of Resistance," in *Words of Fire: An Anthology of African-American Feminist Thought*, edited by Beverly Guy-Sheftall (New York: New Press, 1995), 242.
37. Cherry Smith, "What Is This Thing Called Queer?," in *The Material Queer: A LesBiGay Cultural Studies Reader*, edited by Donald Morton (Boulder, CO: Westview Press, 1996), 281.
38. Smith, "What Is This Thing Called Queer?," 280.
39. Poet on Watch, "An Editor's Notes," in *G.R.I.T.S (Girls Raised in the South): An Anthology of Southern Queer Womyn's Voices & Their Allies*, edited by Poet on Watch and Amber N. Williams (Austin, TX: Freeverse, 2013), ix.
40. Patricia Hill Collins, "Learning from the Outsider Within: The Sociological Significance of *Black Feminist Thought*," *Social Problems* 33, no. 6 (1986): S14.
41. Collins, *Black Feminist Thought*, 184.

192 | Notes to "I Was Silent, But My Brain Was Loud"

42. Carlos L. Dews, "Afterword," in *Out in the South*, edited by Carlos L. Dews and Carolyn Leste Law (Philadelphia, PA: Temple University Press, 2001), 236.

43. Dews, "Afterword," 236–37.

44. E. Patrick Johnson, "'Quare' Studies, or (Almost) Everything I Know about Queer Studies I Learned from My Grandma," in *Black Studies Reader: A Critical Anthology*, edited by E. Patrick Johnson and Mae G. Henderson (Durham, NC: Duke University Press, 2005), 125.

45. Johnson, "'Quare Studies,'" 125.

46. Johnson, "'Quare Studies,'" 125.

47. Bernadette Barton, *Pray the Gay Away: The Extraordinary Lives of Bible Belt Gays* (New York: New York University Press, 2012), 10.

48. Barton, *Pray the Gay Away*, 14.

49. Lincoln and Mamiya, *The Black Church in the African American Experience*, 17.

50. Albert J. Raboteau, *Slave Religion: The "Invisible Institution" in the Antebellum South* (New York: Oxford University Press, 2004), ix.

51. Raboteau coins this "invisible institution" as Black religion under American slavery. Before becoming an autonomous, formal organization, the Christian Black church always operated as an institution "invisible" and separate from the rest of society.

52. Barton, *Pray the Gay Away*, 72.

53. Beverly Greene, "African American Lesbian and Bisexual Women," *Journal of Social Issues* 56, no. 2 (2000): 245, https://doi.org/10.1111/0022-4537.00163.

54. Jehovah's Witnesses define their church as the Kingdom Hall.

55. Johnson, *Sweet Tea*, 2008; Johnson, *Black. Queer. Southern. Women*, 2018.

56. Johnson, *Sweet Tea*, 182.

57. Johnson, *Sweet Tea*, 183.

58. Johnson, *Sweet Tea*, 184.

59. Johnson, *Black. Queer. Southern. Women*, 165.

60. "Sistas" is African American vernacular for the community/communities of Black women.

61. "Brothas" is African American vernacular for the community/communities of Black men.

"I Was Silent, But My Brain Was Loud"

1. Audre Lorde, "The Transformation of Silence into Language and Action," in *Sister Outsider: Essays and Speeches by Audre Lorde* (Berkeley, CA: Crossing Press, 1984), 41.

2. Johnson, "'Quare' Studies," 125.

3. Lorde, "The Transformation of Silence," 41.

4. Lorde, "The Transformation of Silence," 42.
5. Lorde, "The Transformation of Silence," 42.
6. Lorde, "The Transformation of Silence," 41.
7. McKittrick, *Demonic Grounds*, xv.
8. McKittrick, *Demonic Grounds*, xiv.
9. McKittrick, *Demonic Grounds*, xvii.
10. Brundage, *The Southern Past*, 7.
11. Barton, *Pray the Gay Away*, 29.
12. Angela Davis, "Reflections on the Black Woman's Role in the Community of Slaves," *Massachusetts Review* 13, nos. 1 and 2 (1972): 83, https://www.jstor.org/stable/25088201.
13. Patricia Hill Collins, *Black Sexual Politics: African Americans, Gender, and the New Racism* (New York: Routledge, 2005), 91.
14. Collins, *Black Sexual Politics*, 58.
15. C. Eric Lincoln and Lawrence Mamiya, *The Black Church in the African American Experience* (Durham, NC: Duke University Press, 1990), 8.
16. Robin M. Boylorn, *Sweetwater: Black Women and Narratives of Resilience* (New York: Peter Lang), 21.

"The Church Is Not the Building; It's the People"

1. Horace L. Griffin, *Their Own Receive Them Not: African American Lesbians and Gays in Black Churches* (Eugene, OR: Wipf & Stock), viii.
2. When speaking of the Southern Christian Black Church, I am referring to an amalgamation of religious denominations under evangelical Christianity practiced by Southern Black Americans. I refer to these religious denominations and all their variations: Southern Baptist, African Methodist Episcopal, Church of God in Christ, Holiness, United Methodist, and Jehovah's Witnesses. The majority of participants in this study (87 percent) grew up in one or more religious denominations. I refer to how these denominations manifest in the American South and their impact on Southern Black folks. Any time I refer to "the Church," I refer to the Black religious denominations in the South.
3. Griffin, *Their Own Receive Them Not*, 1.
4. Kelly Brown Douglas, *Sexuality and the Black Church: A Womanist Perspective* (New York: Orbis Books, 1999), 105.
5. Paulo Freire, *Pedagogy of the Oppressed* (New York: Continuum, 1970), 63.
6. This position has biblical roots (Ezekiel 33:7) that refers to the watchmen in Jerusalem who stood on the walls of the city to keep inhabitants safe. In the Jehovah's Witness faith, these people provide guidance and prayer to people in the Kingdom Hall. They are the ones who deliver the messages from God to the

people as a method of protecting them. This watchman is seen as a spiritual guide for parishioners, being a "watchman" over their souls.

7. Disfellowship is the process of removing a congregant from fellowship in the Jehovah's Witness faith. In these cases, one is considered to commit some sin that cannot be forgiven by the Church elders. You can either petition to leave or are told to leave the fellowship. If you leave the fellowship, you can no longer associate with any member of the congregation, including family members.

8. Griffin, *Their Own Receive Them Not*, 129.

9. Bettina L. Love, "Examining the Oppressor Within: Lessons Learned by a Northern Researcher in the South," in *Queer South Rising: Voices of a Contested Place*, edited by Reta Ugena Whitlock (Charlotte, NC: Information Age, 2013), 46.

10. Collins, *Black Feminist Thought*, 183.

11. Collins, *Black Feminist Thought*, 185–86.

12. A deaconness is the female version of a deacon, whose responsibility may vary based on the Church. Deacons and deaconesses are often seen as the Church elders and typically exist in the Baptist denomination, acting as the board of directors for the Church, an accountability power. Deacons and deaconesses work closely with the pastor to ensure that the Church operates smoothly. They serve as a checks and balances system to ensure that the pastor maintains Church principles and goals.

13. bell hooks, *Understanding Patriarchy* (Louisville, KY: Louisville Anarchist Federation, 2010), 1.

14. bell hooks, *Communion: Female Search for Love* (New York: William Morrow, 2002), xv.

15. Lincoln and Mamiya, *The Black Church*, 275.

16. Lincoln and Mamiya, *The Black Church*, 275.

17. Evelyn Brooks Higginbotham, *Righteous Discontent: The Women's Movement in the Black Baptist Church, 1880–1920* (Cambridge, MA: Harvard University Press, 1993), 187.

18. Higginbotham, *Righteous Discontent*, 193.

19. Higginbotham, *Righteous Discontent*, 14.

20. During the 1890s, the Black Club movement comprised Black women (namely, Black Church-going women) who believed that education was the best way for Blacks to combat racism and racial uplift. This comprised individuals such as Ida B. Wells, Mary McLeod Bethune, Mary Church Terrell, and Maggie Lena Walker. They believed on the ideas of the National Association of Colored Women of "lifting as we climb" as a charge for racial uplift. See Paula Giddings, *When and Where I Enter: The Impact of Black Women on Race and Sex in America* (New York: Quill William Morrow Press, 1984).

21. Douglas, *Sexuality and the Black Church*, 28.

22. Douglas, *Sexuality and the Black Church*, 27.

23. Collins, *Black Feminist Thought*, 5.

24. Tamura Lomax, *Jezebel Unhinged: Loosing the Black Female Body in Religion and Culture* (Durham, NC: Duke University Press, 2018), 2.
25. Collins, *Black Feminist Thought*, 74.
26. Betty Friedan, *The Feminine Mystique* (New York: Norton, 1963), 15.
27. While Freidan was a pioneer in the second-wave feminist movement, history also reminds us of how she was starkly heteronormative, homophobic, and not accepting of lesbian/queer people in the women's movement in the 1960s. In fact, she called these lesbian/queer people the "lavender menace," because they were considered a problem for the feminist movement. She was afraid that the open involvement of lesbians would somehow hinder the feminist agenda. Because of her comments against lesbian activists involved in the women's movement, lesbian activists made "lavender menace" shirts in protest.
28. Clarke, "Lesbianism: An Act of Resistance," 244.
29. Paul Laurence Dunbar, "We Wear the Mask," in *The Complete Poems of Paul Laurence Dunbar* (New York: Dodd, Mead, 1913), 71.
30. Love, "Examining the Oppressor Within," 49.
31. Barton, *Pray the Gay Away*, 87.
32. Dunbar, "We Wear the Mask," 71.
33. Audre Lorde, *I Am Your Sister: Black Women Organizing across Sexualities* (New York: Kitchen Table Press, 1985), 4.
34. Griffin, *Their Own Receive Them Not*, 59.
35. Griffin, *Their Own Receive Them Not*, 62–63.
36. Griffin, *Their Own Receive Them Not*, 64–65.
37. Jonathan Ned Katz, "The Invention of Heterosexuality," in *Race, Class, and Gender in the United States: An Integrated Study*, 10th ed., edited by Paula S. Rothenberg (New York: Worth Publishers, 2016), 235.
38. These are Southern Black vernacular terms for the masculine-embodied SBQLWP and for a feminine-embodied SBQLWP, respectively. Stud and boi are used in the Southern Black queer female communities.

"The World Is Set Up for Straight Folks"

1. Zora Neale Hurston, *Their Eyes Were Watching God* (New York: First Perennial Classics, 1990), 1.
2. Hurston, *Their Eyes Were Watching God*, 3.
3. Hurston, *Their Eyes Were Watching God*, 3.
4. Lorde, *I Am Your Sister*, 3.
5. Susan Pharr, *Homophobia: A Weapon for Sexism* (Berkeley, CA: Chardon Press, 1997), 17.
6. Collins, *Black Sexual Politics*, 106.

7. Cathy J. Cohen and Tamara Jones, "Fighting Homophobia versus Challenging Heterosexism: 'The Failure to Transform' Revisited," in *Dangerous Liaisons: Blacks, Gays, and the Struggle for Equality*, edited by Eric Brandt (New York: New York University Press, 1999), 90.
8. Collins, *Black Sexual Politics*, 88.
9. I use *heterosexism* and *compulsory heterosexuality* interchangeably.
10. Lorde, *I Am Your Sister*, 4.
11. Lorde, *I Am Your Sister*, 4–5.
12. Lorde, *I Am Your Sister*, 4.
13. Cohen and Jones, "Fighting Homophobia," 88.
14. Cheryl Clarke, "The Failure to Transform," in *Dangerous Liaisons: Blacks, Gays, and the Struggle for Equality*, edited by Eric Brandt (New York: New Press, 1999), 31–44.
15. Cohen and Jones, "Fighting Homophobia," 88–89.
16. Cohen and Jones, "Fighting Homophobia," 90.
17. Collins, *Black Sexual Politics*, 88.
18. Collins, *Black Sexual Politics*, 88–97.
19. Cathy Cohen, "Punks, Bulldaggers, and Welfare Queens: The Radical Potential of Queer Politics?," *GLQ* 3, no. 4 (1997): 440.
20. Cohen, "Punks, Bulldaggers, and Welfare Queens," 440.
21. hooks, *Understanding Patriarchy*, 1.
22. Johnson, *Sweet Tea*, 183.
23. Cohen and Jones, "Fighting Homophobia," 91.
24. Lincoln and Mamiya, *The Black Church*, 107.
25. Lincoln and Mamiya, *The Black Church*, 100.
26. Lincoln and Mamiya, *The Black Church*, 274.
27. Janet Cornelius, *Slave Missions and the Black Church in the Antebellum South* (Columbia: University of South Carolina Press, 1999), 10–11.
28. Jacqueline Grant, "Black Women and the Church" in *But Some of Us Are Brave: Black Women's Studies*, edited by Gloria T. (Akasha) Hull, Patricia Bell-Scott, and Barbara Smith (New York: Feminist Press, 1982); Lincoln and Mamiya, *The Black Church*.
29. Grant, "Black Women and the Church," 141.
30. Collins, *Black Feminist Thought*, 11.
31. Sears, *Growing Up Gay in the South*, 74.
32. Michael Kimmel, "Masculinity as Homophobia: Fear, Shame, and Silence in the Construction of Gender Identity," in *Theorizing Masculinities*, edited by Harry Brod and Michael Kaufman (Thousand Oaks, CA: Sage, 1994), 61.
33. Sears, *Growing Up Gay in the South*, 72–73.
34. Kimmel, "Masculinity as Homophobia," 61.
35. Sears, *Growing Up Gay in the South*, 73.

36. Joan Morgan, *When Chickenheads Come Home to Roost: A Hip-Hop Feminist Breaks It Down* (New York: Simon & Schuster, 1999), 97.
37. Boylorn, *Sweetwater*, 20–21.
38. Higginbotham, *Righteous Discontent*, 199.
39. Collins, *Black Sexual Politics*, 96–97.
40. Collins, *Black Sexual Politics*, 106.
41. Molefi Kete Asante, *Afrocentricity: The Theory of Social Change* (Chicago: African American Images, 2003).
42. Audre Lorde, "Age, Race, Class, and Sex," in *Sister Outsider* (Berkeley, CA: Crossing Press, 1984), 121.
43. Clarke, "The Failure to Transform"; Lorde, "Age, Race, Class, and Sex."
44. Lorde, "Age, Race, Class, and Sex," 121.
45. Pharr, *Homophobia*, 19.
46. Douglas, *Sexuality and the Black Church*, 103–4.
47. Douglas, *Sexuality and the Black Church*, 104.
48. Clarke, "Lesbianism," 246.
49. bell hooks, *Ain't I a Woman: Black Women and Feminism* (Boston: South End Press, 1981), 21.
50. Clarke, "Lesbianism," 243.
51. Cohen and Jones, "Fighting Homophobia," 90.
52. Clarke, "Lesbianism," 246.

"I Am Standing in My Truth"

1. Freire, *Pedagogy of the Oppressed*, 47.
2. Clarke, "Lesbianism: An Act of Resistance," 242.
3. Freire, *Pedagogy of the Oppressed*, 49.
4. Freire, *Pedagogy of the Oppressed*, 49.
5. John Howard, "Introduction: Carryin' On in the Lesbian and Gay South," in *Carryin' On in the Lesbian and Gay South*, edited by John Howard (New York: New York University Press, 1997), 1.
6. Clarke, "Lesbianism as Resistance," 242.
7. Alice Walker, *In Search of Our Mother's Garden: A Womanist Prose* (New York: Harvest Book Harcourt Brace Jovanovich, 1984), xi.
8. Audre Lorde, "Uses of the Erotic: The Erotic as Power," in *Sister Outsider: Essays and Speeches by Audre Lorde* (Berkley, CA: Crossing Press, 1984), 53.
9. Kaila Story, "Not Feminine as in Straight, but Femme as in Queer #AF: The Queer and Black Roots of My Femme Expression/Experience," in *Mouths of Rain: An Anthology of Black Lesbian Thought*, edited by Briona Simone Jones (New York: New Press, 2021), 74.

198 | Notes to The Black Queer Lesbian South

10. Johnson, *Black. Queer. Southern. Women*, 165.
11. Johnson, *Black. Queer. Southern. Women*, 165.
12. Ntozake Shange, *For Colored Girls Who Considered Suicide/When the Rainbow Is Enuf: A Choreopoem* (New York: Collier Books, 1989), 63.

The Black Queer Lesbian South

1. Brundage, *The Southern Past*, 6.
2. Brundage, *The Southern Past*, 7.
3. Brundage, *The Southern Past*, 6.
4. Craig Washington, "Fall Down on Me: Stories of the Club from Black Gay Men in the South," in *Queer South Rising: Voices of a Contested Place*, edited by Reta Ugena Whitlock (Charlotte, NC: Information Age, 2013), 73.
5. *Venus* was small journal publication in Atlanta between January 1995 and November 1996. The magazine was in memory of Venus Landin, co-chair of the African American Lesbian Gay Alliance and well-known lesbian community leader who was murdered by her ex-partner in March 1993.
6. Barton, *Pray the Gay Away*, 209.
7. hooks, *Yearning*, 46.
8. Howard, "Introduction," 5.
9. Cathy Cohen, "Deviance as Resistance: A New Research Agenda for the Study of Black Politics," in *Mouths of Rain: An Anthology of Black Lesbian Thought*, edited by Briona Simone Jones (New York: New Press, 2021), 271.
10. Angela Y. Davis, *Blues Legacies and Black Feminism: Gertrude "Ma" Rainey, Bessie Smith, and Billie Holiday* (New York: Vintage Books, 1998), 38.
11. *Stems* embody both masculine (stud) and feminine (femme) identities. *Aggressive femmes* embody femininity and identify as femmes, but do not fully embody all the traditional aesthetics related to femininity. They appear more aggressive and opinionated within the Black queer lesbian community.
12. Kimmel, "Masculinity as Homophobia," 59.
13. Kimmel, "Masculinity as Homophobia," 61.
14. Kimmel, "Masculinity as Homophobia," 61.

Works Cited

Asante, Molefi Kete. *Afrocentricity: The Theory of Social Change*. Chicago: African American Images, 2003.

Barton, Bernadette. *Pray the Gay Away: The Extraordinary Lives of Bible Belt Gays*. New York: New York University Press, 2012.

Boylorn, Robin M. *Sweetwater: Black Women and Narratives of Resilience*. New York: Peter Lang.

Brundage, W. Fitzhugh. *The Southern Past: A Clash of Race and Memory*. Cambridge, MA: Belknap Press of Harvard University, 2005.

Clarke, Cheryl. "The Failure to Transform." In *Dangerous Liaisons: Blacks, Gays, and the Struggle for Equality*, edited by Eric Brandt, 31–44. New York: New Press, 1999.

Cohen, Cathy J. "Punks, Bulldaggers, and Welfare Queens: The Radical Potential of Queer Politics?" *GLQ* 3, no. 4 (1997): 437–65.

———. "Deviance as Resistance: A New Research Agenda for the Study of Black Politics." In *Mouths of Rain: An Anthology of Black Lesbian Thought*, edited by Briona Simone Jones, 249–79. New York: New Press, 2021.

Cohen, Cathy J., and Tamara Jones, "Fighting Homophobia versus Challenging Heterosexism: 'The Failure to Transform' Revisited." In *Dangerous Liaisons: Blacks, Gays, and the Struggle for Equality*, edited by Eric Brandt, 80–101. New York: New York University Press, 1999.

Collins, Patricia Hill. "Learning from the Outsider Within: The Sociological Significance of Black Feminist Thought." *Social Problems* 33, no. 6 (1986): S14–32.

———. *Black Feminist Thought: Knowledge, Consciousness, and the Politics of Empowerment*. New York: Routledge, 2000.

———. *Black Sexual Politics: African Americans, Gender, and the New Racism*. New York: Routledge, 2005.

Combahee River Collective. "A Black Feminist Statement." In *Words of Fire: An Anthology of African American Feminist Thought*, edited by Beverly Guy-Sheftall, 232–40. New York: New Press, 1995.

Cooper, Anna J. *A Voice from the South*. Xenia, OH: Aldine, 1892.

Cornelius, Janet. *Slave Missions and the Black Church in the Antebellum South*. Columbia: University of South Carolina Press, 1999.

Cutts, Qiana. "My Labels Are [Not] Too Many: My Journey of 'Becoming' a Black, Afrocentric, Southern Lesbian." In *Queer South Rising: Voices of a Contested South*, edited by Reta Ugena Whitlock, 297–325. Charlotte, NC: Information Age, 2013.

Davis, Angela. "Reflections on the Black Woman's Role in Community of Slaves." *Massachusetts Review* 13, nos. 1 and 2 (1972): 81–100. https://www.jstor.org/stable/25088201.

———. *Blues Legacies and Black Feminism: Gertrude "Ma" Rainey, Bessie Smith, and Billie Holliday*. New York: Vintage Books, 1998.

Dews, Carlos L. "Afterword." In *Out in the South*, edited by Carlos L. Dews and Carolyn Leste Law. Philadelphia, PA: Temple University Press, 2001.

Douglas, Kelly Brown. *Sexuality and the Black Church: A Womanist Perspective*. New York: Orbis Books, 1999.

Dunbar, Paul Lawrence. "We Wear the Mask." In *The Complete Poems of Paul Laurence Dunbar*, 71. New York: Dodd, Mead, 1895.

Eaves, LaToya E. "Outside Forces: Black Southern Sexuality." In *Queering the Countryside: New Frontiers in Rural Queer Studies*, edited by Mary L. Gray, Colin R. Johnson, and Brian J. Gilley, 146–57. New York: New York University Press, 2016.

Freire, Paulo. *Pedagogy of the Oppressed*. New York: Continuum, 1970.

Friedan, Betty. *The Feminine Mystique*. New York: Norton, 1963.

Giddings, Paula. *When and Where I Enter: The Impact of Black Women on Race and Sex in America*. New York: Quill William Morrow Press, 1984.

Grant, Jacqueline. "Black Women and the Church." In *But Some of Us Are Brave: Black Women's Studies*, edited by Gloria T. (Akasha) Hull, Patricia Bell-Scott, and Barbara Smith, 141–52. New York: Feminist Press, 1982.

Greene, Beverly. "African American Lesbian and Bisexual Women." *Journal of Social Issues* 56, no. 2 (2000): 239–49. https://doi.org/10.1111/0022-4537.00163

Griffin, Horace L. *Their Own Receive Them Not: African American Lesbians and Gays in Black Churches*. Eugene, OR: Wipf & Stock, 2006.

Halberstam, Jack. *Female Masculinity*. Durham, NC: Duke University Press, 1998.

Higginbotham, Evelyn Brooks. *Righteous Discontent: The Women's Movement in the Black Baptist Church, 1880–1920*. Cambridge, MA: Harvard University Press, 1993.

hooks, bell. *Ain't I a Woman: Black Women and Feminism*. Boston: South End Press, 1981.

———. *Yearning: Race, Gender, and Cultural Politics*. Boston: South End Press, 1990.

———. *Communion: Female Search for Love*. New York: William Morrow, 2002.

———. *Understanding Patriarchy*. Louisville, KY: Louisville Anarchist Federation, 2004.

Howard, John. "Introduction: Carryin' On in the Lesbian and Gay South." In *Carryin' On in the Lesbian and Gay South*, edited by John Howard, 1–12. New York: New York University Press, 1997.

Hudson-Weems, Clenora. *Africana Womanism: Reclaiming Ourselves*. Lambertville, MI: Bedford, 2004.

Hunter, Tera W. *To 'Joy My Freedom: Southern Black Women's Lives and Labors after the Civil War*. Cambridge, MA: Harvard University Press, 1997.

Hurston, Zora Neale. *Their Eyes Were Watching God*. New York: First Perennial Classics, 1990.

Jahn, Janheinz. *Muntu: African Culture and the Western World*. New York: Grove Press, 1990.

Johnson, E. Patrick. "'Quare' Studies, or (Almost) Everything I Know about Queer Studies I Learned from My Grandma." In *Black Studies Reader: A Critical Anthology*, edited by E. Patrick Johnson and Mae G. Henderson, 124–57. Durham, NC: Duke University Press, 2005.

———. *Sweet Tea: Black Gay Men of the South*. Chapel Hill: University of North Carolina Press, 2008.

———. *Black. Queer. Southern. Women: An Oral History*. Chapel Hill: University of North Carolina Press, 2018.

Katz, Jonathan Ned. "The Invention of Heterosexuality." In *Race, Class, and Gender in the United States: An Integrated Study*, 10th ed., edited by Paula S. Rothenberg. New York: Worth, 2016).

Kimmel, Michael. "Masculinity as Homophobia: Fear, Shame, and Silence in the Construction of Gender Identity." In *Theorizing Masculinities*, edited by Harry Brod and Michael Kaufman, 213–19. Thousand Oaks, CA: Sage, 1994.

Lincoln, C. Eric, and Lawrence Mamiya. *The Black Church in the African American Experience*. Durham, NC: Duke University Press, 1990.

Lomax, Tamura. *Jezebel Unhinged: Loosing the Black Female Body in Religion and Culture*. Durham, NC: Duke University Press, 2018.

Lorde, Audre. "Age, Race, Class, and Sex." In *Sister Outsider: Essays and Speeches by Audre Lorde*, 114–23. Berkeley, CA: Crossing Press, 1984.

———. "The Transformation of Silence into Language and Action." In *Sister Outsider: Essays and Speeches by Audre Lorde*, 40–44. Berkeley, CA: Crossing Press, 1984.

———. "Uses of the Erotic: The Erotic as Power." In *Sister Outsider: Essays and Speeches by Audre Lorde*. Berkeley, CA: Crossing Press, 1984.

———. *I Am Your Sister: Black Women Organizing across Sexualities*. New York: Kitchen Table Press, 1985.

Love, Bettina L. "Examining the Oppressor Within: Lessons Learned by a Northern Researcher in the South." In *Queer South Rising: Voices of a Contested Place*, edited by Reta Ugena Whitlock, 41–57. Charlotte, NC: Information Age, 2013.

McKittrick, Katherine. *Demonic Grounds: Black Women and The Cartographies of Struggle*. Minneapolis: University of Minnesota Press, 2006.

Moraga, Cherríe. *Loving in the War Years*. Cambridge, MA: South End Press, 1983.

Morgan, Joan. *When Chickenheads Come Home to Roost: A Hip-Hop Feminist Breaks It Down*. New York: Simon & Schuster, 1999.

Pharr, Susan. *Homophobia: A Weapon for Sexism*. Berkeley, CA: Chardon Press, 1997.

Phillips, Layli. "Introduction—Womanism on Its Own." In *The Womanist Reader*, edited by Layli Phillips. New York: Routledge, 2006.

Poet on Watch. "An Editor's Notes." In *G.R.I.T.S (Girls Raised in the South): An Anthology of Southern Queer Womyn's Voices & Their Allies*, edited by Poet on Watch and Amber N. Williams, ix–xi. Austin, TX: Freeverse, 2013.

Raboteau, Albert J. *Slave Religion: The "Invisible Institution" in the Antebellum South*. New York: Oxford University Press, 2004.

Sears, James T. *Growing Up Gay in the South: Race, Gender, and Journeys of the Spirit*. New York: Harrington Park Press, 1991.

Shange, Ntozake. *For Colored Girls Who Considered Suicide/When the Rainbow Is Enuf: A Choreopoem*. New York: Collier Books, 1989.

Smith, Cherry. "What Is This Thing Called Queer?" In *The Material Queer: A LesBiGay Cultural Studies Reader*, edited by Donald Morton, 277–85. Boulder, CO: Westview Press, 1996.

Stapel, Christopher. "Dismantling Metrocentric and Metronormative Curricula: Toward a Critical Queer Pedagogy of Southern Rural Space and Place." In *Queer South Rising: Voices of a Contested Place*, edited by Reta Ugena Whitlock, 59–72. Charlotte, NC: Information Age, 2013.

Story, Kaila. "Not Feminine as in Straight, but Femme as in Queer #AF: The Queer and Black Roots of My Femme Expression/Experience." In *Mouths of Rain: An Anthology of Black Lesbian Thought*, edited by Briona Simone Jones, 69–75. New York: New Press, 2021.

Walker, Alice. *In Search of Our Mother's Garden: Womanist Prose*. New York: Harcourt Brace Jovanovich, 1983.

Washington, Craig. "Fall Down on Me: Stories of the Club from Black Gay Men in the South." In *Queer South Rising: Voices of a Contested Place*, edited by Reta Ugena Whitlock, 73–89. Charlotte, NC: Information Age, 2013.

Whitlock, Reta Ugena. "Introduction: Loving, Telling, and Reconstructing the South." In *Queer South Rising: Voices of a Contested Place*, edited by Reta Ugena Whitlock, xxi–xl. Charlotte, NC: Information Age, 2013.

Index

Afrocentricity, 128
ancestry, 1, 21; African/Black, 19, 56, 170; connections to, 162–63, 165; Southern Black Church, 32, 160; Southern Black queer, 41, 167, 179, 188
aggressive femmes, 180, 198n11
AIDS/HIV, 25, 108
Allison Chase, 110: "don't ask, don't tell," 55; embodiment, 144, 152; Los Angeles, California, 52
Andy: affirmation, 54; and the Church, 70, 97, 113; coming out, 142; heterosexism, 113; reconciliation, 159; South as homeplace, 48
Angel: bean canning process, 5; finding truth, 145; heterosexism, 109
antebellum South: gender tropes, 121; New South, 151
Ari: racism, 49; traditional notions of femininity, 73
Asante, Molefi, 128
"auntie," 10, 55, 181
authenticity: coming out, 9, 37, 135, 138; family narratives, 12; freedom, 140, 168, 176; heterosexism, 105; reconciliation, 150, 164–65; tropes, 177; truth telling, 145, 165

Baptist: Bynta, 156; Church, 69, 193n2; deacons and deaconesses, 194n12; evangelical Christianity, 31; Fatima, 73; queer affirming, 159; Rami, 70; respectability politics, 80, 82; youth leader, 70
bad woman: Robin Baylorn, 124; sexuality, 124–25; Southern belle, 178; street people, 125. *See also* good woman
Barton, Bernadette: Bible Belt, 55, 126, 172; gender and sexuality, 31, 33; toxic closet, 95
Bible Belt: gays, 172; panopticon, 55, 126
bisexual: gender fluidity, 87–88; Janessa, 75; quare, 29–30; Brooksley Smith, 88
Black: and the Church, 32, 35; enslavement, 5, 61; heteronormative, 110–11, 116; heterosexism, 106, 108; physical space, 49–50, 170; racial uplift, 194n20; racism, 33; sexual deviancy, 127; studs/bois, 154; sundown towns, 191n23
Black Club movement, 194n20; respectability politics, 82
Black liberation, 32, 57, 106; Patricia Hill Collins, 57; whiteness, 128

bois: differences from studs, 182–83; and cishet masculinity, 31, 132–33; Southern gentleman, 153–54; and toxic masculinity, 99. *See also* studs

Boylorn, Robin: archetypes, 125; bad woman, 124, 153; role of the Church, 61

Bree: reconciliation, 159; self-love, 138; tolerance, 97

Brooksley Smith: bisexual, 88; heterosexism, 81; moving to Atlanta, 158

brothas, 40, 192n62

Brundage, W. Fitzhugh: physical space, 170; and the South, 15–16

Byanca: coming out, 140; heterosexism, 113; practice of silence, 44. *See also* coming out narratives

Bynta: Baptist Church, 156; heteronormativity, 51, 111–12; internalized homophobia, 97, 103; reconciliation, 155–56; Southern Black memory, 50. *See also* Sunshine Honeysuckle

Cassie, 3; and the Church, 66; coming out, 87; contradictions of the South, 48; finding self, 145; heteronormativity, 88; heterosexism, 104, 109; motherhood, 95; reconciliation, 164; self-love, 138; snapping beans, 4; truth telling, 164; wearing the mask, 93–94, 96

Catholic, 31, 73

Cayce: duality, 92; embarrassment, 73; Jehovah's Witness watchman, 36, 70, 76; relationship with mother, 78; snapping beans, 5–6; Southern hospitality, 55

chastisement: Byanca, 44; and racial oppression, 95; reconciliation, 155; shame, 94; truth telling, 157

Chicano/Mexican, 24, 154

Christian: Baptist, 31; conservative doctrines and ideologies, 31, 59, 65; enslavement and the Christian Black Church, 32, 192n51; evangelical, 31, 67, 124, 160, 193n2; heterosexism and the Bible, 98; nondenominational Church, 172; reconciliation and, 38, 156–57, 159; silence and, 35; Southern Christian Black Church, 30; Southern Christian Church, 31

Christian Bible, 20, 31, 52; heterosexism, 98; June, 75; Southern belle, 122; studies, 156

Christian fundamentalists, 31

cisgender: binary, 106, 120–21, 152, 155, 184–85; embodiment, 106, 116, 120, 123–24, 144, 152, 184; femininity, 123, 125–26, 149, 152, 179–80; heteronormativity, 32, 60, 66, 81, 83–84, 94, 99–100; heterosexual, 52, 81, 84, 87, 103, 105, 107; identity, 83, 120; lesbian, 144; masculine, 183; normalcies, 120; privilege, 153; tropes, 126; woman, 73, 124

claiming land, 16

Clarke, Cheryl, 25; bisexuality, 88; Black lesbian, 133–34; "Failure to Transform" essay, 107; reconciliation, 148. *See also* bisexuality

Clinton, Bill, 53

closeted, 55, 91–92, 168; duality, 34, 91, 93, 95, 174; heterosexism, 108; relation to prison, 108. *See also* Patricia Hill Collins; coming out

Cochran, Susan, 33

Cohen, Cathy: heteronormativity, 109; heterosexism, 107–8, 114–15, 134; politics of deviancy, 175
Collins, Patricia Hill: Black female domestic workers, 23, 27–28; Black feminist epistemology, 14; Black liberation, 57; Eurocentric knowledge, 13; heterosexism, 106, 108, 126–27; hypersexuality, 105; negative stereotypes, 83; outsider within theory, 28–29, 47, 119; sexual deviancy, 60, 127
coming out narratives, 34–35, 38, 91–92; connection to queerness, 143; racialized sexual queer geography, 92; telling mothers specifically, 74–75; truth telling, 39. *See also* duality; internalized homophobia
condemnation, 69; coming out, 33, 38, 140; "dark cloud," 91; finding truth, 40–41, 145, 167; freedom from, 139; heteronormative, 185; internal, 99, 141; living for others, 138; loss of humanity, 137; process of hiding, 93; reconciliation, 148; self-love, 146; and shame, 66–67, 69, 71, 92, 100; silenced, 63, 65, 135, 174; spiritual grounding, 155–56, 160, 172; weight of guilt, 96–97
Cornelius, Janet, 118
"cousin," 56–57
culture (space), 19
culture of silence, 38–39, 58, 62, 141, 173–74
culture of shame, 38, 57

Davis, Angela Y., 56, 179
dawta, 21, 40, 74, 189n8; paternalistic language, 114; respectability politics, 80

deacon, 35, 67, 118–19, 194n12
deaconess, 75, 194n12
deviance, sexual, 108, 127
Dews, Carlos, 28
disfellowship, 34–36, 70, 76, 92, 158, 194n7. *See also* Jehovah's Witness; Kingdom Hall
domestic workers, 27–28
"don't ask, don't tell" (DADT), 53–55; culture of silence, 62; duality, 93, 95
Douglas, Kelly Brown, 68; dualism, 82; lesbian threat, 131
Du Bois, W. E. B., 28
duality, 34, 38, 51, 83, 174; Cayce, 92; closeted, 34, 91; and coming out process, 139–41; condemnation, 145; "don't ask, don't tell," 93, 95; "fam" connections, 172; heteronormativity, 142; internalized homophobia, 96; Kea, 99; self-hatred, 67, 146; spiritual peace, 157; traumas, 158; truth telling, 147; wearing the mask, 92–95, 146
Dunbar, Paul Laurence, 96; "We Wear the Mask," 93

Eaves, LaToya, 18
elder, 35, 52, 77–78, 118, 150; deacons and deaconesses, 194n12; disfellowship, 194n7; spirituality, 160; terms passed on, 54, 72, 189n8
Endesha, 8; Missionary Baptist Church, 69; queer lesbian actualization, 163; reconciliation, 157, 163, 165; spiritual leader, 157, 172
enslavement: access to food, 5; chattel; Civil War, 15; domestic work, 17; hypersexuality, 105; kinfolk, 55–56; legacy of, 17, 50, 82; mentality,

enslavement *(continued)*
  59–60; role of the Christian Black Church, 32, 192n51; sexual norms, 82, 121; Southern Black Church, 32, 71, 118; Southern gentleman, 122; transatlantic, 17
epistemological: African/Black feminist, 11–14; homeplace, 22; bell hooks, 22; outsider within, 119; resilience, 12; snapping beans, 13; truth telling, 14. *See also* Patricia Hill Collins
Eurocentric, 13, 16
evangelical Christianity, 31, 67, 124, 160, 193n2; ideology, 61, 80; indoctrination, 32; reconciliation, 156–57, 159; spiritual validation, 156. *See also* Bernadette Barton
"existing in two worlds," 91; living a double life, 34, 92, 94

faith: evangelical, 124; Jehovah's Witness, 34, 70, 76, 158, 193, 194n7; E. Patrick Johnson, 160; lessons, 157; reconciliation, 159–60; and religion, 159; Southern Black Church, 67; spiritual journey, 156, 158, 161
family: biological, 55–56, 58–59, 140, 172; kinfolk, 55–56, 58–59
Fatima: Baptist Church, 73; finding truth, 145; grandma's kitchen, 43; heteronormative, 73; looking presentable, 72; sense of belonging, 49; shame, 66
fear: of being connected to whiteness, 130; of being labeled lesbians, 129; of being silenced, 41; "don't ask, don't tell," 55; of family separation, 34; and heteronormativity, 131; of judgment, 138, 148; Audre Lorde, 107, 129; of queerness or gender fluidity, 100, 109, 111; of racial tension, 170; of religious-based chastisement, 44–45, 91; of shaming family, 57, 73–74, 96; silence as response, 44–46, 55, 57, 62
femininity: aggressive femmes, 198n11; Church aesthetics, 72, 92–93; duality, 94; first lady, 117; gender binaries, 155; good woman, 125; heteronormativity, 120–21; heterosexism, 120–21, 149; Janie, 102; masculine-embodied queer lesbian women, 53; reconciliation, 152; shame or embarrassment to family, 73; notions of sexual purity, 124, 126, 149; Southern belle, 123, 153; toxic cisgender heteronormative white, 60; traditional Southern, 71, 178–79; tropes, 121; wearing a mask, 94. *See also* femmes; Southern Black gentlelady
feminist epistemological, 11, 13–14
femmes: aggressive, 198n11; coming out, 144; heteronormativity, 152–53; internalized homophobia, 99; masculinity, 184; Southern belle, 153–54, 179–80; Southern Black, 153, 178–81; tropes, 177–79
first lady: heteronormativity, 116, 118–19, 177; heterosexism, 116; never being enough, 134; notions of sexual purity, 117; and Southern belle, 178–80. *See also* pastor
freedom: authenticity, 8, 168, 176; bisexuality, 88; and US citizenship, 169; coming out, 139; Paulo Freire, 137; from Black heteropatriarchy and heteronormativity, 134; laying of hands, 76; liberation, 137, 140, 147; New South, 151; patriarchy, 35, 82, 84; politics of deviancy, 175; reconciliation, 135, 138, 151,

164–65; Southern Black Church, 32; spiritual practice, 160; truth telling, 145–46, 164–65; urban spaces, 7; whiteness, 127
Freire, Paulo, 69; liberation, 137, 140
Friedan, Betty, 86
"friend," 91; coded language, 90

geography: W. Fitzhugh Brundage, 170; and capitalism, 17; physical place, 19, 21, 168, 171, 174
gender fluidity, 18–19; bisexual, 87–88; embodiment, 73, 143–44; finding truth, 184; gender binaries, 155; heteronormative, 110–11, 120, 125; heterosexuality, 103, 120; Ifa, 160; internalized homophobia, 99–100; and the term lesbian, 26, 89; notions of sexual purity, 82, 126; and the term "queer," 25, 27, 89; reconciliation, 149; shame, 88–89; culture of silence, 33, 46; Southern Black Church, 66–68, 80–81, 91; "white person's thang," 127. *See also* cisgender, binary; "don't ask, don't tell"; shame
gender-nonconforming: binary, 53; coming out, 143–44; heterosexism, 105; interlocutors, 26; pressure to embody the Southern feminine aesthetics, 73, 94; toxic masculinity, 131–33; tropes, 39; visibility of, 184; wearing the mask, 95
gender norms, 25; binary, 120, 126; heteronormativity, 110; oppressive, 181; Southern Black Church, 35–36, 78; shame, 36; toxic, 40; tropes, 132, 178
Gilroy, Paul, *The Black Atlantic*, 50
good ol' boy: heteronormativity, 123; masculinity, 154; patriarchy, 120, 132; trope, 121, 177, 182–83

good woman: heteronormativity, 124; marriage, 125; Southern belle, 125, 178; trope, 177, 179. *See also* bad woman
grandma and 'em, 10, 12–13, 59, 175–76; duality, 140; heteronormativity, 150; home, 21; knowledge and wisdom, 10, 13–14, 20–21; laughter, 44; never being enough, 134; pleasing, 74; reconciliation, 150, 155–56, 158, 160; snapping beans, 1, 8–9, 11–14, 45; spiritual grounding, 156–57; truth telling, 14, 146–47
grandma's kitchen, 1, 43, 46, 48, 63, 144–46; as Black feminist epistemological space, 13
Grant, Jacqueline, 118
green beans, 1, 3–4; canning and storing, 2, 5–6, 188; flavor, 4–6, 190n4; growing process, 5; other beans, 4; snapping beans, 5–8, 11, 47, 57, 175
Greene, Beverly, 33

heathens, 61
heteronormative: Bynta, 51, 111–12; Cassie, 88; cisgender, 32, 60, 66, 81, 83–84, 94, 99–100; Cathy Cohen, 109; condemnation, 185; duality, 142; femmes, 152–53; first lady, 116, 118–19, 177; freedom from, 134; gender and sexual fluidity, 81, 84, 110–11, 120, 125; gender norms, 110; good ol' boy, 123; good woman, 124; grandma and 'em, 150; June, 91; Leah, 111; Maezah, 111; monogamy, 111, 123, 130; pastor, 116, 118–19, 177; sin, 119; Southern Black persons, 110–11, 116; Vanessa, 109; white, 60

heterosexism: Andy, 113; Angel, 109; authenticity, 105; Black Southern, 106, 108; Brooksley Smith, 81; Byanca, 113; Cassie, 104, 109; Christian Bible, 98; Cathy Cohen, 107–8, 114–15; Patricia Hill Collins, 106, 108, 126–27; femininity, 120–21, 149; first lady, 116; gendered roles; gender-nonconforming, 105; gendered value system, 106; indoctrination, 106; interlocutors defining, 104–5, 109; Tamara Jones, 106–8, 114; June, 143; Kea, 104; Kris, 119; LaDawn, 109; Leah, 113; Audre Lorde, 104, 106–7; Makeda, 104; Marie Dylan, 104, 120; monogamy, 61, 80, 104, 106, 114, 120; pastor, 116; Remi, 106, 116, 120; separation from, 108, 127; sin, 119; Star, 134; Sweet, 104, 120; Tené, 80, 111; Toni, 110; cisgender identity; and monogamy

heterosexual: cisgender, 52, 81, 84, 87, 103, 105, 107; gender fluidity, 103, 120; Suzanne Pharr, 105, 114

Higginbotham, Evelyn B., 80, 82, 125. *See also* respectability politics

homeplace: African/Black ancestry, 19, 56; contradictions of, 21, 48, 51, 63; duality, 94; epistemological, 22; "fam," 172–73; joy, 186; and liberation, 140; narrative, 22; sense of belonging, 3, 6, 21; site of resistance, 22, 173; South as homeplace, 48, 162, 168; racialized sexual geography, 20; Southern Black femme, 181; truth telling, 177; wearing the mask, 94

homophobia: condemnation, 156; duality, 39, 140, 157; internalized, 96–97, 99–100, 145; reconciliation, 160. *See also* self-hatred

homosexuality: and abomination, 45, 65, 75; "devil," 68; gender and sexual fluidity, 67, 84; heterosexism, 109, 114; notions of sexual deviance; queerness and whiteness, 89, 127–28, 130, 155; Suzanne Pharr, 105; sexual deviancy, 127; sin, 31, 97; Southern belle, 152

hooks, bell: homeplace, 22, 173, 181; shame and patriarchy, 76–77, 112, 133; *Yearning: Race, Gender, and Cultural Politics*, 22

Howard, John, 174

Hudson-Weems, Clenora, 24

Hunter, Tera W., 17

Hurston, Zora Neale, 101; *Their Eyes Were Watching God*, 102; townsfolk, 103, 134–35

in-between woman, 124–26, 177. *See also* bad woman; good woman

indoctrination, 31–32, 77; culture of silence, 53; femme identity, 181; heterosexism, 106; patriarchy, 77, 112; tropes, 121

insiders, 27–29; racialized sexual queer geography, 38, 47. *See also* Patricia Hill Collins

interlocutors: Black history and identity, 50, 128; canning and storing beans, 5–6; with children, 95; about conversations and questions, 2, 7, 10; defining heterosexism, 104–5, 109; defining sexual and queer identities, 22; gender-nonconforming, 26; homeplace, 21; Jehovah's Witness ideologies, 34; queer, 26–27, 30, 144, 189n1; responses from, 11

internalized homophobia: condemnation, 96, 156; duality, 38–39, 140, 157; need for a faith practice, 157, 160; physical harm, 99; self-hatred, 96, 100; standing in one's truth, 145; toxic binary norms, 99

Jae: condemnation, 97–98; masculine embodied, 73, 94, 131; perceived threat to Southern Black cishet men, 94; self-love, 145; sense of belonging, 48–49; shame for mother, 57

Janessa: bisexual, 75; coming out, 75, 78; laying of hands, 76; mother's role in the Church, 74; sense of belonging, 49; snapping beans in silence, 5, 46

Jehovah's Witness: Cayce, 36, 70, 76; disfellowship, 34–35, 70, 76, 92, 158, 194n7; Kea, 70, 76, 92; Kingdom Hall, 192n54; reconciliation, 158; James Sears, 34; Southern Black Church, 193n2; watchmen, 193n6

Jezebel: duality, 83; gender binary, 60; hypersexual, 60, 83; trope, 24, 82–83

Jim and Jane Crow, 3, 50

Johnson, E. Patrick: Church as nurturing space, 115, 160; defining Southernness, 1; quare theory, 29–30, 89; Southern Black Church, 35–36; spiritual grounding, 156. *See also* quare

Jones, Tamara: Black liberation, 106; heterosexism, 106–8, 114

Jordan, June, 25

joy: freedom, 165; reclaimed, 139; reconciliation, 157, 161; and thriving, 137, 185–86; and trauma, 21, 177

June: Black history, 50; heteronormative, 91; heterosexism, 143; homophobia, 51, 75, 83; mother's role in the Church, 74; queer lesbian actualization, 142; reconciliation, 158; shame, 91, 144

Katz, Jonathan Ned, 98

Kea: complex relationship with the South, 48, 96; heterosexism, 104; internalized homophobia, 60, 99; Jehovah's Witness watchman, 70, 76, 96; participation in the Church, 70; shame from Church, 76, 86, 92; socialization of gender normalcy, 120–21; threat from mother, 36, 76

Kendra, 69

Kimmel, Michael: "heroic artisan," 122, 183; historic construction of manhood, 181, 183

Kingdom Hall, 192n54; disfellowship, 34–35, 70, 76, 158. *See also* Jehovah's Witness

Kris: heterosexism, 119; self-love, 138; sense of belonging, 49; shame, 74, 90

LaDawn: heterosexism, 109; passing, 73; sense of belonging, 56, 58; shame, 83, 90, 105–6; silence, 58

Leah: coming out, 142; heteronormative, 111; heterosexism, 113; masculine embodied, 94; Minnesota, 50; moving to the South, 50; spiritual validation, 156; sexual fluidity, 84

Leila, 138

lesbian: baiting, 129; cisgender, 144; Cheryl Clarke, 133–34; Endesha, 163; fear of being labeled, 129; femininity, 53; gender fluidity, 26, 89; June, 142; notions evil, 133; racialized sexual queer geography, 26, 37; respectability politics, 125;

lesbian *(continued)*
self-naming and the term queer, 24–26; separation of mothers and daughters, 78–79; Shay, 125; perceived threat by, 131; truth telling, 147, 164. *See also* queer lesbian actualization
Lincoln, C. Eric, *The Black Church in the African American Experience*, 31–32. *See also* Mamiya, Lawrence H.
living a double life, 34, 92, 94; Kea, 96
Lomax, Tamura, 83
Lorde, Audre, 25; erotic as power, 152; heterosexism, 104, 106–7; homophobia, 96, 106, 129; *I Am Your Sister*; silence, 45–46, 128
Love, Bettina, active coping, 73, 94
lynching, 3, 50, 191n23

Maezah: Church musician, 70; coming out, 142–43; finding truth, 145; heteronormativity, 111; heteropatriarchy, 112, 130; queerness, 89; sexual fluidity, 88–89, 126–27; snapping beans, 3
Makeda: "don't ask, don't tell," 54; finding truth, 145; heterosexism, 104; masculine embodied, 154; reconciliation, 158; social gathering spaces, 172
Mamiya, Lawrence H., *The Black Church in the African American Experience*, 31–32
mammy, 24; asexual, 60, 87; trope, 82–83
Marie Dylan: coming out, 147; culture of silence, 46; "don't ask, don't tell," 54; duality, 51; heterosexism, 104, 120; sense of belonging, 49; "slave mentality," 59

masculine embodied: femininity, 53; Jae, 73, 94, 131; Leah, 94; Makeda, 154
masculinity: bois, 31, 132–33; cisgender; 183; femmes, 184; gender-nonconforming, 131–33; generational norms; good ol' boy, 154; Southern good ol' boi, 182; Southern stud, 183; stud as threat to cishet, 131–33; toxic, 99
Mays, Vickie, 33
McKittrick, Katherine: connection to enslavement, 50; geography, 16–17, 49; multidimensional South, 47
memory: pain and silence, 46; racialized geographic space, 17; of safety, 8; snapping beans, 14, 43; Southern Black history, 15–16, 49–50, 59, 170. *See also* grandma's kitchen
Methodist, 31, 159; African Methodist Episcopal Church, 87, 193n2
misogyny, 25, 177
monogamy: feminine identity, 178; heteronormative, 111, 123, 130; heterosexism, 61, 80, 104, 106, 114, 120; policing Black sexuality, 108, 114; polyamory, 147; and queerness, 110; shame, 80
Moraga, Cherríe, 154; *Loving in the War Years*, 24
Morgan, Joan, 122, 124. *See also* Southern belle
mothas, 78
myths, 23–24, 107, 142, 150

naming and renaming: bisexual, 87; gender fluidity, 26, 89; heterosexism, 24; and the term lesbian, 24–26, 37, 87, 131; and the term queer, 25, 27, 27, 30, 37, 89; and the term quare, 30; queer lesbian

actualization, 87, 149; racialized sexual queer geography, 22–23, 37; reconciliation, 23, 163; and self-defining, 23–24; shame, 85–89; truth telling, 146. *See also* bisexual; Patricia Hill Collins; Clenora Hudson-Weems
Neile, 145
Nelson, James B., 82
New South, 151; gender fluidity, 185; narrative, 155; perspective, 38; place and space, 39; reality, 175
Nina Simone, 50
Nommo, 24
nondenominational: Christian Church, 172; megachurches, 31
Nyx, 110

Onika Rose, 105, 164
outsiders, 1, 25, 27, 53, 129–30, 173; outsider within, 28–29, 38, 47, 63, 119, 155; racialized sexual queer geography, 27–29, 38, 47. *See also* Patricia Hill Collins

pastor: church mothas, 78; and deacons and deaconesses, 75, 194n12; Endesha, 157; fear among parishioners, 45; hegemony, 67, 117; heteronormativity, 116, 118–19, 177; heterosexism, 116; historical knowledge, 98; hypocrisy and, 84; pulpit as "man's space," 115, 117, 123; queer or LGBTQIA+, 159, 172; reconciliation, 156; sexual autonomy, 35. *See also* first lady
patriarchal dualism, 82
patriarchy: freedom, 35, 82, 84; good ol' boy, 120, 132; heterosexism; bell hooks, 76–77, 112, 133; indoctrination, 77, 112; shame and, 76–77; Southern Black mother, 77, 79, 103; Southern gentleman, 60, 183
Paulette, 97
Pentecostal, 31, 159
pew position, 118
Pharr, Suzanne: compulsory heterosexuality, 105, 114; lesbian baiting, 129
physical place: connection between geography and culture (space), 19; finding space, 174; sense of belonging, 21, 168, 171; social control, 170; and spiritual space, 171
Poet on Watch, 26–27
polyamory, 147
postbellum America, 27
pronouns: "he," 183; "they/them," 68, 88, 97

quare: E. Patrick Johnson, 29–30, 89; and the term queer, 30; outsider within, 38; racialized sexual queer geography, 29–30; theory and framework, 29–30, 89
queer: Baptist, 159; coming out narratives, 143; Endesha, 163; fear of, 100, 109, 111; femininity, 53; interlocutors, 26–27, 30, 144, 189n1; June, 142; Maezah, 89; monogamy and, 110; pastor, 159, 172; racialized sexual geography, 30; reconciliation, 163; respectability politics, 125; self-naming and the term lesbian, 24–26; separation of mothers and daughters, 78–79; gender and sexual fluidity, 8, 14, 25–27, 89; Shay, 125; Southern Black ancestry, 41, 167, 179, 188; Toni, 27; truth telling, 147, 164; whiteness and homosexuality, 89, 127, 130, 155

queer lesbian actualization: coming out, 87, 146; internal homophobia, 67; liberation, 137; life changes, 142; reconciliation, 163; relationship with mothers, 75; role of the Church, 66; spiritual validation, 156; truth telling, 147, 164. *See also* bisexuality

Raboteau, Albert J., 32, 192n51
racialized sexual queer geography: challenges Southern traditional geography, 18, 26, 39, 51; coming out narratives, 92; duality, 92; heteronormativity, 19; homophobia, 19; insider/outsider positionality, 27–29, 38, 47; lesbian, 26, 37; naming and renaming, 22–23, 37; outsider within, 29, 37–38, 47; quare, 29–30; queerness and queer embodiment in a specific geography, 18, 28, 30, 178; silence, 51; trauma, 51
Rainey, Ma, 179
reclamation, 162, 185; affirmation, 2; Black femmes, 153, 181; home, 163
reconciliation: Andy, 159; authenticity, 150, 164–65; Bree, 159; Bynta, 155–56; Cassie, 164; chastisement, 155; Cheryl Clarke, 148; condemnation, 148; Endesha, 157, 163, 165; evangelical Christianity, 156–57, 159; faith, 159–60; femininity, 152; freedom and, 135, 138, 151, 164–65; gender fluidity, 149; grandma and 'em, 150, 155–56, 158, 160; homophobia, 160; Civil War; identity; Jehovah's Witness, 158; joy, 157, 161; June, 158; Makeda, 158; pastor, 156; queer lesbian actualization, 163; Reign, 156, 160; separation and, 158; Shay, 151, 162; Southern Christian Black Church, 38; Star, 158; spiritual, 158–60. *See also* truth telling
Reign: coming out, 141; reconciliation, 156, 160; truth telling, 146
Remi: duality, 92; heterosexism, 106, 116, 120; shame, 68, 90; Southern Baptist youth leader, 70; Southern hospitality, 52
respectability politics, 72; cisgender feminine embodiment, 120; clothing, 72; first lady, 117; notions of sexual purity, 78, 82; queer lesbianism, 125; shame, 80, 84; Southern belle, 123

same-gender loving, 25
Sapphire, 24, 82
Sears, James T.: *Growing Up Gay in the South*, 34; Southern belle, 121, 123–24; Southern good ol' boy, 121–22, 182–83; Southern gentleman, 121, 182; tropes of the South, 125, 177; US South, 15–16
self-affirmation, 145–46
self-defining, 23
self-destructive, 69
self-discovery, 36, 147, 156
self-harm, 69
self-hatred: Church trauma, 68; condemnation, 91, 145; duality, 67, 146; internalized homophobia, 38, 96, 98, 100; spiritual validation, 160–61
self-love: Bree, 138; Cassie, 138; condemnation, 146; Jae, 145; Kris, 138; Star, 138, 146; Tisha, 138; Toni, 138
self-naming: and self-defining, 23; terms lesbian and queer, 24–26

separation: between Church and families, 66, 155, 158; between Church and state, 113; Black families and enslavement, 56; from mother, 78–79; heterosexism, 108, 127; reconciliation, 158. *See also* shame

sermon, 118; homophobic, 65–66, 75; spiritual validation, 156

sexual fluidity: cisgender heteronormativity, 81, 84, 110; culture of silence, 44, 54; queerness, 14, 26, 89; racialized sexual geography, 18, 111; shame, 80, 84, 89; "white person's thang," 127. *See also* cisgender, binary; "don't ask, don't tell"; gender fluidity; quare theory; shame

shame: chastisement, 94; condemnation, 66–67, 69, 71, 92, 100; culture of, 38, 57; Fatima, 66; femininity, 73; gender fluidity, 88–89; gender norms, 36; Kea, 76, 86, 92; Kris, 74, 90; Jae, 57; June, 91, 144; LaDawn, 83, 90, 105–6; monogamy, 80; and patriarchy, 76–77, 112, 133; Remi, 68, 90; respectability politics, 80, 84; sexual fluidity, 80, 84, 89; Shay, 86; Star, 95; Vanessa, 80

Shange, Ntozake, *For Colored Girls Who Considered Suicide/When the Rainbow Is Enuf*, 161

Shay: reconciliation, 151, 162; reconnecting with family, 66, 163; queer lesbians, 125; shame, 86

silence: Byanca, 44; condemnation and, 63, 65, 135, 174; culture of, 38–39, 46, 58, 62, 141, 173–74; "don't ask, don't tell," 62; fear and, 41, 44–46, 55, 57, 62; gender and sexual fluidity, 33, 44, 46, 54; indoctrination, 53; LaDawn, 58; Audre Lorde, 45–46, 128; memory, 46; notion of respect; oppressive; snapping beans, 5, 46; Southern Christian Black Church, 35; therapeutic

sin: condemnation, 97; disfellowship, 76, 194n7; evangelical shame, 67; "hate the sin, love the sinner," 33, 59, 65, 97–98; heteronormativity, 119; heterosexism, 119; perceived, 97–98; Southern Black mothers, 79. *See also* disfellowship; shame

sistas, 40, 192n61

Smith, Barbara, 25

Smith, Bessie, 179

Smith, Cherry, 25–26

South as backward, 6–7, 20, 60, 62, 79

Southern belle, 60, 122–23; cisgender binary embodiment, 121, 123–24; good woman, 125; homosexuality, 152; James Sears, 121–22; trope, 153–54, 177–78. *See also* Joan Morgan

Southern Black mother, 20; being drawn to the South, 21; notions of purity, 95; patriarchy, 77, 79, 103; separation from queer lesbian daughters, 78–79; shaming, 74–75, 79

Southern Black personality (SBP), 102–4, 138; compulsory heterosexuality, 105; femme, 39, 178–80; heteronormative, 110–11, 116; heterosexism, 105; Zora Neale Hurston's townsfolk, 103, 134–35

Southern Black femme, 39, 178–80; homeplace, 181; Southern studs and good ol' bois, 183

Southern Black gentlelady, 178
Southern Black nonbinary person, 178
Southern Christian Black Church, 30; African practices, 17; antebellum South, 32, 193n2; code of silence, 35; condemnation, 38, 45, 63, 65; homophobia, 33; racial impact, 33, 192n51; reconciliation, 38; James Sears, 34–35; toxic traits, 139
Southern Christian Church, 31
Southern gentleman: aristocratic lineage, 117; mental labor, 122; Southern gentlelady, 122, 182–83; Southern patriarchy, 60, 183; trope, 177, 182
Southern good ol' boi: masculinity, 182; trope, 178
Southern stud: masculinity, 183; trope, 178
spirituality: African-centered, 128, 160; Black mothers, 77; faith practice, 157–58, 160; reconciliation, 158–60; redefined, 155–56; separate from religion, 36, 158, 160; Southern lineage, 162–63; and trauma, 36
"standing in my truth": coming out, 14; Fatima, 145
Stapel, Christopher, 6, 62
Star: duality, 94; heterosexism, 134; internalized homophobia, 97; self-love, 138, 146; shame from mother, 95; spiritual reconciliation, 158; truth telling, 145, 147; wearing the mask
stems, 180, 198n11
Story, Kaila, 153
studs: differences from bois, 182–83; internalized homophobia, 99; Southern gentleman, 153–54; threat to cishet masculinity, 131–33; toxic expectations, 99, 154. *See also* bois

Sumter, South Carolina, 2, 43, 56. *See also* grandma's kitchen
sundown towns, 17, 191n23
Sunshine Honeysuckle: canning beans, 6; coming out, 141–42; relationship with Bynta, 111–12; resilience, 138; sense of belonging, 48. *See also* Bynta
Sweet: heterosexism, 104, 120; wearing the mask, 94

Tené: heterosexism, 80, 111; homophobia, 111
Tisha: living for others, 138, 146; self-love, 138; sense of belonging, 48; Southern Black Church, 70
Toni: future generations, 173; heterosexism, 110; internal validation, 161; moving to Atlanta, 50–51, 58; Ohio, 50, 162; self-love, 138; spiritual practices, 160, 162; and the term queer, 27
Torrey: coming out, 142; embodiment, 87; "slave mentality," 59–60
toxic practices, 38
trans or transgendered, 30, 59
transatlantic slavery, 17
trauma, 21, 177; the Church and self-hatred, 68; duality, 158; and joy, 21, 177; spirituality, 36
truth telling: authenticity, 145, 165; Cassie, 164; chastisement, 157; coming out narratives, 39; duality, 147; epistemological, 14; freedom, 145–46, 164–65; grandma and 'em, 14, 146–47; homeplace, 177; Reign, 146; queer lesbian actualization, 147, 164; Star, 145, 147. *See also* reconciliation

Vanessa: future generations, 173; heteronormative, 109; shame, 80

Venus magazine, 171, 198n5

Walker, Alice, 5; womanism, 29, 150
Washington, Craig, 171
welfare queen, 82–83
white: gender and sexual fluidity, 127; heteronormative, 60; toxic cisgender heteronormative, 60; "white person's thang," 127

whiteness: Black liberation, 128; challenging, 154; coming out, 148; fear of, 130; freedom, 127; and homosexuality and queerness, 89, 127, 130, 155
Whitlock, Reta Ugena, 15

youth leader, 70